Translating the Bible into Action

Second Edition

Translating the Bible into Action

How the Bible Can Be Relevant in All Languages and Cultures

Second Edition

Margaret Hill and Harriet Hill

© 2022 Margaret Hill and Harriet Hill

Published 2022 by Langham Global Library
An imprint of Langham Publishing
www.langhampublishing.org

Langham Publishing and its imprints are a ministry of Langham Partnership

Langham Partnership
PO Box 296, Carlisle, Cumbria, CA3 9WZ, UK
www.langham.org

ISBNs:
978-1-83973-671-1 Print
978-1-83973-681-0 ePub
978-1-83973-682-7 Mobi
978-1-83973-683-4 PDF

Margaret Hill and Harriet Hill have asserted their rights under the Copyright, Designs and Patents Act, 1988 to be identified as the Authors of this work.

All rights reserved. No part of this publication may be reproduced, stored in a retrieval system or transmitted, in any form or by any means, electronic, mechanical, photocopying, recording or otherwise, without the prior written permission of the publisher or the Copyright Licensing Agency.

Requests to reuse content from Langham Publishing are processed through PLSclear. Please visit www.plsclear.com to complete your request.

All Scripture quotations, unless otherwise indicated, are taken from the Holy Bible, New International Version®, NIV®. Copyright ©1973, 1978, 1984, 2011 by Biblica, Inc.™ Used by permission of Zondervan.

Scripture quotations marked (GNT) are from the Good News Translation in Today's English Version-Second Edition Copyright © 1992 by American Bible Society. Used by Permission.

Scripture quotations marked (NASB) are taken from the New American Standard Bible®, Copyright © 1960, 1962, 1963, 1968, 1971, 1972, 1973, 1975, 1977, 1995 by The Lockman Foundation. Used by permission.

Scripture quotations marked (NLT) are taken from the Holy Bible, New Living Translation, copyright © 1996, 2004, 2007, 2013, 2015 by Tyndale House Foundation. Used by permission of Tyndale House Publishers, Inc., Carol Stream, Illinois 60188. All rights reserved.

Scripture quotations marked (RSV) are from Revised Standard Version of the Bible, copyright © 1946, 1952, and 1971 National Council of the Churches of Christ in the United States of America. Used by permission. All rights reserved.

British Library Cataloguing-in-Publication Data
A catalogue record for this book is available from the British Library

ISBN: 978-1-83973-671-1

Cover & Book Design: projectluz.com

Langham Partnership actively supports theological dialogue and an author's right to publish but does not necessarily endorse the views and opinions set forth here or in works referenced within this publication, nor can we guarantee technical and grammatical correctness. Langham Partnership does not accept any responsibility or liability to persons or property as a consequence of the reading, use or interpretation of its published content.

Contents

Preface vii
Acknowledgements xiii
What We Believe xv
1 Barriers to Engaging with Scripture............................ 1
2 Using Appropriate Scripture Products 11
3 Language in the Plan of God................................... 21
4 Culture in the Plan of God 29
5 Mother-Tongue Scripture Use and Church Growth 39
6 Using Scripture in Multilingual Churches 45
7 Helping Interpreters Perform Well........................... 53
8 Multi-Ethnic Churches 61
9 Identifying Relevant Issues 67
10 Providing Necessary Background Information 77
11 Preparing Bible Studies 91
12 Preparing Sermons... 101
13 Meditating on God's Word 107
14 Trauma Healing 113
15 HIV/AIDS and the Church..................................... 119
16 Bible Storying 127
17 Preparing for Good News Encounters..................... 139
18 Engaging People with Scripture in Evangelism 147
19 How Muslims Use the Bible 153
20 Engaging Hindus with the Bible............................. 161
21 Engaging Children and Youth with Scripture 169
22 Family Prayers... 181
23 Using the Bible in Our Digital World 187

24	Engaging People with Scripture through Music and Dance	197
25	Engaging People with Scripture through Drama	205
26	Engaging People with Scripture through the Visual Arts and Media	215
27	Mother-Tongue Reading and Writing for Literates	227
28	Basic Literacy and Scripture	237
29	Research, Marketing, and Distribution	245
30	How to Bring about Change	257
31	Preparing for Scripture Engagement Seminars	269

Appendix 1: Good News for Muslims 279
Appendix 2: Researching Song Styles 283
Appendix 3: Example of Sunday School Lesson 285
Appendix 4: Recording Scripture and Dramas 287
Appendix 5: Answers 291

Preface

When Jesus was born on earth, God was translated into our human world. God doesn't require us to abandon our language and culture to relate to him; he came and made his home among us. This act of God's translation of himself continues today as the gospel is expressed in local languages and lived out in local cultures. God speaks our languages, enters our homes, sings our tunes, and brings healing to everyone and every culture that is willing to receive it. It is the nature of Christianity to express itself in the local language and culture, and in so doing it affirms the cultural and linguistic identity of all people. The result is a multilingual, multicultural church.

For too long the church has ignored its cultural and linguistic diversity. For too long it has tried to impose a universal code of thought and conduct on its members. It has not grappled adequately with the theological and practical implications of the diversity of languages and cultures in the plan of God. Some have dominated without realizing it, while others have been trodden under foot.

The church needs to encourage people to communicate with God in their own language. It needs to encourage them to integrate their Christian and cultural identities so that their worldview is transformed to reflect the values of God's kingdom. Each linguistic and cultural group has its own unique work to do in this regard.

This book has been developed to respond to this need. It has evolved over a period of thirty years in workshops and courses with church leaders from a myriad of languages and cultures. Some have been marginalized until very recently and are just now hearing God speak to them through his word in their language for the first time. They are awed by the experience of affirmation. It tingles throughout their bodies and deep down in their souls. Good news of the best variety. This book has helped them embrace their God-given identity and interact with their new Scriptures in ways that are meaningful. Others have been in positions of power, unaware of the discrimination those from minority languages experience. This book has helped them address the diversity of languages and cultures in their churches in ways that affirm the identity and dignity of all people. It helps them minister to all of their members effectively.

Since all churches speak at least one language and have at least one culture, this book is relevant to all.

We begin by identifying common barriers to Scripture engagement, and then discuss theological foundations of this translated faith. The book then explores how multilingual churches can maintain unity in Christ and celebrate the diversity of their membership. It goes on to help people use Scripture in relevant ways: identifying relevant cultural issues, preparing Bible studies and sermons, addressing human concerns, and doing meditation. It gives help on sharing faith through storying and "good news encounters." It addresses sharing faith with Muslims and Hindus, with children and youth, and in the home. It explores the use of music, drama, the visual arts, and digital media. It helps those needing literacy programmes and gives advice about research, marketing, and how to introduce change. The materials in this book can be used in many ways, but one way that is especially effective is to use them in local Scripture engagement seminars. The final chapter in the book explains how to organize and run such seminars.

Talking about Language

We refer to languages in various ways throughout this book. We use the term "mother tongue" to refer to the first language(s) people learn when they are small children. This language is also referred to as our "language of identity" because it shapes who we are. Often, children learn their first language from their mother, and this is why it is commonly referred to as the "mother tongue." In reality, though, children may actually learn their first language from their father, or they may learn two languages at the same time, one from their mother and another from their father.

We use the terms "minority language" or "local language" to refer to languages that are spoken by relatively small ethnic groups. We use the term "majority language" to refer to languages that are spoken by the majority of people in a nation or region, such as French, English, Chinese, or Swahili. In some societies, people speak more than one majority language.

Everyone has a mother tongue. For some, it is a minority language. For others, it is a majority language. Majority-language speakers, who tend to have power and wealth, often marginalize minority languages and the people who speak them. Since language and identity are often closely linked, this marginalization can affect the core of a person's being.

How to Use This Book

Chapters from this book can be used in weekly meetings of a church or community, or a selection of chapters can be used in a seminar that lasts several days. The materials are designed so that participants can teach what they have learned to others, so begin with those who can train others. Those passing on what they have learned will learn better, and more people will benefit.

Most of the chapters in this book can be taught in an hour or two, but they can also be used over an extended period of time. For example, once a group has learned to do Bible studies, they can then work on creating a stock of them. In a seminar, it's usually possible to cover between two and three chapters per day. Schedule a series of seminars over time and cover additional chapters each time. Only those who have used what they learned in their churches should be invited to attend the follow-up seminar. Over time, you can complete the whole book. The churches will benefit as their members become well nourished in their faith.

Whether using this book in an hour's meeting or in a week-long seminar, you'll need to select what you will be able to cover. First read all the chapters and then select those most relevant for your situation. Within the chapters you select, you will also need to decide which exercises, discussions, and assignments you can fit into the time you have available. Give participants enough new ideas to keep them interested, and enough interaction with those ideas to develop new attitudes and practices.

Stories and Participatory Learning

Everybody loves a *story*, so each chapter begins with a story about Pastor Simon and his imaginary adventures in the land of Sanatu (see the map on page xviii). The story sets the theme for the chapter, and the discussion questions that follow get participants involved in the topic.

Each chapter has several main teaching points. These are interspersed with group discussion questions and exercises because people learn best when they participate in the learning process. When teaching, observe the ten-minute rule: no one should teach for more than ten minutes without having a discussion or exercise of some sort. As much as possible, the course is designed to draw out what the participants already know. Often new ideas result from this interaction.

Some *discussions* take place in the large group. Others take place in small groups of various sorts. The kind of small group is indicated by a symbol. The table below lists the kinds of groups, their symbols, and how they function.

Type of Exercise	Symbol	Directions for Discussion or Exercise
Stories		The story can be read aloud, either by one person or by several people taking it in turn. Alternatively one person can learn the story in advance and tell it to the group. Or participants can present a drama, based on the story.
Teaching Questions		1. Ask the whole group the question(s). Give them time to think before answering. This will help you to understand what they already know and get them interested in the topic. 2. Write their responses on a board or flip chart. 3. Then look at the points listed in the book. If any are relevant to the situation but have not been mentioned, add them to the discussion.
Large-Group Exercise		Let the whole group do the exercise together. Encourage as many people as possible to participate. This is an opportunity to brainstorm and think up new solutions.
Small-Group Discussion		1. Read over the questions or exercise with all the participants. 2. Divide the participants into groups of four or five. Unless a special type of group is indicated in the instructions, put people of different backgrounds together. Vary the mix of the groups over the course of the seminar. 3. Give the small groups enough time to discuss the questions or do the exercise. 4. Bring the groups back together. Have one spokesperson for each group share the group's conclusions with the large group. If time is limited, allow each group to say one thing rather than give a summary of their discussion. Or ask them to give feedback on just one of the questions. 5. You may want to write the findings on the board or on large sheets of paper.

Special Small Groups		
Church		Divide participants into groups of four to six by the types of churches they attend, such as Catholic, Baptist, Pentecostal, Lutheran. This is indicated when discussions or exercises discuss the policies and practices of each kind of church.
Language		Divide participants into groups of four to six according to the languages they speak. This is indicated when the discussion or exercise deals with issues within a language community.

Assignments are given towards the end of each chapter. These provide additional interaction with the ideas presented in the chapter. Most often, participants do these on their own in writing. This individual feedback allows the leader to see how each participant is absorbing the materials.

At the end of each chapter, some *key readings and websites* are listed. Many of the readings are at a basic level and enhance the teaching of the chapter. If the book is used for a credited course, participants should read some of the readings for each chapter. Many of the articles can be found at www.scripture-engagement.org.

Acknowledgements

First Edition

This book is a written version of an oral tradition that has been passed down by many around the world over the past fifteen years. We thank all those who had a hand in shaping it. In particular, we would like to thank Rick Brown, Dave Cochran, Mary Crickmore, Bettina Gottschlich, John Lindley, Kirby O'Brien, David Payne, Michelle Petersen, David Presson, Michael Rynkiewich, Lamin Sanneh, Brian Schrag, Stephen Tucker, Andrew Walls, and Kathie Watters. The following copyright holders have given permission for the use of photographs and/or artwork in this book: Rolf Buehler, Craig Duddles, Harriet Hill, Margaret Hill, Ralph Hill, Joyce Hyde, Rick Krowchenko, Elria Kwant, Pieter Kwant, Michael McMillan, Kirby O'Brien, Hugh Steven, and Wycliffe Bible Translators.

Harriet Hill & Margaret Hill

Second Edition

This second edition had many contributors. Special thanks to those who put so much time and energy into the revision. Extra-special thanks are due to Lynley Hatcher who spent many hours editing the chapters and collecting material from various people. Margaret Hill also contributed greatly by reviewing and editing the entire manuscript. The writers of new sections include Lalit Kumar, Richard Margetts, and John Oo. Those who edited existing sections include Ed Beach, Andrea Ciccarelli, Maik Gibson, David Gray, Rachel Hanna, Tim Hatcher, Brian Kelly, Matt Menger, Katherine O'Donnell, John Ommani, Nathan Payne, Michelle Peterson, Justin Randolph, Tanya Spronk, and Kathie Watters.

What We Believe . . .

1. God wants to communicate with us in a way we can understand.

2. In the past, God sent his Son – his Word made flesh – to this world to save us. Today, he communicates with us by his word, the Bible.

3. The incarnation shows us the way God wants to reach us: he comes and lives in our communities.

4. The diversity of languages and cultures is compatible with the plan of God. Our unity is based on love, not similarity.

5. Christianity can be expressed in all languages and lived out in all cultures. None is excluded; all need to be transformed by the gospel.

6. God wants the gospel to penetrate people's worldviews and most often this is done best in the mother tongue.

7. In order for us fully to know our identity in Christ, we must integrate our past into what we are becoming in Christ. This includes our language and culture.

8. Churches cannot last long – nor can Christians mature in their faith – without the word of God in a language people understand.

9. Church leaders need to be sure that all members of their congregations are fed spiritually, regardless of their social class, gender, or age.

10. The more church leaders encourage the use of Scripture in appropriate languages and media, the more the members will use it.

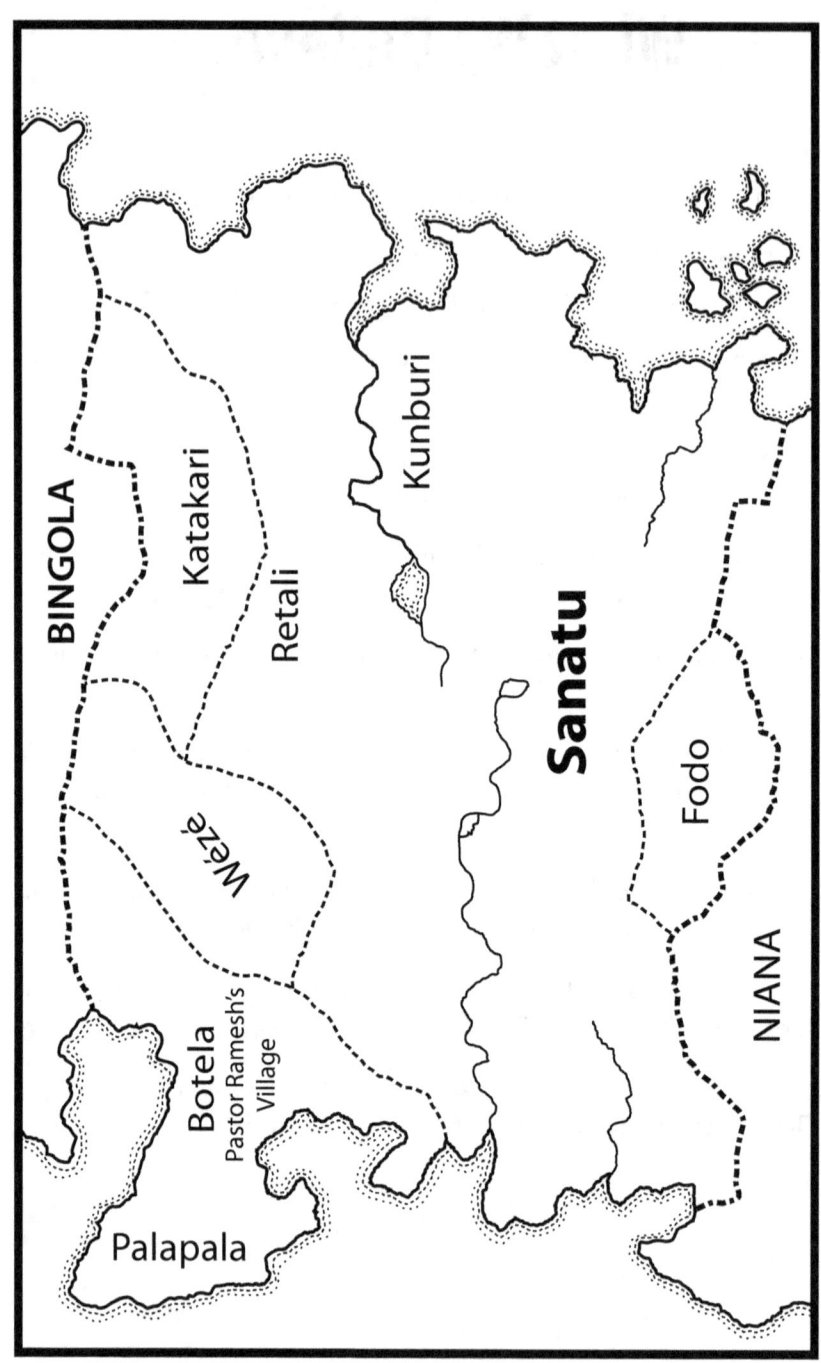

The land of Sanatu, where Pastor Simon lives

1

Barriers to Engaging with Scripture

Introduction

The vast majority of church leaders in the world would say that their faith is based on the Bible. They would also say that it is important for their church members to read and understand the Bible. But what is the reality? Few ordinary church members in any country study the Bible and apply its truths to their lives. Why is the reality so different from the ideal? This chapter looks at some of the barriers that keep people from reading and engaging with Scripture. The rest of this book proposes ways to address each barrier.

PASTOR SIMON'S WORRYING DISCOVERY

Simon Nga is the pastor of a large church in the northern area of Sanatu. The major language there is Kisanu, the official language is English, and the local language is Palapala. The New Testament was recently published in Palapala. Each Sunday about five hundred people come to the morning service. About 90 percent speak Palapala, but the service and Bible readings are all in Kisanu or English. Some people carry a large English Bible and a few have a copy of the new Palapala New Testament with its bright green cover.

Pastor Simon is continuing his studies at a local theological college. This term he is taking a weekly course on Christian education in the church. As part of this course, he has to design a questionnaire in Palapala to study the level of Bible knowledge among his church members. These are some of his questions:

- Who is Jesus?
- What was the work of the twelve apostles Jesus chose?
- Why did God send a flood at the time when Noah built the ark?

- What is the Bible?
- Can you tell me one verse you have memorized from the Psalms?

Pastor Simon gave copies of the survey to fifty of his church members who had been coming to church for at least ten years. Thirty were able to write in the answers themselves. Twenty of them were not literate and so he read the questions to them and wrote down their answers.

Pastor Simon got back forty-one of the questionnaires. When he added up the results, the totals horrified him. Thirty-five people had fewer than half of the answers right. A number of them had only one or two answers right, yet they had been sitting in his church Sunday after Sunday. Pastor Simon began to think about this. "I've been teaching these people the Bible for years, and yet they seem to have been asleep! What should I do?" he wondered.

Soon after this, Pastor Simon received an invitation to go to a seminar for church leaders to learn to use the Palapala New Testament. He was doubtful about the idea, but since the top denominational leaders had sent the invitation, he agreed to go along. At the conference, he began to learn to read in Palapala, and he found that the Scriptures came alive for him in a new way.

"When I get back home," he thought, "I'm going to use Palapala for the New Testament readings in the service. Maybe then people will understand the Bible better."

1. What are some of the barriers that prevent people from engaging with the Bible? First think of barriers that apply to engaging with the Bible in any language. Additional barriers prevent people from engaging with Scripture in minority languages, and we'll address these later.
2. List the barriers on a large sheet of paper. After the lists have been made, ask one member of each group to share their list with all the participants. After all the groups have shared, talk about any of the points below that are relevant but have not been mentioned. Finish by making a composite list of all the barriers, and display it as a poster on the wall.

1. General Barriers to Engaging with Scripture

A. Literacy Barrier

Printed Scriptures are effective when people know how to read and like to do so. But many people prefer to communicate using oral rather than written means, so they don't know how to read. Even if literacy classes were available, people may not be interested in attending them. In some cases, those who do learn to read may still prefer oral means of communication and soon lose their new skills. In other cases, people may want to learn to read, but they are hindered by poor eyesight or other problems. If Scripture is only presented in written form to people who do not know how to read or do not like to read, this is a serious barrier. (See chapters 2, 16, 23, 24, 25, and 26.)

B. Relevance Barrier

People may not find the Bible to be relevant to their everyday lives. They may read or listen to the Bible for a short time because their pastor said they should, but they won't continue if they don't find that it helps them. In fact, the Bible is relevant to all aspects of our lives, but people may need help to understand it and to apply it to their lives. (See chapters 9, 14, 15, and 17.)

C. Context Barrier

The Bible was written for people who lived at least two thousand years ago in cultures that were very different from ours today. The biblical authors didn't have to describe their culture in detail because their readers knew all about it. But today most of us know very little about the cultures of the Bible, and this makes it hard for us to understand the biblical authors' meaning. Yet often there is little material to help people gain this background knowledge, especially in countries in the Majority World. (See chapter 10.)

D. Distribution Barrier

People may want to read or listen to the Bible, but they may not be able to get a copy. This distribution barrier is so significant that the British and Foreign Bible Society (one of the members of the United Bible Society) was founded as a response to it. In 1802, a poor Welsh girl named Mary Jones saved up her money for months and walked many miles to buy a Bible. When she arrived at the bookshop, she found that they had sold out. The bookshop owner decided that he would start an organization to make Bibles available to every person in a language they understood at a price they could afford. Lack of good distribution channels can be a serious barrier to the use of Scripture. (See chapter 29.)

E. Language Barrier

People may have trouble engaging with the Bible if they read or hear it in a language they don't understand well. They may know a language well enough to buy produce at the market but not well enough to understand the Bible. Even if they understand the language, it may not be a language of their heart – a language that they use in the most intimate parts of their lives. For God's word to engage us deeply, we need to understand it and meditate on its truths in a language we understand well that touches our hearts. Otherwise, our engagement with it will be superficial, and we may lose interest in Scripture. (See chapters 3, 5, and 8.)

F. Translation Barrier

Sometimes people reject translations because they do not correspond to the expectations or needs of the community.

- People may not like the style of the translation.
- The medium in which Scripture is presented may not fit the community's preferences. For example, a printed translation would not be appropriate for a primarily oral community. Or Scripture in audio form will not be used if people don't have a way to play the recordings. Many people would enjoy reading or listening to Scripture on mobile phones (see chapter 23).
- A translation may be too old for people to easily understand. Translations need to be revised regularly because languages change over time and writing systems can also change. Those that were done more than twenty-five years ago may be difficult for people to understand.
- Reluctance to change may be a problem. People almost always reject revisions of old translations at first, because they are used to the old translation and consider it holy.

2. Barriers to Engaging with Minority-Language Scripture

Certain barriers keep people from using Scripture in their mother tongue if they speak a minority language.

1. What are the specific barriers to using the available minority-language Scriptures? List them on a large piece of paper.
2. After the lists have been made, ask one member of each group to share their list with the large group. (Add any of the points below that are relevant but have not been mentioned.) Finish by making a composite list of all the barriers, and display it as a poster on the wall.

A. Multilingualism Barrier

In many places, churches are made up of speakers of many different languages. Church leaders may use a neutral language in an effort to be fair to everyone. They may fear that using the local languages will divide the church. Meanwhile, the people may not understand the deeper spiritual truths being taught because they don't understand the language being used well enough, or it may not be a language of their heart. (See chapters 6, 7, and 8.)

B. Language Attitude Barrier

Minority ethnic groups may consider their language to be inferior. This attitude may have developed due to pressures from the larger society. For example, in some places people may have been punished as children at school for speaking their mother tongue even when playing in the playground. Attitudes learned as a child go very deep. If people feel ashamed of their language, they will not want to use mother-tongue Scriptures. (See chapters 3, 4, and 6.)

C. Church Leader Barrier

If church leaders do not encourage their congregations to use mother-tongue Scriptures, this will present a serious barrier. Church leaders may not use mother-tongue Scriptures for a variety of reasons. They may fear that they will not be able to read the mother tongue aloud properly. Or they may think that the majority language is more "holy." Or they may have received all their theological education in a majority language and not know how to express biblical concepts in their own language. Or they may not be from the same language group and may not have learned the local language. (See chapters 3, 4, 5, 6, 12, and 27.)

If a church has a tradition of using Scripture in a majority language, it may present an enormous barrier to the use of the minority-language Scripture. Changing a long-established tradition is a difficult and slow process. (See chapters 30 and 31.)

D. Community-Ownership Barrier

If churches feel that the translation in the minority language does not belong to them, they may not use it. This can happen where a translation has been done without inviting all the churches that use the language to participate in the translation process. Some denominations may feel that they have been left out if the translation team did not include someone from their church. People who speak a different dialect from the one used in the translation may feel that they have been ignored. The lack of local ownership can be a barrier to people engaging with the minority-language Scripture. (See chapters 2, 6, and 30.)

E. Economic Barrier

Minority-language Scriptures are expensive to publish, so Bible translation agencies subsidize them to make them affordable. But in times of extreme economic distress, even subsidized prices may be too high, and the majority-language Scriptures may be cheaper. Churches may not be willing to be involved in distributing minority-language Scriptures because they do not usually generate a profit. (See chapter 29.)

F. Translation Barrier

While translations of the Bible into any language face challenges, minority-language translations face some additional ones:

- Sometimes people are not interested in the first Bible books that were translated. If people's first exposure to mother-tongue Scripture is negative, they may reject it for the long term. For example, Muslims may reject the entire translation if the first book published is Luke's Gospel. The order in which materials are translated affects Scripture use.

Dialect differences may present barriers in two ways:
- The translation may not have been done in the dialect that the majority of the language group understands.
- Although people might be able to understand the dialect used in the translation, they may not want to use it for social reasons. For example, they may see the speakers of the dialect as enemies or as inferior. (See chapter 2.)

G. Writing System Barrier

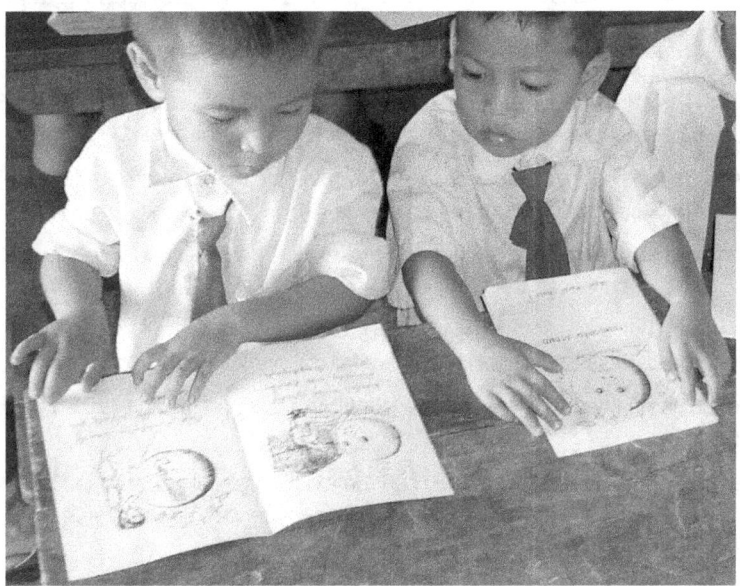

The way a language is written can make it difficult to read. In general, each meaningful sound should be represented by a separate letter in the alphabet. If this isn't done, a language may be hard to read. English is a good example of a language that does not have enough letters. It has five letters for vowels, but there are twenty-one distinct vowel sounds. Tonal languages may need to have the tone marked on certain words or else people will stumble and have to reread sentences.

With enough education in a language, it's possible for people to learn to read it even if it has an inadequate alphabet. However, if little education is available in a language with an inadequate alphabet, most people won't be able to learn to read it.

People may reject the way their language is written even if it is linguistically correct because it doesn't look like the majority language or simply because they don't want their language written that way. Developing a writing system that is easy to use and accepted by the people takes time but is essential for people to read the translated Scripture.

Some languages are harder to read than others. For example, one language in East Democratic Republic of Congo has forty-eight separate symbols for consonants alone. This makes learning to read quite difficult, but it isn't an insurmountable barrier to the use of the Scriptures in that language. (See chapters 27 and 28.)

1. Put the list of barriers you compiled in the first of the previous two exercises in front of the group and read it through again.
2. Ask everyone to choose four barriers they think are the most important in their area. Don't discuss solutions to these problems yet.
3. Read out each item and ask for a show of hands for those who vote for that barrier. It may be good to ask them to shut their eyes before voting, so others don't influence them.
4. Mark the barriers in order of importance to the participants.
5. Do the same thing with the second list of barriers (to engaging with mother-tongue Scriptures).
6. Put these two lists up where they can remain throughout the seminar. Be sure that the barriers considered the most important by most people are covered well during seminar teaching and discussion sessions.

Assignments

1. Design a questionnaire to test the Bible knowledge of the members of your own church. Give the questionnaire to twenty members and see how much people have understood from the sermons and Bible teaching.
2. If you have a church with members who speak the same mother tongue as well as the majority language, carry out a mini survey to compare how well people understand Bible passages in each language.
   (a) Choose two Bible passages with a similar level of difficulty – for example, Mark 10:46–52 and Mark 1:40–45.
   (b) Read the first passage to six people in the majority language, and ask questions to see what they have understood.

(c) Then read the second passage in the mother tongue, and ask questions to see what they have understood.

(d) Then do the same thing the opposite way round with six more people: read the first passage in the mother tongue and the second in the majority language. Compare the results.

(e) Do people understand one language better than the other? Think about what this might mean for church services and Scripture reading.

3. Another way to find out which language communicates best is to teach two subjects with a similar level of difficulty to the same group. The first week, teach in the majority language; and the next week, teach in the mother tongue. Each time give them a quiz to find out how much they have understood. Compare the results.

Readings

Beine, David K. "Views about Scripture: A Key to a Well-Used Book?" *Notes on Sociolinguistics* 6, no. 1 (2001): 5–15. https://scripture-engagement.org/wp-content/uploads/2020/09/Beine-D-2001-Views-about-Scripture.pdf.

Brichoux, Felicia. "Please Don't Speak My Language!" *Notes on Scripture in Use and Language Programs* 18 (1988): 27–37.

Dye, T. Wayne. "The Eight Conditions of Scripture Engagement: Social and Cultural Factors Necessary for Vernacular Bible Translation to Achieve Maximum Effect." 2009. https://scripture-engagement.org/content/eight-conditions-scripture-engagement/.

Hatcher, R. Timothy. "Eight Conditions Questionnaire." https://scripture-engagement.org/questionaire/eight-conditions-scripture-engagement/.

Hill, Margaret. "The Use and Lack of Use of Translated Scriptures." *Scripture in Use Today* 1 (2000): 12–16. https://scripture-engagement.org/content/use-and-lack-use-translated-scriptures/.

Payne, David L. "On Promoting Vernacular Scriptures Where a National Language Translation Is Venerated." *Notes on Literature in Use and Language Programs* 17 (1988): 18–23. https://scripture-engagement.org/content/promoting-vernacular-scriptures-where-national-language-translation-venerated/.

Welser, Marcia. "Assessing Scripture Use Conditions with the Welser Scale." 2009. https://scripture-engagement.org/content/assessing-scripture-use-conditions-welser-scale/.

Wilson, J. D. "What It Takes to Reach People in Oral Cultures." *Evangelical Missions Quarterly* 27, no. 2 (1991): 154–59. https://missionexus.org/what-it-takes-to-reach-people-in-oral-cultures/.

2

Using Appropriate Scripture Products

Introduction

The process of translating Scripture involves many choices. Church leaders need to understand the options and issues involved in translation so that they can make wise choices about Scripture products for their communities. This chapter discusses some of the options and suggests ways of designing relevant Scripture products.

TRANSLATION CHALLENGES IN SANATU

Pastor Simon was at a conference for all the pastors from his denomination in the northern region of their country. On the second day, representatives from Bible translation agencies gave the pastors some news about the ongoing Bible translation projects in ten languages of Sanatu. The pastors listened with great interest and at the end asked many questions.

Pastor Lambo spoke first. "Almost all the people I work with are illiterate; they are also followers of Islam. The translation team has produced a very nice Gospel of Luke with illustrations, but no one wants to buy or read it. If they'd discussed it with us, we would have asked for some Old Testament stories in audio form and certainly no illustrations! Now what can we do?"

Pastor Mark also had a problem. "We have a translation of the whole New Testament in our language, but it was done by a small team of people who didn't consult with us or with the Catholics. They only worked with a small denomination that has four churches. Now the Catholics are saying they want to do their own translation. What can we do?"

Then Pastor Raji shared his problem. "We have a translation in the local language, but a lot of people don't like it. When they compare it with the English or the Kisanu translation, they find that there is a lot added into it. Now they don't trust it."

Finally, Pastor Yeti asked about the Bible in Weze. He said, "This translation was published in 1952. We don't speak that way anymore. When we use this translation in church, people find it hard to understand. What can we do?"

1. Divide into four groups. Have each group take one of the problems expressed by the pastors and discuss solutions.
2. Have you experienced similar problems? If so, discuss them.

1. Working with Church Leaders on Translation Programme Issues

Church leaders decide which Bible translations and Scripture products are used in their churches, so it is very important to involve them in making decisions about translation projects. Since a translation is shared by all the churches in a language community, top leaders from all the major churches represented in the community should be involved. If there are no churches in the area, leaders from churches or missions that are interested in beginning ministry there should be consulted. Translators need to educate these church leaders about translation issues so that they can make informed decisions. The more those who will be using the Scripture products are involved in the decision-making, the more likely it will be that they use those products when they are completed. This section looks at programme issues.

A. Choice of Translators

Churches can be involved in translation projects by supplying translators and reviewers. Ideally, each of the major churches interested in having mother-tongue Scripture should propose three to five candidates who fulfil certain criteria, such as educational level, character qualities, and spiritual engagement. If possible, a Bible translation agency should hold an assessment course for these candidates. The leader of the course can assess the abilities of each participant and give the results to the church leaders. They can make the final selection based on the candidates' performance on the course as well as other factors, such as their character, availability, and so forth. The candidates who are not chosen to be translators can serve as reviewers.

B. Establishing Review Committees

Review committees check the initial drafts of the translation produced by the translation team. They are one of the best ways of establishing local ownership.

Those organizing the translation project should invite all denominations in the area to send representatives to a training course of three to five days. On this course, participants learn basic translation principles and start reviewing some draft translation work to be sure it sounds natural in the language. A number of review committees can be established in major centres of the language area.

2. Working with Church Leaders on Translation Product Issues

Many decisions must be made about the kind of translation product that would be appropriate for a community. These must be considered carefully because the more Scripture products match the community's needs and expectations, the more likely it is they will be used.

A. Selection of Medium

What may seem like lack of interest in Scripture may actually be lack of interest in the medium in which it is presented. Scriptures can be prepared in a variety of print, audio, or audio-visual media. For example, Scripture passages can be printed in short booklets, in diglot versions, in cartoon form, and so on. Audio Scriptures can include local music or drama. Films can be used, for example the *Jesus* film or the Lumo Project. Scripture apps or websites can be developed so that Bible passages can be read or listened to on mobile phones. Clips of Bible videos can be part of apps and websites. Social media platforms can promote Scripture as well or be used for Bible studies. Show church leaders examples of a variety of products to help them decide the kind(s) of product(s) and platform(s) appropriate for their community. Scripture engagement will increase if the medium matches the community's preferences.

B. Selection of Biblical Passages

Certain biblical passages will be more relevant to a community than others, and it is important to start with those that attract people's attention. Examples include the following:

- Passages needed for the evangelistic track of the Bible storying programme (see chapters 16 and 18).
- Passages with high appeal to Muslim communities (see chapter 19).

- For liturgical churches, the gospel passages for the next liturgical year; for example, if you are in Year B, translate the passages for Year C.
- Luke's Gospel: this is appropriate where there are plans to record the *Jesus* film.

C. Selection of the Kind of Translation

Church leaders need to understand the different kinds of Bible translations and their goals. Over time, translators have had different ideas about what made a good translation. Long ago, people thought that they should translate each word of the original text with a word in the receptor language. This is referred to as a word-for-word translation. This approach often led to awkward constructions that were difficult to read. People had to get used to this strange form of their language to understand the meaning. The King James Bible is the nearest to this type of translation in English.

Later, people understood that the meaning of the original needs to be expressed in the receptor language, regardless of whether it takes the same number of words or not. This is referred to as a "dynamic equivalence" translation. The idea was that the effect of the translation should be equivalent to that of the original, and the translation should follow the natural structures of the language. Most Bibles translated into English recently have used this translation model, with some taking more liberties to express the meaning than others.

More recently, people have realized that the author's meaning isn't found in the text alone, but in the interplay of the text with the background information that the text brings to mind. For example, when Matthew wrote that Jesus associated with tax collectors, he expected his audience to know how much Jews despised them. Giving audiences the biblical text in their language is only half the task. If they do not have the background information that the original readers had, they will not understand all of the intended meaning. They may use their own background information and misunderstand the meaning, or they may not have any background information and so understand very little or none of the intended meaning.

Translators can solve this problem of background information in two ways:
- They can keep their translation as close to the original as possible and expect the audience to learn the background information

that is different from their own. This is referred to as a "reference translation."
- They can adapt the text to their audience's context. This makes the text easier for their audience to understand, but every adaptation changes the meaning in some way. This is referred to as a "contextualized translation."

For example, imagine translating "Give us this day our daily bread" for an ethnic group whose staple food is rice. If there is a local word for "bread," translators can use it and then supply in a footnote the information that bread was the staple food for Jews. Or they can translate "Give us this day our daily rice," with the option of including a footnote explaining that the text literally said "bread." This would be easier for their audience to understand immediately using their own background knowledge, but it is not as close to the original meaning. Of course, for cultures that have bread as their staple food, there would be no difficulty translating the verse.

Different kinds of translations are useful for different purposes. A reference translation is best for those who want to know what the original author communicated as exactly as possible and who are willing to learn the original background information. A contextualized translation is better for those who want a translation that is easier to understand without having to learn the original context and who are less concerned about the author's exact meaning. The kind of translation that is done needs to match the audience's needs and expectations. If it doesn't, they will not be satisfied, and the translation may not be used.

1. Have you noticed any differences in translations that you have used?
2. What kind of translation do you think would be best for your church?

> The more closely Scripture products match a community's needs and expectations, the more likely it is they will be used.

D. Understanding Differences in Translations

One thing that can look very different between translations is idioms. In an idiom several words together mean something quite different from the meaning of the individual words. For example, in referring to a rebellious son, someone might say, "He broke his mother's heart." This does not mean that the son literally attacked his mother and smashed her heart with an axe or that her heart fell into pieces like a broken glass, but that he made his mother very sad. Translators need to communicate the meaning of the idiom, not the meaning of the individual words. For example, a translation of this into Ngbaka would say, "He caused that his mother's liver sat down." Many idioms in the Bible come from the Hebrew culture. If these are translated literally, often they make little sense.

Many ideas that were known in biblical times may not be known by certain audiences today – for example, snow, Roman soldiers' armour, the sea, or ships. Translators may have to use a descriptive phrase to translate these concepts – for example, "a large animal called a camel." They may use a more general term – for example, "flowers" instead of "lilies" (Matt 6:28). In certain cases, they may be able to substitute a known object for an unknown one. For example, they may substitute a leopard for a lion in 1 Peter 5:8, since the focus is on a dangerous animal.

In each of the passages below, the King James Version has retained the form of the original text rather than translating the meaning. What do the passages below mean in modern English? You may need to look at the context of each verse.

1. Mark 2:19 – Can the children of the bridechamber fast, while the bridegroom is with them?
2. Acts 18:6 – Your blood *be* upon your own heads; I[1] *am* clean: from[2] henceforth I will go unto the Gentiles.[3]
3. Acts 2:37 – Now when they heard *this*, they were pricked in their heart.
4. Matthew 3:8 – Bring forth therefore fruits meet[4] for repentance.[5]

E. Key Biblical Terms

When a translation project is underway, leaders from all the churches need to be involved in decisions about translating key biblical terms such as Holy Spirit, grace, the cross, repentance, glory, eternal life, God, or angels. A Scripture engagement seminar is a good time to discuss decisions about terms like these.

---

1. ch. 20:26 (Gk.). Comp. Ezek. 3:18, 19, and 33:9.

2. See ch. 28:28.

3. *The Holy Bible: King James Version*, Electronic Edition of the 1900 Authorized Version. (Bellingham, WA: Logos Research Systems, Inc., 2009), Ac 18:6.

4. Or, *answerable to amendment of life*. Acts 26:20.

5. *The Holy Bible: King James Version*, Electronic Edition of the 1900 Authorized Version. (Bellingham, WA: Logos Research Systems, Inc., 2009), Mt 3:8.

The group may have to deal with a number of issues. Certain concepts may be difficult to express in the local language. Or two or more denominations may use different terms for certain biblical terms, and they may not want to change.

It may take a long time, much discussion, and careful study to reach agreement, and this may block progress on the translation. Often a compromise is the only solution. For example, in a large language in the Democratic Republic of Congo, Catholics and Protestants had different terms for "Holy Spirit." They knew they had to have one Bible for everyone to use, so they had to come to an agreement on the term used in the translation. After much discussion, their solution was to take the word for "holy" from the Catholics and the word for "Spirit" from the Protestants! Ten years later, no one remembered the original terms.

If a translation is already published, then it is equally important to help the church leaders understand and learn to use the terms in the translation. A booklet of key biblical terms is a useful tool. (See chapter 7.)

1. Are any terms in your mother-tongue Scriptures still unresolved? What are they?
2. How can the discussion on these terms be moved forward?
3. Pick four biblical terms that cause problems in your language, and discuss what you understand by them. When you are with others from your community, ask them what they understand by these terms.

F. Formatting Options

The format of Scripture products affects whether people buy and use them. Church leaders need to help decide whether the product will be produced in print, in audio format, on the web, in a Scripture app, or in a variety of these media.

If the product is to be printed, then the question of illustrations, colour of cover, layout, and so forth should be decided together. The font needs to be large enough for people to read in poor light. Wide margins around the text will also make it easier to read.

For audio Scripture, packaging is important. Church leaders need to decide about any music that is used. Some communities may want to use local music while others may want to use pre-recorded music provided by recording agencies. Scripture websites and apps should be appealing and include attractive content such as music, video, and culturally pleasing artwork. Content should be shareable on social media platforms.

Think of a new translation of Scripture in your country. This might be a new translation of the Bible in a majority or minority language.

1. Have people accepted the new product?
2. If not, why do they reject it?

3. Working with Church Leaders on Language Issues

Certain language issues affect whether Scripture will be used or not. Here are some of the main areas.

A. The Writing System

Basic questions about the writing system should be settled before work on the translation begins, but often it takes years of discussion before issues are fully resolved. Two areas that may need to be discussed are word boundaries and the spelling of proper names. Scripture engagement seminars may be a good place to discuss these things.

Typically, word boundary issues involve grammar – for example, whether the pronoun is written attached to the verb or separately, or whether compound words are written as one or two words. The way these words are written is a matter of opinion, but people may have very strong opinions! These things need to be discussed thoroughly.

Names need to be spelled the same way throughout Scripture, so it's important to establish rules for spelling them early on in the translation programme. There are over a thousand proper names in the New Testament, and more than six thousand in the Old Testament. If names – especially important names like "Jesus" – are spelled in ways that certain churches do not accept, they may reject the translation altogether.

B. Dialect Issues

The church leaders of an area need to agree about the dialect to be used in their translation. This may require many hours of discussion and possibly help from linguists. After a decision is made, church leaders from dialects other than the one selected need to promote the mother-tongue Scriptures. They can teach people to read the Scriptures aloud using the pronunciation of their own dialect. For example, if the dialect used in the translation has some words beginning with "f," and another dialect pronounces the same words with a "p," people in that dialect should pronounce the words with a "p" when reading aloud. English is a very good example of one written form that serves many oral dialects.

1. Which of the above points have all the churches in your language area discussed already?
2. Which ones have been neglected so far?
3. If the translation project is still underway in your language, do you have any denominations not involved in it? What could you do to bring them into the process?

Assignments

1. Ilea is a translation project leader who wants to get the Bible translated as quickly as possible. He doesn't feel he has time to talk with church leaders about translation issues. List some reasons why he should take time to involve them.
2. Which of the subjects in this chapter do you think are the most important to cover in Scripture engagement seminars in your area? Why?
3. Translate a paragraph that is not Scripture from English into your language. You can use an information leaflet or a paragraph from a magazine or newspaper. Write down the problems you encounter.

Readings

Beekman, John. "Anthropology and the Translation of the New Testament Key Terms." *Notes on Translation* 80 (1980): 32–42. https://scripture-engagement.org/wp-content/uploads/2008/10/Beekman-J-1980-Anthropology-and-NT-Key-Terms.pdf.

Glover, Warren. "Diglot New Testaments: Pros and Cons." *Notes on Scripture Use* 2 (1982): 14–16. Revised 2009. https://scripture-engagement.org/wp-content/uploads/2020/09/Glover-W-1982-Diglot-NTs.pdf.

Gutt, Ernst-August. "From Translation to Effective Communication." *Notes on Translation* 2, no. 1 (1988): 24–40. Revised 2009. https://scripture-engagement.org/wp-content/uploads/2020/09/Gutt-1988-From-Translation-to-Effective-Communication.pdf.

Headland, Edna. *Key Terms of the Bible Course: Student Handbook*. SIL International, 2013. https://scripture-engagement.org/wp-content/uploads/2020/09/Headland-E-2013-Key-Terms-Manual-English.pdf.

Hill, Harriet. *The Bible at Cultural Crossroads*. Manchester: St Jerome Publishing, 2006, 1–12, 53–60.

Hill, Harriet, et al. *Bible Translation Basics*. Dallas: SIL International, 2011.

Margetts, Richard. *Which Audio Player? Listening to the Translated Scriptures: A Review of Today's Digital Audio Players*. 4th ed. 2019. https://scripture-engagement.org/wp-content/uploads/2020/09/Margetts-R-2019-Which-Audio-Player-2019-11-05.pdf.

Simons, Gary. "The Lectionary Approach in Scripture Translation." *The Bible Translator* 35, no. 2 (1984): 216–23. http://www.ubs-translations.org/tbt/1984/02/TBT198402.html?seq=18.

"Social Media for Missions: An Introductory Guide." Mobile Ministry Forum, 2018. https://scripture-engagement.org/content/social-media-missions/.

Titrud, Kermit. "Diglots in the Philippine Context." *Notes on Literature and Language Programs* 42 (1994): 23–28. Revised 2008. https://scripture-engagement.org/wp-content/uploads/2008/11/Titrud-K-1994-Diglots-in-the-Philippine-Context.pdf.

Other Resources

http://www.biblesociety.org – This is the site of the United Bible Societies.

http://www.wycliffe.net – This is the site of Wycliffe International.

http://www.scripture-engagement.org – This website has many helpful articles on Scripture engagement on a variety of topics.

http://www.emdc.online/home – This website has a variety of Scripture engagement resources including online courses and tools to assess Scripture engagement in your community.

https://software.sil.org/scriptureappbuilder/ – Scripture App Builder.

3

Language in the Plan of God

Introduction

Christians need to have access to Scripture in a language they understand and that also speaks to their hearts. When people's mother tongue is a minority language, they may think that it is inferior to majority languages and not appropriate for communicating with God. This chapter looks at what we believe the Bible teaches about language and discusses some ways to raise the status of marginalized languages.

GOD SPEAKS PALAPALA

Read aloud the following paragraph, and then have two people perform this scene.

Pastor Simon came back from his seminar full of new ideas about using Palapala in church services and other church meetings. At the seminar he had been amazed to discover how much better he understood Ephesians in his own language. Now he could see a way to help his congregation improve their understanding of the Bible and of their faith. He looked up who was scheduled to lead the service that Sunday and found that it was Mr. Amani, so he went to visit him to discuss changing the language for the Sunday service.

    Simon: Good morning! How are you and your family?

    Amani: We are all fine. How are you doing, and did you return well from Retali?

    Simon: Yes, everyone is well, and I had no problem on the road.

    Amani: Come and sit down and drink some tea.

    Simon: I've come to tell you about what I learned at the seminar and also to discuss the service for this Sunday. During the seminar, we learned to read Palapala, and I found that reading the New Testament in Palapala really spoke to my heart. Almost everyone who comes to our church is a Palapala like us, so I would like us to use much more of our own language in the service, and also our New Testament readings should be from Palapala. I've brought some copies of the New Testament back with me.

Amani: Well, I find this a shocking idea! Why would we want to use Palapala to talk to God? Using Palapala in church would pollute the place! Surely we should use a respectable language like English! Anyway, you know it's the prayers that are said in English that really work.

Simon: We learned on the seminar that all languages are the same in God's sight and that English – or even Kisanu – isn't any better than Palapala. God made them all, and they are all good and beautiful. Besides, God wants us to understand what he's saying. I thought I understood Ephesians, but when I heard it in Palapala, I realized that I was missing a lot of what Paul was saying.

Amani: Understand? Are we supposed to understand God's word? That would take all of the power out of it!

Simon: I know some religions teach that the less you understand, the more powerful the holy words are, but Christianity is different. God wants us to understand him and know him very well. He is powerful, but he also wants to be very close to us.

Amani: Really? Are you sure?

Simon: Yes. When Jesus came to this world as a baby, he learned to speak the language of his village. If he had been born in a Palapala village, he would have learned Palapala, not Kisanu. When someone speaks our language, we know they understand us and care about us. When I hear Scripture in Palapala, God seems to be one of us, not a foreigner.

Amani: Well, these are all new ideas to me.

What do people in your area believe is the best language to use to communicate with God?

1. Theological Foundations

The use of minority-language Scriptures depends on a good understanding of how God communicates with us. In the next three chapters we will develop a theological foundation for using minority-language Scriptures. Refer to "What We Believe . . ." at the beginning of this book to find these beliefs listed.

A. God Wants to Communicate with Us in a Way We Can Understand

We know that God wants to communicate with us because he sent his Son to this earth to live with people (John 1:14). Jesus spoke the languages of the people he lived with so that they could understand him. He also lived in their culture and communicated in the context of that culture. For example, he spoke about vineyards and fishing and shepherds as well as Roman coins and Old Testament passages.

Today he communicates with us by his word, the Bible. The good news needs to be understandable to those who receive it, which means that it needs to be expressed in a language people know well and identify with. Where their culture is different from that of Jesus's day, they will also need to understand the cultural background information they are missing.

Many religions use magical rituals that ordinary people are not meant to understand. They may say prayers in a foreign language because it seems more holy. The fact that most people do not understand the prayers makes them seem powerful. Christianity is not like that. God wants to communicate with us in a way we can understand.

The Bible teaches that it is important to understand its message. Understanding the Bible leads to power in many areas of life, such as the power to live a righteous life. Understanding the Bible can empower us to live peacefully in community with each other. It can help us have strength to follow God's instructions.

1. Find some passages in the Bible that teach us that God wants us to understand Scripture. (For some answers, see 1. p. 291.)
2. In your culture, do people view religion as something they should understand? Explain.

B. The Incarnation Shows That God Comes to Us and Lives with Us

By using our language, Christ shows that he identifies with us. In many religions, people strive to reach God to be accepted by him. They may consider their way of life too lowly for God. But God doesn't have this attitude. Although he is completely holy, he sent his Son Jesus to live among us in this world. Rather than polluting his divine nature, Jesus healed the brokenness of the people and cultures he touched. When we have Scripture in our language, God is translated into our world. He connects with who we are in our deepest identity.

1. How do people in your community feel about God speaking their mother tongue?
2. Discuss the scene at the beginning of this session. Act out a continuation of it showing what Pastor Simon could say to help Amani understand that God speaks his language.

C. The Diversity of Languages and Cultures Is Part of the Plan of God

Collect leaves and flowers from different plants. Take time to look at them closely and then ask the following questions:
1. How is each one different?
2. What does this teach you about God's creation?

God didn't create just one kind of flower but many. In the same way, God created a variety of languages and cultures. We know that this variety will continue to the end of this world because Revelation 7:9 says that people from every language will stand before God's throne at the end of time: "After this I looked, and there before me was a great multitude that no one could count, from every nation, tribe, people and language, standing before the throne and before the Lamb."

The modern world relies on standardization. For example, in a factory each part of a car needs to be made identically so that all the parts fit together. Creativity is not allowed on the assembly line. People have tried to apply the way factories work to all of life, which leads them to think it is more practical for everyone to speak the same language.

God's creation is not like this. No two people or cultures are the same. God created each one in its own special way. The church is not united by making everyone the same, but by respecting the diversity of its members. Each person and each group bring their praise to God in the way that only they can. If they neglect praising God in their language and using their cultural forms, the variety of praise that Revelation 7:9 speaks of will be incomplete and the church will be the poorer for it.

1. Are there ways in which people in your community are shamed for speaking their mother tongue?
2. Are there ways in which people in your community are honoured when they speak the majority language?
3. How can churches affirm the variety of languages God created?

D. No Language or Culture Is Holier Than Another

1. Show a King James Bible, a majority-language Bible (for example, Swahili), and a Bible or New Testament in a local language. Ask the group: which of these Bibles is the most holy? Discuss the replies briefly without drawing any conclusions.
2. When Jesus was born, four languages were used in Israel:
   - Latin was the prestigious language of the colonial authorities.
   - Greek was the language of education, communication, and trade.
   - Aramaic was the language used in the homes of the Jews.
   - Hebrew was the language of the Jewish Scriptures and religious studies.

   Which language do you think Jesus usually used?

Most scholars think that Jesus usually spoke Aramaic, the language ordinary people used in everyday life. He also knew Hebrew and probably spoke Greek too.

If any language were the best to use to speak to God, it would have been the language that Jesus used, but apart from a few isolated words and phrases, we don't have a record of his original words. We only have translations of them.

> God wants to communicate with us in the language we use in our everyday lives.

On the day of Pentecost, people heard the good news in their own languages (Acts 2:5–11). They probably understood Greek, but God performed this miracle to show that he values the mother tongue, even for people who may know other languages.

In the first centuries of the Western church, the Bible was translated into Latin so that ordinary people could understand it. Over time, people stopped speaking Latin, but the church continued to use the Latin Bible because they thought it was a holy, powerful language. When ordinary people couldn't understand Scripture, the church became weak.

Later on, individuals in Europe began to translate the Bible into their native languages. In England in the late 1300s John Wycliffe decided to translate the Bible into English because he wanted ordinary people to understand it. The church leaders said to Wycliffe, "How can you convey the word of God in a barbaric language like English?" Finally, in the 1500s, the Bible became much more widely available for people in England and Europe to understand in their own languages and for the church to be strengthened.

No language is holier than another. All are capable of expressing the message of the Bible. People are always adding new concepts to their culture and finding ways of expressing them. If people lack a biblical concept, they can learn it and develop a way of expressing it in their language.

1. What language(s) do people in your community think the Bible was written in?
2. What translation(s) of the Bible do people use in your churches? Why do they use these translations? Are they able to understand them well?
3. Do you think English is a barbaric language or a language of high status? Why do you think people's views of English changed over the centuries?
4. When people can't understand Scripture, what effect does this have on their faith and their church?

2. Increasing the Status of a Language

If people have a low view of their language, how can it be improved?
List responses on the board. (Add any of the following points that are relevant but have not been mentioned.)

The following activities can encourage people to feel good about using their own language.

- Teach Christians that God values all languages and cultures.
- Teach Scripture engagement courses in seminaries and other Bible institutions.
- Introduce the language into the school system.
- Associate the language with modern life, such as radio, DVDs, Internet, television, and mobile phones. Have celebrities from the ethnic group perform in it and promote it.
- Publish in the language: New Testaments, Bibles, dictionaries, notices, websites, apps, and so on.
- Hold competitions using the language – reciting Bible memory verses, reading Scripture aloud, singing songs, and so on.

- Teach people to pray in their language. Help them learn useful phrases such as "Lord," "praise God," "Our Father in heaven," "heal," "in Jesus's name," and so on.

1. If your mother tongue is a minority language that is marginalized, which of the above ideas might you like to try to increase its status? What other ideas can you think of?
2. How can churches create an atmosphere of respect for all the languages and cultures represented in their congregations?

Assignments

1. Think of a church you know where many church members speak a minority language. Write a letter to the pastor to convince him or her that it is important to use the Scriptures in the mother tongue of the people.
2. Look up the following passages and write down what they say about the use of the mother tongue: Revelation 7:9–10; Acts 2:5–11; Esther 8:9.
3. Read "What We Believe . . ." at the beginning of this book. Underline the parts you think are the most important for your situation.
4. List five phrases in your language that would be helpful for someone from your area to learn who usually prays in another language.

Readings

Bediako, Kwame. "The Doctrine of Christ and the Significance of Vernacular Terminology." *International Bulletin of Missionary Research* (July 1998): 110–11.
Gottschlich, Bettina. "Transformational Scripture Engagement among the Budu of Congo-Kinshasa." PhD diss., Fuller Theological Seminary, 2012. https://scripture-engagement.org/content/transformational-scripture-engagement-among-budu-congo-kinshasa/.
Grudem, Wayne. "The Perspicuity of Scripture." *Themelios* 34, no. 3 (2009): 288–308. http://themelios.thegospelcoalition.org/article/the-perspicuity-of-scripture.
Lewis, Melvyn Paul, and Gary F. Simons. "Assessing Endangerment: Expanding Fishman's GIDS." *Revue Roumaine de Linguistique* 55, no. 2 (2010). DOI: 10.1017/CBO9780511783364.003. https://www.researchgate.net/publication/228384852_Assessing_endangerment_Expanding_Fishman%27s_GIDS.
McKinney, Carol. "Which Language: Trade or Minority?" *Missiology* 18 (1990): 279–90.
Peterson, Eugene. *Eat This Book: A Conversation in the Art of Spiritual Reading*. Grand Rapids, MI: Eerdmans, 2009.

Quakenbush, J. Stephen, and Gary F. Simons, eds. "Language and Identity in a Multilingual, Migrating World." SIL International, 2019. https://scripture-engagement.org/content/language-identity-multilingual-migrating-world.

Sanneh, Lamin. "Gospel and Culture: Ramifying Effects of Scriptural Translation." In *Bible Translation and the Spread of the Church*, ed. P. Stine, 1–23. Leiden: Brill, 1990.

Slocum, Marianna. "Goal: Vernacular Scriptures in Use." *Notes on Scripture in Use* 15 (1987): 7–11. https://scripture-engagement.org/wp-content/uploads/2020/09/Slocum-M-1987-Paez-Scriptures-in-Use.pdf.

Walls, Andrew. "The Translation Principle in Christian History." In *Bible Translation and the Spread of the Church*, ed. P. Stine, 24–39. Leiden: Brill, 1990.

Other Resources

http://www.worldmap.org/ – The World Missions Atlas Project gives the reader a flavour of the efforts being made to reach people all over the world. It shows the extent of Bible translation. This is a legacy site that documents Mapping Christian Missions between 1995 and 2005.

4

Culture in the Plan of God

Introduction

Sometimes people are told that they need to reject their culture and adopt a "biblical" culture when they become Christians. But this isn't possible. We can't escape our culture. Whether openly or in secret, it remains a part of our life and identity. Rather than trying to escape it, we need to express our faith in and through our culture. When we do, we're able to live out our faith genuinely and in a way that is attractive to others around us.

SAMUEL EVANGELIZES IN ANOTHER CULTURE

Act out this skit.

A Sanatu evangelist, Samuel, is from the south of the country. He has recently returned from being trained by a large Western organization and plans to reach all the lost people in the Palapala area in one month. He has just arrived in Pastor Simon's village, where he finds two men eating. Their names are Ata and Babu. They are sitting on stools under a tree, eating from one pot with their hands.

> Samuel: Hello, hello. I have come to tell you that God loves you. Yes, God, who created the whole world, loves you. He loves everyone in the whole world. He loves Africans, Americans, Chinese, everyone. Yes, God loves you. Do you accept Jesus, his Son, as your saviour?
>
> Ata: Hello. Sit down. Eat.
>
> Samuel: Thank you. (Scowls at the food, almost afraid of it.) As I was saying, do you accept Jesus as your saviour?
>
> Ata (confused, overwhelmed, and wanting to please the visitor): Yes.
>
> Samuel: Praise God! You're Christians now.

Ata (looks surprised, a bit afraid): Yes . . .?

Samuel (suddenly realizing a problem): But why are you eating outside? Christians eat indoors. Now that you are Christians, you'll have to eat your meals inside your house. That's how Christians eat.

Ata: Inside? It's hot and dark in there. There's no room to eat. Here under the mango tree we get the breeze.

Samuel: No, Christians always eat indoors. God wants them to. And where is your cutlery?

Ata: Cutlery?

Samuel: Yes, you know, knife, fork, and spoon. Why on earth are you eating with your hands? That's primitive and pagan. Christians use cutlery when they eat. Here, use this fork.

(Ata tries to get his food to his mouth with a fork. He's clumsy. The food drops off.)

Samuel: Let me help you. We'll have to have fork lessons in this church, I can see. (Finally gets food into Ata's mouth.) And where are your plates? You can't eat from one pot any more. Christians use plates. And they eat at a table. Here, let me show you. (He takes Ata to a table already prepared and sits him down at it. There is a plate, glass, knife, fork, and spoon.) This is how Christians eat. (He models how to eat.)

Ata (bewildered, protests): But . . .

Samuel: And why are you eating with your friend? Where is your wife?

Ata: My wives eat together, I eat with my friends, and the children eat over there together. I'll call my wives.

Samuel: Wives?

Ata (proudly): Yes, I have three wives.

Samuel: Ooh la la! We'll think about that once we finish the cutlery lessons (overcome with how many problems he's encountering). Choose one wife, and eat your meals with her and your children at this table. You'll need to buy a plate, glass, and cutlery for each one. That's the way Christians eat.

Ata: Where am I going to find all that money? What can I do?

Samuel: I've got to go now, but I want you to know that God loves you very much. He really does. He loves you. (Rushes off.)

1. How do you think Ata and Babu felt about God when Samuel left?
2. What problems do you think Samuel had?
3. Is it possible for a person to be fully a part of his or her culture and fully Christian? If so, how?

1. God Created Us to Live in a Culture

God created us to live in a cultural context. A person can't live without a culture any more than a fish can live without water. Culture isn't bad; it's essential for life. Just as the variety of languages is part of God's plan, so is the variety of cultures.

1. What will happen to a fish if it leaves the water?
2. What can happen to people who try to leave their culture or are forced to do so?

2. Christianity Can Be Lived out in Any Culture

Sometimes people think that one culture is better than another culture. This can mean that some people are arrogant and prideful about their culture while people from another culture may feel shame about theirs. However, God made people in every culture and values all cultures.

Are some cultures superior to others? Or does each culture have something unique and wonderful to contribute?

Sometimes people think that all Christians are moving from their heathen past into one "biblical" culture. They think that eventually all Christians around the world will look and act the same, like the early Christians. This concept is not correct. It's not possible, for the simple reason that there is no one biblical culture. The cultural background of nomadic Abraham was very different from that of the Israelites at the time of the kings. In the New Testament, Jews were under a colonial power, Rome, and the culture changed again. Many of the early Christians were Greeks living in yet another culture.

When people refer to the biblical culture, which one do they mean?

The early church had to deal with the question of culture. One issue they faced was whether Greek Christians had to adopt Jewish culture to be saved. Some Jews thought that they did. For example, they thought that Greek males had to be circumcised and obey the Jewish rules about food and the Sabbath. After all, these were the cultural norms given by God in the Old Testament. When this was discussed at the church council in Jerusalem, the apostles decided that Greek believers didn't need to adopt Jewish culture to be Christian (Acts 15). At the same time, Jewish Christians were to continue in their way of life. Each lived out their faith in their cultural context.

3. The Gospel Transforms and Redeems Cultures

Some people feel that if their culture changes, it will be destroyed. They feel that if any part of a culture is replaced with something else, the culture will no longer function. This is true of machines but not of cultures. Cultures change all the time as people respond to changes in their environment.

1. Did any of you become a Christian after the age of twenty?
2. When you became a Christian, did people still recognize you?
3. What was different about you?

When we become Christians, others can still recognize us, but we change as God gradually transforms us into his likeness so that we become all he created us to be. We keep our personal identity. In the same way, we keep our cultural identity as Christians, but God transforms the way we live out our cultures so that we can be all that God created us to be. Christians should be recognizably Manlinke or Teke or Akha but transformed. We should not try to forget our culture but rather keep the good parts of it.

"Therefore, if any one is in Christ, he is a new creation; the old has passed away, behold, the new has come" (2 Cor 5:17 RSV). How do you understand this verse?

Sometimes people think this verse means that we should reject our culture. Actually, this passage is referring to letting go of old prejudices and attitudes, the negative parts of culture. Christians need to work out how to live their Christian faith in their culture. Then their Christian and cultural identities can be integrated into one, and their witness to others within their culture will be much more genuine and appealing.

1. In the past, when the Baju of Nigeria became Christian, they were required to say the following: "I repent: I renounce my culture. I will follow Christ."[1] Do you agree with this? Why or why not?

2. Can you think of one custom or belief in your culture that is compatible with Christianity but is not accepted by the church? Discuss this with others.

4. When the Gospel Is Expressed in Our Mother Tongue, It Penetrates Our Worldview

Show a net, either a real one or an illustration from a publication or drawn on a blackboard, an overhead transparency, or a device. Then place or draw another net over it. Then tell the group, "A language is like a net thrown over reality. Another language is another net. It is rare that the holes in the two nets fall in exactly the same places."[2]

---

1. See McKinney, "Conversion to Christianity," 147–65.
2. Translated into English from *Nouveau Testament Interlinéaire Grec/Français* (Swindon: British and Foreign Bible Society, 1993).

Different cultures put different "nets" on reality. For example, some cultures have one word for both brothers and male cousins, and one word for both fathers and uncles. Others have separate words for these categories. The categories our culture uses are the glasses through which we perceive reality. When the gospel is expressed in our mother tongue, it penetrates our categories, which represent our deepest sense of reality.

5. Important Truths for Different Worldviews

Many of us are used to understanding and expressing the gospel in an individualistic way: "God loves *me* and sent his Son to die for *me*." This is not how the Bible normally explains the gospel, nor is it appropriate for many worldviews around the world. Three main categories of worldviews are honour–shame, power–fear, and innocence–guilt. Individualistic cultures tend to focus on innocence and guilt. Most collectivist cultures contain a combination of honour–shame and power–fear elements as well as a small amount of innocence–guilt. The Bible comes from the Middle East. It was therefore written in a context with honour–shame and power–fear ideas.

In contexts where honour–shame plays a key role, the identity of a person is mainly tied to his or her family, clan, and wider society. People like to stay connected with their family and want their family to take pride in them. They like earning honour for their family rather than for themselves. Those who are old are honoured for their wisdom, and those who are rich are honoured for the help they give to those who work for them and for their generosity to their family. For people with such worldviews, it is as important to be part of a community as it is to have a personal faith. *Belonging* is as important as believing. The most important truth for people in these honour–shame contexts is that Jesus, although shamed when he suffered, was honoured by his resurrection and ascension. After the ascension, he took the highest position of honour at his Father's right-hand side. He shares that honour with us. We are brothers and sisters "in Christ." New believers need to belong to a Christian community that shows loyalty to one another. It is very important for them to understand that they belong to this community through Christ's work on their behalf. A key passage for worldviews containing an honour–shame perspective is Ephesians 2:11–22, part of which is as follows:

> Consequently, you are no longer foreigners and strangers, but fellow citizens with God's people and also members of his household, built on the foundation of the apostles and prophets,

with Christ Jesus himself as the chief cornerstone. In him the whole building is joined together and rises to become a holy temple in the Lord.

People in communities where power–fear is important, on the other hand, are interested in controlling the spirits or gods. Children are often given amulets to wear to protect them from harmful spirits. Sacrifices are made to cleanse their house and make sure that a family's future is happy and nothing bad happens to them. Some of these groups have mediums who are supposed to be able to contact the spirit world for them. These groups often have fortune tellers too. The most important truth for people in contexts where power–fear is the driving force is that Jesus Christ has won the *victory* over all the powers of evil, sin, and death. He has proved this by his resurrection and ascension to the side of his Father. A key passage for people with power–fear worldviews is Ephesians 1:15–23, which contains the following verses:

> . . . his incomparably great power for us who believe. That power is the same as the mighty strength he exerted when he raised Christ from the dead and seated him at his right hand in the heavenly realms, far above all rule and authority, power and dominion, and every name that is invoked, not only in the present age but also in the one to come.

In practice, most worldviews around the world contain elements of both honour–shame and power–fear. They might even have some individualistic innocence–guilt within them, but that isn't the most important part of their worldview. Therefore, explanations of the good news that are based only on an innocence–guilt perspective are not as likely to impact people as much as those that talk about *belonging* and *victory*.

People need to be able to understand and make sense of truths from Scripture. Therefore, it's important that we study the worldview of those we are seeking to reach to make sure we are sharing good news that is both biblical and relevant to them. Also, the way that we serve in these communities needs to be adapted to the context. In a place where most people's background is power–fear, we will want to pray with people for their healing and deliverance. In a place where people are mainly interested in honour–shame, we will want to build a strong community. People learn as much from what we do as from what we say.

Worldview	Worst Thing That Can Happen	Best Thing That Can Happen through Christ
Honour–shame	Be shamed in front of the community, bring shame on family	Be an honourable part of a Christian community
Power–fear	Be controlled by evil spirits or unseen forces	Know and feel that Christ has conquered all the forces of evil
Innocence–guilt	Be overwhelmed by personal sin	Find personal forgiveness for sins

1. What is the most important worldview in your people group (honour–shame, power–fear, or innocence–guilt)?
2. With this worldview in mind, how will you explain the gospel to both believers and unbelievers within your people group?
3. Read Ephesians chapters 1–2. Which parts of Ephesians 1–2 would be most helpful for those in your people group?

6. Christianity Is Expressed Differently in Different Cultures

1. How many of you have kissed your brother in Christ today? Why not? Do you claim to obey the Bible?
2. 1 Peter 5:14 says, "Greet one another with a kiss of love," and Romans 16:16 repeats this command: "Greet one another with a holy kiss." Do you now feel guilty for not kissing your brother today? Why not?

Actions can have different meanings in different cultures. For example:

- *The left hand:* In much of Africa, to give something to someone with the left hand is considered a serious insult. In the UK, no particular meaning is associated with the left hand.
- *Looking someone in the eyes:* This is a sign of respect in many cultures in the West, especially when children are being corrected by their parents. It is a sign of disrespect in many cultures in Africa and Asia.
- *Standing up to speak in a meeting:* This is sign of respect among the Adioukrou of Côte d'Ivoire, but it is a sign of disrespect among the Kouya, also of Côte d'Ivoire.

The Bible Was Written for Everyone but Not to Everyone

Each book of the Bible is addressed to a specific group of people in a specific cultural context. We are "listening in" on words that were originally addressed to someone else. When we apply Scripture to our lives, it is the underlying principle of each passage that we should apply. Three questions help us:

- What did this mean to the people who first received the message?
- What is the underlying principle or the lesson to be learned?
- How can it be applied to our situation?

Cultures change with time so the meaning of an action does not always remain the same. This is true both of modern cultures and of biblical cultures.

1. How were people selected for leadership roles in the Old Testament (1 Sam 10:1)?
2. How were people selected for leadership roles in the New Testament (Acts 1:21–26)?
3. What was the meaning associated with anointing someone with oil in James 5:14?

Choose two of the following passages. Try to find out what each passage meant in its original context. First, discuss the underlying principle communicated in each one. Then propose a way this could be lived out in your culture. (For sample answers, see 2. p.291.)

1. John 13:14–15 – Washing each other's feet.
2. Exodus 23:19 – Don't boil a kid in its mother's milk.
3. 1 Timothy 2:8; 1 Kings 8:22 – Raise your hands to pray.
4. Leviticus 19:13 – Pay wages daily.

7. Christians Are United by Love, Not by Similarity

Two Christians can have different ways of living out their faith and both can be valid (Rom 14:14–16). When Christians from different cultures are together, out of love they should refrain from doing things that may offend others or cause them to lose their faith. For example, when Christians from the West visit certain places in Africa, they should be careful not to use their left hand to greet or to give things to someone. Paul adopted other people's customs in order to be able to bring them to Christ (1 Cor 9:20–22).

What unites Christians is not that they adopt the same customs but that they are united in love (John 17:21) and in their faith in the cross of Jesus Christ (Gal 6:14–15).

Think of an occasion in the past when you have been with people of another culture. Have you done something in a different way out of love for those people?

Assignments

1. Identify a Western practice taught in your church that is confusing, offensive, or has a wrong meaning in your culture.
2. Can we adopt a "biblical Christian" culture today? Give some reasons for your answer.

Readings

Dye, T. Wayne. "Toward a Cross-Cultural Definition of Sin." *Missiology* 4 (1976): 27–41.

Finifrock, Monica, and Albert Kathenya. "Swallowed in His Love: A Look at How the Mother-Tongue Scriptures Shed Light on an Age-Old Rite of Passage among the Tharaka People of Kenya." *Scripture in Use Today* 12 (2006): 3–11. https://scripture-engagement.org/wp-content/uploads/2020/09/Finifrock-Kathenya-2006-Swallowed-in-his-love.pdf.

Georges, Jayson. *The 3D Gospel: Ministry in Guilt, Shame and Fear Cultures.* N.p.: Timē Press, 2014.

Hayward, D. "Measuring Contextualization in Church and Missions." *International Journal of Frontier Missions* 12, no. 3 (1995): 135–38. http://ijfm.org/PDFs_IJFM/12_3_PDFs/05_Hayward.pdf.

McKinney, Carol. "Conversion to Christianity: A Baju Case Study." *Missiology* 22, no. 2 (1994): 147–65.

Nagai, Y. "Being Indigenous as Well as Christian: A Case of Maiwala Christians in Papua New Guinea." *Missiology* 27, no. 3 (1999): 393–402.

Neeley, Paul. "Creating a Farm Blessing Church Service." *Notes on Scripture in Use* 41 (1994): 36–38.

Perry, C. "'Bhai-Tika' and 'Tij Braka': A Case Study in the Contextualization of Two Nepal Festivals." *Missiology* 18, no. 2 (1990): 177–83.

Priest, Robert J. "Missionary Elenctics: Conscience and Culture." *Missiology* 22, no. 3 (1994): 292–315.

Walls, Andrew. "Africa and Christian Identity." *Mission Focus* 4, no. 7 (1978): 11–13.

———. "African Christianity in the History of Religions." In *The Cross-Cultural Process in Christian History*, 116–35. Maryknoll, NY: Orbis, 2002.

———. "The Gospel as Prisoner and Liberator of Culture." In *The Missionary Movement in Christian History: Studies in the Transmission of Faith*, 3–15. Maryknoll, NY: Orbis, 1996.

5

Mother-Tongue Scripture Use and Church Growth

Introduction

The rapid spread of Christianity in many parts of the world has all too often resulted in what has been called "Christianity a mile long and an inch deep." People may have accepted Christ as their Lord and saviour, but they may not know much about him or live in ways that honour him. The amount of Scripture churches use and the language of the Scriptures they use may contribute to this situation. If people can't read or hear Scripture in a language they understand, their spiritual growth will suffer. This chapter looks at the role language plays in helping Christians grow in their faith and suggests ways to increase the amount of Scripture used in churches.

REACHING THE WEZE

The Weze people live near the area where Pastor Simon works. They number about eighty thousand, and they have been very resistant to the gospel. The only church in the area belongs to Pastor Simon's denomination. The Bible Society has started a translation project in Weze. Genesis, Exodus, and Luke are available, but few people are using them.

One week, Pastor Simon went to a regional church leaders' meeting with Yeti, the pastor of the Weze church. During the meetings, the leaders discussed reaching unreached people groups. Everyone agreed that the Weze was an unreached people group because less than 2 percent of the population considered themselves Christians of any type. They discussed at great length ways of evangelizing the Weze.

Finally Pastor Yeti told a sad story. He said, "Last year there was a big evangelistic campaign in the area, and a well-known evangelist from abroad conducted the meetings. Many people went along out of curiosity, and some came forward at the end to say that they wanted to follow Christ. The evangelist and his team gave them very nice English Bibles, but hardly anyone understood English, and most didn't know how to read. Now, one year later, a few of those people are in my church, but many lost interest after the campaign was over. I think now it will be harder to get them to come to any other evangelistic meetings."

Yeti continued, "My church services are in Kisanu, and I worry that at least half the congregation do not really understand what is being said. Several of the new converts have been attracted away from my church to a new cult that has just come into the area. What can I do?"

That evening Pastor Simon had a long chat with Yeti and told him about his experiences when he changed from using Kisanu to Palapala and how everyone understood the service now. Yeti went home with a lot to think and pray about.

1. What effect has the language(s) used in your church had on the success or failure of its ministry?
2. Have you ever tried to use different languages for different parts of your church service?

1. The Role of Language in Church Growth

If mother-tongue Scriptures are to be used, church leaders need to understand their importance and model their use. Often someone in a language group needs to champion this cause and share the vision with the other church leaders.

A. Christians Cannot Mature in Their Faith Unless They Have Access to the Bible in a Language They Understand

An important part of our growth as Christians comes by knowing God's word. It is our spiritual food that makes our faith grow strong. For example, when the Kasena New Testament in Ghana was published in the 1980s, people were finally able to understand God's word and the church grew both in faith and in numbers.[1]

In some places, Christians hear only a few verses of the Bible on Sunday read by the pastor in a language they barely understand. This isn't enough to make them strong in their faith, and they are much more likely to follow false teaching of sects or leave the church altogether.

Sometimes, even though people do not understand the majority language well, they like it more than their mother tongue. In this case, either they need help to learn the majority language better, or they need to value their mother

---

1. See Howell, *Religious Itinerary of a Ghanaian People*, 178–81.

tongue more. To grow as Christians, they need to hear or read God's word in a language they understand well and like to use.

B. No Church Can Last Long without Scripture in a Language the People Understand

Missionaries who went to China in the early 1900s translated the Bible into Chinese. In 1951, the Communists chased out all the missionaries, but in the twenty years that followed, the church multiplied 500 percent! There were 4 million Christians in China in 1951. Today it is estimated that there are over 100 million Christians in China. The people's faith was sustained by the Bible in their language, even through times of persecution.

By contrast, the northern part of Africa was the centre of Christianity in the first few centuries AD. The church leaders used Latin and didn't translate into the local languages of Punic and Berber, even though only the very educated church members knew Latin. When Islam swept across that part of Africa from AD 600 to 900, the church virtually disappeared. The lack of Scriptures in the local languages played a significant role in the church's downfall. By contrast, the churches in Egypt and Ethiopia experienced many of the same pressures, but they had Scripture in their languages and have survived to this day.[2]

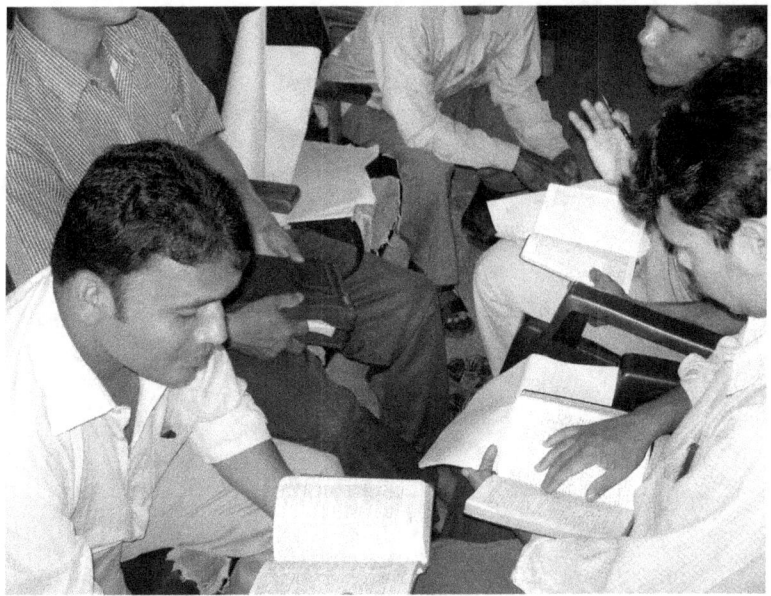

---

2. See Shenk, "Demise of the Church in North Africa," 31–154.

C. Church Leaders Must See That All Members of Their Congregations, Regardless of Their Social Class, Gender, or Age, Receive Spiritual Food in a Language They Understand Well

Imagine a typical family that comes to your church on Sunday morning. Mr. Gambu, the father, has an office job at the local hospital. His wife, Mary, went to school for six years but has forgotten most of what she learned there. Her mother is living with them and speaks very little of the majority language. They have six children ranging from Caroline, who is just finishing secondary school, to little Emmanuel, who is five years old.

Imagine them walking out of the church at the end of the service. What spiritual food have they received? If the whole service and the readings were in the majority language, then Mr. Gambu and the two oldest children have had a good meal, his wife has had a little snack, and the grandmother and the younger children have had no spiritual food at all!

1. Which group in your church is most neglected?
2. How can they be fed spiritually?

D. The More Church Leaders Encourage People to Use the Scriptures in Their Mother Tongue, the More the Members Will Use Them

Act out this scene.

Some church members are sitting in a room when a young man rushes in with Scripture booklets in a local language and says how great they are. He tries to sell copies, but the people don't take much notice of him and don't buy his booklets. Then the head pastor arrives wearing a long robe and says much the same thing. Everyone promptly buys the booklets and tries to read them.

1. How can pastors help or hinder people using Scripture in their language?
2. Why might pastors be afraid or unwilling to use the mother-tongue Scriptures in church? (After taking the group's responses, add any of the reasons below that have not been mentioned.)
3. Finally, discuss possible solutions to the problems you have identified.

Pastors may be afraid to use their mother tongue in church for many different reasons.

- They may be afraid to read aloud in their own language in church because they can't read it fluently.

- They may feel that people will look up to them more if they use the majority language.
- They may not know how to express biblical concepts in the mother tongue.
- They may belong to a different language group from that of their congregation.
- They don't like change of any sort.

2. Increasing Scripture Use in Church Meetings

Church leaders need to offer their members generous amounts of Scripture during their Sunday services and other weekly, monthly, or yearly meetings. Churches vary in their traditions in this regard. Liturgical churches have a fixed order of readings for the services throughout the year. In non-liturgical churches, preachers choose freely the Scripture passage they use each week. Either method can work well to provide people with Scripture.

1. How much Scripture is read or heard in the average Sunday service in your churches?
2. How much Scripture is read or heard in other meetings during the week?
3. In what other ways is Scripture communicated in your church (drama, Bible stories, Scripture songs)?
4. Have each church group report back to the whole group. Help them to see the advantages and disadvantages of their present practices.

How can we help our congregations to hear more Scripture during the church service?

Assignments

1. Have some of your church members left the church or joined sects? What do you think you could do to stop this?
2. Look at the history of a church in your area. Trace its growth and the languages it has used through the years.

Readings

Howell, Allison M. *The Religious Itinerary of a Ghanaian People: The Kasena and the Christian Gospel*. Achimota, Ghana: Africa Christian Press, 2001, 178–81.

Senavoe, Juliana. "The Effects of Non-Translation of the Scriptures among the Guan of Southern Ghana: Some Preliminary Findings." *Journal of African Christian Thought* 5, no. 1 (2002): 48–60.

Shenk, C. E. "The Demise of the Church in North Africa and Nubia and Its Survival in Egypt and Ethiopia: A Question of Contextualization?" *Missiology* 21, no. 2 (1993): 31–154.

Tripp, Martha D. "Encouraging Scripture Use among the Amuesha." *Notes on Scripture in Use* 8 (1984): 15–21. https://scripture-engagement.org/content/encouraging-scripture-use-among-amuesha.

Woodward, Mark. "The Impact of Vernacular Scriptures: Assessing the Benefit of Local Language Scriptures among the Bilingual Malila and Nyiha Communities of Tanzania." MA diss., Redcliffe College, UK, 2014. https://scripture-engagement.org/content/impact-vernacular-scriptures/.

Other Resources

www.emdc.online – A Scripture engagement website with many courses and other resources.

www.scripture-engagement.org – A website with many articles and resources.

6

Using Scripture in Multilingual Churches

Introduction

Using Scripture in a local language works wonderfully in communities where everyone uses that language as their mother tongue, but more and more communities and churches are multilingual. Does this mean that churches must abandon Scriptures in local languages in favour of those in majority languages? This chapter addresses the issue of language use in multilingual churches.

JOHN MARK'S MULTILINGUAL CHURCH

Pastor Simon was travelling again and arrived in a small Palapala village right on the edge of the language area. The Catholic catechist Lambo had asked him to visit John Mark, one of the new catechists in his area. Lambo had told Pastor Simon that John Mark was having problems in his church and could do with some help.

John Mark was very happy to see Pastor Simon, and they discussed all sorts of things. Eventually they talked about the languages they used in church services and meetings. John Mark said, "Lambo has been talking to me for months about using Palapala in church. The bishop is also telling us that the Sunday Mass should be in the language of the people. I attended a seminar last year, and I know how to read it, but here we are having some big problems.

"My big question is, how do we keep the unity of the church and yet feed the people spiritually in a language they understand well? As I was telling you, we already have problems with divisions within the church. There is a small but influential group of people from a neighbouring group, the Weze. They understand Palapala, but if I conducted the service in it, they would feel that I was showing favouritism to my people and dividing the church. They would rather continue to use Kisanu because it's neutral for all of us. Then there is the local headmaster and a couple of other families from the south who don't understand Palapala at all. On the other hand, at least thirty people in the congregation do not understand the service when we have it in Kisanu. So what should I do?"

1. What would you say to John Mark?
2. Do you have similar issues in your area?

1. Multilingualism

How many languages do you speak?
As communities become more and more multilingual, so does the church. Church leaders need to understand multilingualism so that they can communicate the gospel effectively.

READ ABOUT KOFFI AND NOGBOU

Koffi grew up in a small village speaking his mother tongue, Palapala. At school, he learned English. Now he uses English at his job in a government office, as well as at home. Little by little, he is forgetting Palapala.

Nogbou grew up with Koffi in the same village. Like Koffi, he learned English in school and now uses it at his work. When he finishes work and relaxes with friends or family, he prefers to use his mother tongue. He continues to speak both languages well.

1. Which case do you think is more likely to occur in your area? Why?
2. Why do you think Nogbou still uses his mother tongue at home and with friends?

A. Using Different Languages in Different Contexts

In multilingual societies, people use different languages in different settings and for different purposes. In some cases, like Koffi's, people gradually abandon one language in favour of another. In other cases, like Nogbou's, people use a majority language in formal situations, such as in offices or schools, and their mother tongue in more intimate situations, such as with family and friends. This is referred to as "diglossia," a situation in which a majority language and a mother tongue can continue to be spoken for centuries without one being lost at the expense of the other.

A quick way to find out if people are abandoning their language is to listen to the language children use at home and when they play together. If most children no longer speak their parents' language, it is in danger of dying out. Within a generation, it may no longer be the language of the ethnic group. If children continue to learn and use their parents' language, even though many people are able to speak the majority language as well, it is not in danger of dying out.

B. The Two Functions of Language

Language has two functions:
- It allows people to communicate with others.
- It allows people to identify with a social group.

When Jesus came to earth, he spoke the language of the people he lived with. This allowed him both to communicate with them and to identify with them. Languages are like tools. Just as people use different tools for different tasks, people may use different languages to accomplish different goals. They want to use the most effective and most appropriate language for the situation.

Our choice of language also shows with whom we want to identify. In the past, Bible translation organizations determined where separate translations were needed by measuring whether people in one area could understand a text recorded in another area. Now they realize that people's attitude towards a language is as important as their ability to understand it. If people want to identify with a culture, they will want to use its language. If they don't like a culture, they won't use its language.

READ JAMES'S STORY

James grew up in a village where his mother tongue was used all the time and most people only knew a bit of English. He was bright and learned to speak English well at school. While he was away at secondary school, he became serious about his faith in Jesus and began the process of becoming a lay preacher.

The New Testament had been translated into his language, but he hadn't taken the time to learn to read it. When he returned to his village for the school holidays, the church elders asked him to preach the very first Sunday. He was delighted and prepared with great care. The congregation was made up of villagers: older men and women, and many children who were either too young for school or simply didn't go. The service was conducted in the mother tongue, but when James preached, he used English and had someone interpret his message.

1. What language would have been easiest for James's audience to understand?
2. Why do you think James preached in English?
3. With whom did James want to identify?

4. When you hear a stranger speaking your language, how does it affect your relationship with that person?
5. In many churches, the only part of the service that is conducted in the mother tongue is the announcements. Why might this be? What does this indicate?

2. Language Policy in Your Church

Every organization has a set of established practices about the language(s) it uses. This is known as its language policy. Sometimes language policies are stated explicitly, as in schools and offices, but sometimes they can only be observed, as in many churches or homes. Here is an example of a church language policy from a denomination in Burkina Faso.

> We will encourage the use of translations in local languages in all the churches to include:
> - The reading of the Bible in local languages in the church services and prayer meetings.
> - Bible studies in the local languages.
> - Reading of Scripture in local languages when visiting the sick and the elderly.
>
> We will prepare Bible school students to use Scriptures in local languages by:
> - Teaching the system the government has established to write the extra letters needed by local languages.
> - Teaching students to read and write proficiently in their own languages.

Churches need to be sure that their language policy allows all their members to grow in their faith. No one should leave church spiritually hungry. Here are some principles that can help churches to address the issues of multilingualism.

- A church must recognize its multi-ethnic composition. Since ethnic differences among people can lead to tension and violence, the church may be tempted to establish its unity by ignoring such differences. Pastors who do this often use majority-language

Scriptures. This often brings a superficial unity and doesn't resolve ethnic tensions which may continue below the surface. Churches cannot grow if they ignore their multi-ethnic composition. Rather than ignoring these differences, the church needs to address them and meet the needs of each ethnic group within the congregation. Each group must have a way to participate in the life of the church.

- A church must value its multi-ethnic composition and lead every ethnic group to appreciate the others. This goes beyond simply tolerating one another.
- A church must recognize and rejoice in its multi-ethnic unity in Christ. Jesus spoke of our diversity in our unity when he said, "I have other sheep that are not of this sheepfold. I must bring them also. They too will listen to my voice, and there shall be one flock and one shepherd" (John 10:16).[1]

The church can have a prophetic voice in the world by celebrating its diversity and demonstrating that, in Christ, differences do not lead to divisions and violence. If Christians cannot love one another across ethnic boundaries, who can?

1. Church leaders often find it hard to keep the balance between creating a sense of unity between Christians from different languages and ensuring that all members are being fed spiritually in a language they understand well. In the churches of your denomination, which of these two do you think is the most neglected? Explain why you think this is the case.

2. Read James 2:1–4, 9. Make up short drama scenes of a church welcoming a wealthy visitor who does not speak the local language. Have some groups show a good way to welcome the visitor and meet the needs of the congregation, and other groups show a negative way that leaves most of the people without being fed spiritually. Present these to the whole group at a convenient time.

> No one should leave church spiritually hungry.

---

1. See Tippett, "Dynamics of the Bicultural Church," 360–70.

50 Translating the Bible into Action

The languages used in your church reflect its language policy, even if it isn't stated explicitly. Divide into church groups, and fill out the following form to discover your church's language(s) policy.

Name of church: _____		
Language(s) spoken by people in the congregation: _____		
What languages are normally used in the following situations? If there are times when other languages are used, note these.		
Sunday service	**Monolingual context**	**Multilingual situation**
Bible reading		
Liturgy		
Preaching		
Announcements		
Songs		
Other activities		
Bible studies		
Prayer meetings		
Youth meetings		
Sunday school		
Other		

Now discuss these questions:

1. What languages are represented in your churches?
2. Does your church meet the needs of each ethnic group represented in the congregation?
3. Does your church maintain the unity of the congregation?
4. What changes would you recommend?
5. How does your church decide where to assign pastors (priests) and evangelists?
    (a) It assigns them to areas where they speak the language, when possible.
    (b) It assigns them to areas without thinking about language issues.
    (c) It intentionally assigns them outside the area where their language is spoken.
    (d) It encourages them to learn the local language if they do not already speak it.
    (e) Other?
6. Does your church require leaders to be able to read their mother tongue?

7. If a translation programme is underway, is the church involved in it in some way? If so, how is it involved? If not, how could it be?
8. How can your church welcome an important guest who doesn't speak the local language and still feed the rest of the congregation?

3. Dual-Language Bible Studies / Listening Groups

Many multilinguals like to use words from all of the languages they speak. This helps them understand more and express themselves well. Dual-language Bible studies follow this natural pattern. In a dual-language Bible study, the group reads the Bible passage or listens to it in both the majority language and the local language. The members understand the Bible passage better this way. They discuss the passage in whichever language or mix of languages they like. This helps them apply it more deeply to their lives.

Dual-language Bible studies work best if everyone in the group knows both languages. If there are monolingual people in the group, this can cause difficulties. The monolinguals don't understand everything that is being said and sometimes ask for interpretation. When arranging a dual-language Bible study, try to make sure that all the members know both languages.

Assignment

Imagine that a leader in your church feels that using local languages in the church service will increase ethnic tension and divide the church. Write a letter to this leader telling him or her if you agree or disagree, and explain how you feel the church can maintain its unity while meeting the spiritual needs of all the members.

Readings

Fast, Anicka. "Managing Linguistic Diversity in the Church: Language Ideological Contestation within a Shared Moral Framework in South-Western Burkina Faso." *Language Documentation and Description* 6 (2009): 161–212.

Hanawalt, C., B. Varenkamp, C. Lahn, and D. Eberhard. *A Guide for Planning the Future of Our Language*. Dallas: SIL International, 2016.

Harris, Sue. A. "Why Compete? Creating New Functions for Traditional-Language Literature Use." *Notes on Sociolinguistics* 2, no. 4 (1997): 181–87. http://www.scripture-engagement.org/content/why-compete-creating-new-functions-use-new-testament.

Hatcher, Timothy, and Sangsok Son. "Translanguaging: Leveraging Multilingualism for Scripture Engagement." *The Bible Translator*, 2021.

Jackson, Amy. "Small Groups in a Bilingual Church." SmallGroups.com. 2014. https://www.smallgroups.com/articles/2014/small-groups-in-bilingual-church.html.

Lewis, Melvyn, and Gary Simons. "Assessing Endangerment: Expanding Fishman's GIDS." *Revue Roumaine de Linguistique* 55, no. 2 (2010). DOI: 10.1017/CBO9780511783364.003. https://www.researchgate.net/publication/228384852_Assessing_endangerment_Expanding_Fishman%27s_GIDS.

Lewis, M. Paul, Gary F. Simons, and G. Richard Tucker. *Sustaining Language Use: Perspectives on Community-Based Language Development.* Dallas: SIL International, 2016.

Ommani, John L. "Engaging African Multilingualism with Scripture." 2021. https://scripture-engagement.org/content/engaging-african-multilingualism-with-scripture.

Son, Sangsok. "Translanguaging, Identity, and Education in Our Multilingual World." In *Language and Identity in a Multilingual, Migrating World*, eds. J. Stephen Quakenbush and Gary F. Simons, 123–42. N.p.: Pike Centre/SIL International, 2019.

Tippett, Alan R. "The Dynamics of the Bicultural Church." In *Introduction to Missiology*, 360–70. Pasadena, CA: William Carey, 1987.

Trudell, Joel. "Bible Translation and Social Literacies among Four Nso' Churches in Cameroon: An Ethnographic Study." PhD diss., University of Edinburgh, 2004.

Other Resources

A long but good example of a language policy is that of the Catholic Church: http://www.vatican.va/roman_curia/congregations/ccdds/documents/rc_con_ccdds_doc_20010507_liturgiam-authenticam_en.html

This site has materials about multilingualism. Some are in other major languages in addition to English

https://missionexus.org/sil-international-takes-a-serious-look-at-multilingualism-and-migration/

7

Helping Interpreters Perform Well

Introduction

In multilingual churches, there will always be a need for good oral interpretation. Visiting pastors who do not speak the local language want what they say to be communicated clearly and correctly. As multilingualism increases, the role of the interpreter will also increase. This chapter discusses how to help interpreters do their job well.

INTERPRETATION GONE WRONG

One month, Pastor Simon was asked to make a pastoral visit to a new church in a large town. It was in the Palapala area, but this town had attracted people from all over Sanatu because it had some large plantations, a bottling factory, and a number of secondary schools. Pastor Simon arrived on a Saturday and stayed in the home of the young pastor, Thomas. He was invited to preach the next day at the main Sunday service. Thomas explained that the sermon had to be in Kisanu because many of the people in the church were from other areas and didn't understand Palapala. They had interpreters who translated the readings, the announcements, and the sermon into Palapala.

The next morning when the church service was about to begin, Pastor Simon saw Thomas running around trying to find someone. Pastor Simon asked what the problem was, and Thomas explained he was having difficulty finding interpreters. In the end he found a couple of young men who were willing to help. The service began with a couple of hymns in Kisanu, and then some short songs in Palapala using local music. Pastor Simon was amused to see how everyone seemed to wake up when they sang in Palapala!

The Scripture reading was taken from Galatians 5. A deacon read the passage aloud from the Kisanu Bible, then the interpreter stood up to interpret. "Wait a minute!" thought Pastor Simon. "Why aren't they using the printed New Testament in Palapala?"

As the interpreter spoke, Pastor Simon became more and more agitated. They came to the passage that says, "The acts of the flesh are obvious: sexual immorality, impurity and debauchery; idolatry and witchcraft." The interpreter simply said, "We do bad things like bad sex and other bad things," rather than listing the different sins in the passage. Later on he interpreted "will not inherit the kingdom of God" as "will not get lots of good things." By this time, Pastor Simon was wondering how well his sermon would be interpreted.

When it was time for the sermon, the first thing Pastor Simon did was to read Galatians 5 in both Palapala and Kisanu. Then he tried very hard to speak in short sentences and to keep his Kisanu clear. This helped the young man interpreting to some extent, but he still didn't interpret some things correctly, especially when Pastor Simon used biblical terms such as "save," "temple," or "apostle." That night, Pastor Simon and Thomas had a long discussion about the whole problem of interpretation and how Thomas could help his interpreters do a better job.

1. When do you think interpreters should be used? When should they not be used?
2. What advice would you give to Pastor Thomas about the choice, training, and preparation of interpreters?
3. Share some experiences of people making mistakes when doing oral interpretation of Scripture or sermons.

1. Types of Interpretation

In multilingual churches, the best way for everyone to receive spiritual nourishment from the service may be to have the main part of the service in the majority language and have the service interpreted into one or more of the local languages. If printed Scriptures are available in the local language, the interpreter should read them. If the interpreter is not literate, someone else should read the passage. If no one can read the mother tongue, either the Scriptures need to be recorded so people can listen to them, or the community needs to start literacy courses.

1. What kinds of interpretation have you observed?
2. What are the advantages and disadvantages of each kind?

A. Translation Sentence by Sentence

Sentence-by-sentence translation is probably the most common form of interpretation. The speaker and the interpreter stand at the front of the church side by side. After each sentence the speaker pauses, allowing the interpreter to provide a translation. The disadvantage of this type of interpretation is that it takes up a lot of time. If the pastor preaches for thirty minutes, then with interpretation the sermon will take an hour! It takes even longer if it is interpreted into more than one language.

B. Simultaneous Translation

Simultaneous translation is the most difficult sort of interpretation. While the main speaker is talking, the interpreter listens and at the same time speaks the message in the second language. This takes practice! In some situations, an interpreter whispers to a group of people at the back of the church. In other situations, the interpreter sits in a booth equipped with headphones and a microphone and those needing the translation hear it by using headphones. The disadvantage of this type of interpretation is that interpreters need to be very skilled to interpret what has just been said while still listening to what is being said now.

C. Summary Translation

Sometimes the sermon or other information may be followed by a summary in a second language. This may be done by the speaker or by an interpreter. The disadvantage of this type of interpretation is that the speakers of the second language will not get as much from a summary of the sermon as those who understand the full sermon. In addition, giving a summary that includes all the main points requires a fair degree of skill.

1. In your own church, which methods of interpretation have been used? Do you think any other methods should be used in certain situations?
2. Some churches have found that, rather than having interpretation into two or more languages, it is better to have separate services on the Sunday morning – for example, an 8 a.m. English service with interpretation into Hausa and a 10 a.m. service in Fulani. Discuss if this would be helpful in your church.
3. How do you choose interpreters?

2. Choosing Interpreters

In the story at the beginning of the chapter, Pastor Thomas was trying to find interpreters at the last minute. This does not normally produce good results. Churches should choose and train a group of interpreters, so they are well prepared. Someone who wants to do this work should have the following abilities:

- A good level of understanding of both languages.
- Good verbal ability: some people are able to express themselves better than others. Often people who are known to be good storytellers have good verbal ability and a wide vocabulary. Women are often stronger in this area than men.
- A good Christian lifestyle: interpreters are seen as co-preachers with the main speaker, so it is not good to have someone who is known to be living an immoral life filling this role.
- Literacy in both languages involved in the interpretation: it is helpful if the person chosen can already read and write both languages. However, this is not as important as the first three abilities because people can learn to read and write if they are motivated to do so.

1. What types of people usually serve as interpreters in your church?
2. Can you think of others who might become interpreters?
3. What do you think is the most important qualification of a good interpreter?

> Churches should choose and train a group of interpreters.

3. Training Interpreters

Once identified, interpreters need to be trained in basic principles of interpretation and in handling concepts that are difficult or not well known. If a translation programme is underway, interpreters and reviewers can be trained together in basic translation principles using lessons from a translation manual.

A. Knowledge of Basic Translation Principles

Interpreters need to understand the following:

- How communication works and the important role that context plays. (See chapter 10.)
- That translation doesn't involve translating one word exactly for another word. Interpreters learn this best by doing exercises where they are required to express an idea in several different ways. (See chapter 2.)
- The differences between oral and written translations. A good interpreter uses the normal oral forms of the language and does not sound like a book!

B. Difficult and Unknown Concepts

Translators and church leaders have put a great deal of study, thought, and discussion into the selection of the terms used in their translation. If a language already has a translation of Scripture, interpreters should use the terms that have been used in it for key concepts. A booklet listing these terms can be an enormous help to interpreters. It should give the following information for each one:

- The term in the majority language.
- The term translated into the local language.
- An explanation of its meaning in Scripture, including any useful background information.

> *An example of text from a booklet explaining difficult biblical concepts*
>
> Priest – *ngangga 'da Gale*
> Used to describe priests in the Bible. This was a group of people that first came into being at the time of Moses. The first priest was Aaron. One of their main tasks was to sacrifice animals to God. Do not confuse this term with *sango* – used for modern-day Catholic priests.
>
> righteous – *wi bolo zu*
> This term describes a person who is upright before God and obeys his commandments – literally, a straight head.
>
> Temple – *ga toa da Gale*
> Literally this means the big house of God. This is the phrase used for the big building in Jerusalem where the priests offered sacrifices to God. The temple mentioned in Luke had been built by King Herod.

Sometimes interpreters have to translate concepts that the audience does not know. The way the interpreter translates the term depends on what the speaker said. For example, supposing that you live in a tropical climate, how would you translate "snow"? If it is used as a figure of speech such as "Your sins will be as white as snow," you might translate it as "completely cleansed." On the other hand, if a visiting speaker starts by saying, "When I left my home country, it was snowing," you can say that it was very cold.

 Do you have any helps like this for interpreters? If not, who could prepare them?

C. Knowing the Important Things to Communicate

Interpreters can't translate exactly what the speaker says because usually there isn't enough time to do so, and no interpreter, however good, remembers every detail of what was said. Interpreters need to recognize what is most important and only translate that.

Interpreters also need to know their audience. They may need to act as cultural mediators, providing background information that they know their audience needs. For example, if a preacher casually speaks about Solomon's wisdom without explaining who Solomon was, a good interpreter may decide to slip in a sentence quickly saying, "Solomon was a king who received special wisdom from God after he prayed for it."

When people have studied good interpreters, they have found that they have a speech style that is different from normal speech. Often good interpreters repeat nouns more and use pronouns less. They also use linking words more than normal. Interpreters can be encouraged to do these things to help their audience understand them more easily.

D. Opportunities for Practice

The best way to train interpreters is to have them listen to good examples and then start to interpret in a non-threatening situation where they can receive feedback. New interpreters should start interpreting for a small group rather than in a church service. They should begin by translating into their own tongue from another language because this is usually easier than translating into another language.

Divide into groups of three people who all speak the same two languages. Have one person give a short talk about a subject set by the seminar leader – for example, public transport in the country, or how to run a Sunday school. Have the second person translate into the second language sentence by sentence. Have the third person make notes on the quality of the translation. After ten minutes, have the note-taker share his or her observations with the interpreter, and then have the group switch roles and repeat the exercise.

4. Making Interpretation Easier

What are some ways speakers can help interpreters?
Get feedback from the group (and then mention any of the points below that haven't already been stated).

Churches can do the following things to help interpreters:
- Post a list in the church so that interpreters know beforehand when it is their turn to serve.
- Meet with interpreters before the service and go over an outline of the talk. Check that they have all the Scripture portions needed.
- Show your appreciation for the interpreters. It is good to acknowledge their hard work in front of the whole church from time to time.

Speakers can do the following things to help interpreters:
- Speak in short, complete sentences with simple structures.

- Wait for the interpreter to finish before starting the next sentence.
- Avoid alliteration, such as "I am going to talk to you about three 'Ss' – saved, sanctified, and sent."
- Avoid any information that depends on a play on words, such as "Today we will look at the four 'for's' found at the beginning of Romans 8."
- Avoid cultural references that are not understood by part of the audience, such as "Tonight, as I looked at the big jumbo jet . . ."

Assignments

1. If you speak more than one language, observe two situations where interpreters are translating between them. Write about the positive and negative qualities of the interpreters you observe.
2. Think about a multilingual church that you know. When do you think it is best to divide people into ethnic groups for meetings, and when should interpreters be used?
3. Take a story in English and translate it orally into another language. Make a recording of your translation. Play it back sentence by sentence and decide how you could improve.

Readings

Kalik, Jill. "Spontaneous Translators: Notes and Queries." *Scripture in Use Today* 5: 32–37.

8

Multi-Ethnic Churches

Introduction

Multilingual churches are generally multi-ethnic churches because people who speak different languages usually represent different cultures. This can lead to tension because, consciously or subconsciously, people tend to think their culture's way of doing things is the right way, and they tend to judge others by their own standards. Pastors in multi-ethnic churches need to help church members identify their ethnocentrism and understand one another better.

TENSIONS BETWEEN THE MBANI AND THE PALAPALA

Pastor Simon was asked by his church office to visit a church in his denomination that was about 80 kilometres south of his village. It was still in the area where Palapala was spoken but was very near to the southern language of Mbani. The Mbani people were quite different from the Palapala. They were cattle herders while the Palapala people were farmers. There seemed to be a serious problem between Yeli, the pastor, and some of his church members. Pastor Simon was asked to visit and see if he could help them be reconciled.

Pastor Simon had a terrible journey to get to Yeli's village. The first minibus he took broke down, and the next one got stuck in the mud! By the time he arrived at Yeli's village, he was very tired and dirty. When he got off the minibus, he just wanted to clean up and rest, but a group of men wanted to talk to him immediately. They whisked him off to the church compound. As soon as they had finished their greetings, the men started talking about Pastor Yeli. They complained about the use of the church farm, the collection for the poor, and the languages used in the church. Pastor Simon just listened to them and didn't try to give any answers or suggestions. He realized that they were all Mbani. After about an hour, he excused himself and went to find Pastor Yeli's house.

Pastor Yeli was also eager to talk to Pastor Simon about the troubles in the church, but he saw that Pastor Simon needed a good night's sleep first.

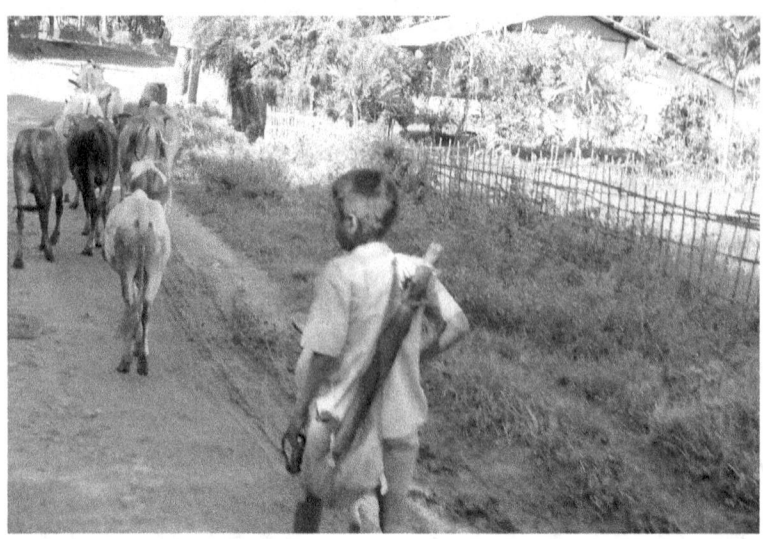

The next day, they settled down to discuss the problem. "It all started with a funeral," Yeli said. "The headmaster of the local primary school died suddenly, and his widow asked the church to help with the funeral arrangements. Mr. Yu and Mr. Gali, two of our deacons, agreed to make the arrangements. When they started doing this, Mr. Ketele and Mr. Rati intervened and said they were doing it all wrong. We finally agreed a compromise, but from that point onwards we had two camps in the church. If Mr. Yu suggested anything, like selling the vegetables from the church garden, Mr. Ketele would be sure to tell everyone that this was a wrong thing to do and that the food should all be given to the poor. Mr. Yu and Mr. Gali always support my suggestions, but the other two leaders are automatically against anything I suggest. These men just can't get along with each other."

Pastor Simon thought about the whole situation for a while and then asked, "What language groups do these four men come from? Last night I noticed that all the men talking to me were Mbani."

Yeli replied: "Mr. Yu and Mr. Gali are Palapala like us; Mr. Ketele and Mr. Rati are Mbani."

"Well, I think you have an ethnic conflict here, rather than an interpersonal problem," said Pastor Simon. "Let's arrange to meet with these four men and with a couple of other mature leaders, one Palapala and one Mbani."

1. If you were Pastor Simon, how would you lead the meeting with these men from the two groups?

2. What underlying problems between the two groups were probably causing the ethnic tension?

1. Ethnic Tensions in the Early Church

Ethnic tensions are not new to the church. The early church was multi-ethnic and experienced ethnic tension. The seeds of this tension were sown centuries earlier when Israel was conquered by Assyria and Babylon. Many Jews were deported to other countries. There they were influenced by the Greek culture of their hosts, also known as Hellenistic culture, and began speaking Greek. The Jews who had been left in their homeland continued speaking their mother tongue, Hebrew or Aramaic. Life was difficult for them, and they tended to be poor, while many of those who lived outside the homeland became wealthy. These two groups didn't get along very well with each other.

Even if Jews had lived most of their lives elsewhere, they preferred to be buried in their homeland, so many of them moved back to Israel in their old age. Often the men died before their wives, and this left a lot of Greek-speaking widows in the Jerusalem church. The Jews were renowned for the excellent way they cared for their widows, but the number of widows became more than the homeland Jews could take care of. Tension developed along ethnic lines. Acts 6:1–7 tells what happened.

Read Acts 6:1–7 and discuss the following questions:
1. Did the early church consider this problem important? How do we know?
2. What action did they take?
3. Were the seven men selected all ethnic Jews?
4. What was the result of their action?
5. What can we learn from this passage about dealing with ethnic tension in the church?

2. Culture and Worldview

Think about the following three statements:
- Every person is like all other people.
- Every person is like some other people.
- Every person is like no other person.

In what ways are all three of the above statements true?
(After the discussion, mention any of the points below that did not come up.)

We all . . .
- have bodies, and live and die like other people.

- are more similar to people from our group than to those from other groups.
- are unique as individuals.

We all learn our culture as small children, and for the rest of our lives we perceive the world through it. We consider the way we've learned to do things and to think about life to be normal. When people from different cultures meet, their perceptions of what is normal are not the same. These differences can occur at various levels, such as . . .

- the visible level – for example, clothing styles and cooking pots;
- the level of our minds – that is, the beliefs and thoughts that we can express; for example, the way we think a good wife should behave or how we think malaria is spread;
- our worldview level – that is, the things we hold strongly but are often unaware of. These are much more difficult to identify. We notice them only when we are with people who think differently. For example, those who assume that people are entitled to a private life realize that they make this assumption only when they are exposed to a culture where privacy is considered antisocial.

Until we can understand people from their cultural perspective, we will interpret their behaviour according to the patterns of our own culture and misunderstand them. For example, an African attending a conference in the United States went outside in the early evening to socialize, just as he would do at home. He didn't find anyone outside and concluded that Americans were not sociable. When he went into the building, he found people talking together. Then he realized that they socialize inside rather than outside.

Another example is from West Africa. At a seminar, most of the participants believed that people from a certain ethnic group ate their dead. They based this belief on the fact that the villages of this ethnic group didn't have cemeteries. When this was shared openly, the participants from the ethnic group explained that they bury their dead in their compounds, not in cemeteries. Suddenly, everyone realized that they weren't so strange after all.

1. Think of a stereotype or generalization you have of another culture – for example, that Americans are noisy, or that British people drink tea all the time.
2. Think about an incident you've experienced which either illustrates or challenges this stereotype.

3. Reducing Ethnic Tension

In multi-ethnic churches, church leaders need to help their people understand each other's culture so that they do not make negative value judgements about each other. Without this kind of understanding, the church will find it difficult to experience their unity in Christ.

To identify your own ethnocentrism, follow this process:

1. Notice when you make value judgements – that is, when you feel that something is strange and can explain it only by saying something like, "The Kisanu are stupid/slow/proud/ . . ."

2. Analyse the situation in which you make this sort of judgement. Remember the details of the experience in slow motion. Stick to what happened. Avoid interpreting the situation.

3. Imagine a context in which this behaviour would not be strange. Propose a possible explanation of why the person might have acted in this way.

4. Check your explanation. See if it occurs anywhere else in the culture. Talk to the person about it, if you can.

Assignments

1. Try to discover your own ethnocentrism using the method described above over a period of several days. Write down two situations in which you've sensed tension with someone from another culture. Propose an explanation for that person's behaviour, and see if it is confirmed. Report back to the large group.
2. Describe some of the most common reasons for ethnic tension in your church or area. Propose ways you think the church can address these.

Readings

Carroll, Raymonde. *Cultural Misunderstandings: The French–American Experience.* Translated by C. Volk. Chicago: University of Chicago Press, 1988.

———. *Evidences invisibles: Américains et Français au quotidien.* Paris: Seuil, 1991.

Huang, Jianbo. "Being Christians in Urbanizing China: The Epistemological Tensions of the Rural Churches in the City." *Current Anthropology* 55, Supplement 10 (2014): S238–S247. https://www.journals.uchicago.edu/doi/pdf/10.1086/677882.

Keyworth, Stephen, Sarah Fegredo, Colin Pye, Jonathan Somerville, and Ruth Whiter, eds. *Baptists Together: Many Cultures, One Church.* Spring 2018. https://www.baptist.org.uk/Publisher/File.aspx?id=202007&view=download.

Pasquale, Michael, and Nathan L. K. Bierma. *Every Tribe and Tongue: A Biblical Vision for Language in Society*. Eugene, OR: Pickwick, 2011.

Patten, Malcolm. *Leading a Multicultural Church*. London: SPCK, 2016.

Rynkiewich, M. *Soul, Self and Society: A Postmodern Anthropology for Mission in a Postcolonial World*. Eugene, OR: Cascade, 2011.

9

Identifying Relevant Issues

Introduction

Sometimes people aren't interested in Scripture because they see no connection between it and their lives. They may attend church but continue to use traditional means to address the real issues of their lives. To help people connect their Christian faith with daily life, pastors need to understand the issues they are facing and help them think through how to respond appropriately with Scripture. This takes some research and reflection. In this chapter, we will explore how to do this.

A QUARREL BREAKS OUT

It was the end of the Sunday morning service, and groups of people were standing around chatting. Pastor Simon was greeting people and asking about those who were sick when he noticed a group of men having an intense discussion. As various other people started to join them, two of the men began yelling at each other. It looked as though they might even start a fight, so Pastor Simon felt it was time to investigate.

As he walked towards the group, he heard people shouting, "They must go!" Others were yelling, "No, it's not a Christian thing to do!" After a few minutes, he understood what the dispute was all about. Traditionally, every three years, Palapala boys between ten and fifteen years of age were taken into the bush for special initiation ceremonies, referred to as the *gaza*. While they were away, the elders taught the boys many things and circumcised them.

The local chief had recently announced that the boys would be going into the bush for the *gaza* the following month. The men were discussing whether or not Christian parents should send their boys. Pastor Simon soon realized that the discussion was turning into a quarrel, and he quickly suggested that the deacons and elders of the church should meet to discuss this properly the following evening. After a few final loud comments, people began to drift away.

The following evening, Pastor Simon sat down with nine men of the church. He hadn't invited the deaconesses this time, so that the men could talk more freely about this sensitive issue. They began by praying for God's wisdom, and then Pastor Simon said that the first thing they should do was to share their experiences of the *gaza* and to understand properly what it involved. All had been to some version of the *gaza*, though Pastor Simon and three others had been to a shorter one for schoolboys. They all had vivid memories of being beaten and starved and of the pain they were expected to endure without crying out. They remembered some positive things as well, such as learning which plants were poisonous and which could treat illness. They also remembered the way they were made to call on various spirits and divinities to give them strength. As they discussed the *gaza*, they agreed that its main purpose was to turn boys into men.

After a while, Pastor Simon fetched a blackboard and put it in front of them. He said, "Let's list the various things that happen at the *gaza*. We'll have one column for good things, one column for things that are definitely forbidden in the Bible, and a third column for things that are not very good but not forbidden either."

After much discussion they had long lists. Some of the good things were learning about plants of the forest, learning to obey your elders, bonding together as an age group, and learning to endure hardship. Some of the bad things were calling on spirits other than God for help, learning that women were inferior and should be beaten to make them obedient, and learning how to be cruel to others. Some neutral things they listed were learning to endure pain without crying and learning how to sing falsetto!

"Now," said Pastor Simon, "how could we help the boys of the church learn these good things and how to be a good Palapala Christian man without also learning the things that are not acceptable for a Christian?"

1. What happens when important issues in life are not addressed by the church?
2. Are there any cultural issues your church has addressed successfully? Explain.

1. Identify a Relevant Issue

The first step in identifying the issues that are problems for people is to spend time talking with the people, listening for the needs they have. The things people are struggling with may be different from what you expect, so listen carefully with an open mind.

What cultural issues are difficult for Christians in your area?
List the answers on the board. (Add any topics from the list below that are relevant but have not already been mentioned.)

Areas in which Christians may encounter problems include the following:

- Various cultural rituals and beliefs surrounding important transitions in life, such as birth, initiation, marriage, and death.

Identifying Relevant Issues 69

- Dealing with illness, misfortune, and suffering as a Christian.
- Witchcraft and fear of supernatural powers and spirit beings.
- Marriage and divorce.
- Interpersonal conflict and how to resolve it.
- Various forms of injustice and how to respond to it.

If different kinds of churches are meeting together for a Scripture engagement course, work on subjects that they can all agree on rather than addressing subjects on which they might differ, such as the significance of baptism or what exactly will happen at the end of the world.

2. Study the Issue without Judging

After selecting an issue to address, you first need to understand it thoroughly. For example, if Christians are going to a traditional healer, you need to find out why they are doing so. Ask yourself questions like these: What needs do they have? What other solutions are available to them when they are ill or have problems? Who or what do they think causes illness? Who is going to the healer? What exactly does the healer do? What power does he use?

The various aspects of behaviour can be compared to the parts of a tree. We see the branches and leaves, but there is an equally large root system underneath the ground that supports the tree. Visible practices are like the leaves. Things we believe and can explain to someone are like the branches. Beliefs, values, and attitudes that underlie our actions are like the roots. We take them so much for granted that we are hardly aware of them. They are invisible even to us but sustain our practices and beliefs.

Often the church addresses only the visible practices and behaviours without addressing the root causes of an issue. They may chop off the branches of certain practices, but in no time the stump has sprouted anew and people are back to their old practices again. For example, telling people they should not engage in sexual relations outside marriage is not likely to be effective if men believe they will get ill if they don't have sex and there is a ban on sexual relations for a long period after women give birth.

To get to the root causes, ask people why they behave as they do. For every layer of practice or thought you uncover, ask why, until they have no more explanations. For example, here is a series of questions and explanations for why some people go to traditional healers.

- Why do people go to healers (a practice, like the visible leaves)?

    Because they are ill.

- Why do they think they became ill (beliefs they can explain, like the branches)?

    Because someone has cursed them.

- Why do they think someone has cursed them (underlying beliefs, like the roots)?

    Because the person was jealous of their good fortune.

- What happens if they don't go to healers (consequences for not following tradition)?

    People might blame family for the sickness if they do not go.

One underlying cause of going to healers, then, is the belief that jealousy causes illness. Telling people to go to a hospital rather than a traditional healer may not be effective if they believe their illness is due to jealousy. The consequences of not going to a traditional healer are that people might suspect that the family does not care for their loved one, or they might even suspect that a member of the family is responsible for the curse.

Research the issue thoroughly. Often we are impatient and want to deal with issues before we understand them, and so we never get to the root causes. If a doctor has only a superficial understanding of a patient's condition, the doctor may prescribe the wrong treatment and only make the patient worse rather than curing him or her. In the same way, we need to take time to understand an issue without making any judgement or rushing to find a solution. You may find, for example, that people go to traditional healers because they can't afford other medical treatment, or are obliged to do so by their extended family members, or because they don't believe that Jesus can help them. The better you understand an issue, the better you can respond to it. Have people verbalize their beliefs as Pastor Simon's church did in the example about *gaza*. Saying them out loud helps them fully understand their beliefs and the underlying beliefs.

Use the mother tongue for this research, especially for key concepts, so that you know what you're referring to. Two Africans were very surprised one day after a very long discussion about demons to find that they weren't talking about the same thing at all. When speaking English, they both used the word "demon," but one used it to refer to ancestor spirits, who were generally helpful, while the other used it to refer to malicious bush spirits. When they began using their local terms, they were finally able to understand each other.

Select a topic that would be relevant in your church. Then work through the following questions.

1. What practices are involved – that is, what can you observe?
2. What beliefs are involved – that is, what explanations do people give?
3. What are the roots that sustain the practices? Ask why, why, why, until you have uncovered root causes.
4. What happens if they do not participate in the practice – that is, what are the consequences that people face for not participating?

3. Determine What Is True

Once you understand an issue, you can begin to sort truth from error. God reveals himself through the body of Christ working together, so involve in this process other pastors, theologians, and those who have a good understanding of the language and culture. It will take time, study, and reflection to do this well. A concordance can be helpful, but be sure to study verses in their context.

Scripture is an important source of truth, but we also learn things from other sources. For example, science rather than Scripture tells us that malaria is caused by a parasite in the blood. Some topics will draw heavily on science or other sources, and others will draw primarily on Scripture.

Scripture does not directly address issues that were not known in the cultures the biblical authors were addressing. For example, the kind of unconscious soul-eating witchcraft found in many parts of Africa was not known in cultures biblical authors were addressing. The word "witchcraft" in the Bible refers to those who used conscious magical means to accomplish their goals. For topics the Scripture does not address directly, find other passages in Scripture that address them indirectly. For example, if the underlying causes of witchcraft are jealousy and the fear of spiritual attack, look for passages that speak to these issues.

1. Listed below are some beliefs underlying witchcraft from one ethnic group in Africa. Have each small group take one belief and determine how the Bible addresses it, whether to affirm it, modify it, or challenge it. Give Bible references that support your claims. (For sample answers, see 3. p. 292.)

    - If witchcraft didn't exist, the world would be perfect: only very old people would die, and there would be no illness, sterility, or misfortune.
    - Spirits and spiritual forces are more powerful than humans.
    - Evil is stronger than good.
    - Misfortune is due to others, not to any fault of mine. For example, if I drive while I'm drunk, crash my car, and kill a passenger, it's because someone was working witchcraft on me, not because of my drunk driving.
    - People need to protect themselves from spiritual attack.
    - A person can become a soul-eating witch without wanting to and can do evil without knowing it.
    - It is right and necessary to take vengeance on those who harm family members.

2. Determine what Scripture says about the topic you identified earlier as relevant for your church. Verbalize the Scripture that speaks to the underlying reason for the practice.

4. Respond to the Issue Biblically

As you work with other church leaders to understand and analyse an issue, you may find that the church has condemned certain practices that are actually acceptable for Christians. For example, early missionaries condemned some musical instruments that may actually be quite acceptable to use in Christian worship today.

You may discover that some beliefs and practices need to be modified to be acceptable for Christians. For example, it is very appropriate for Christian boys to be initiated and become men, but the prayers offered during the traditional initiation ceremonies need to be directed to God, not to other divinities. You may find other practices need to be completely condemned by Christians. For example, it is not acceptable for Christians to abandon the tenth child born to a family because they think the child will bring bad luck.

Whenever a belief or practice is discouraged, it needs to be replaced with something that carries out the good functions of the original belief or practice. This is referred to as a "functional substitute." For example, in an area where drunkenness was a problem, one church prohibited beer at church festivals. However, rather than letting people go thirsty or taking the festive spirit out of these events, or worse, having them drink beer in secret, the church served Coca-Cola instead. This made everyone happy because they associated Coca-Cola with parties. If the functions of a belief or practice are not satisfied in some way, people will probably continue with the old practices and beliefs undercover. Nature abhors a vacuum.

It is very important that believers support each other at times when traditional religious practices are expected. It is difficult to resist pressure when family or friends expect participation. The Bible says we are to "carry each other's burdens." For adapted practices or substitutes to work, believers will have to support each other and help each other to stand firm when social pressure comes. It is best to work through this process with as many believers as possible. The more leaders and believers accept the adapted practice or the substitute from the beginning, the more likely it is to succeed. Build as much unity among believers as possible.

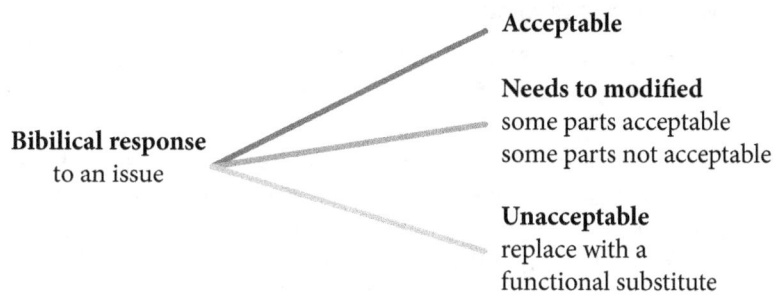

What are some functions of male initiation ceremonies?
Take answers from the group. (Add any from the list below that have not already been mentioned.)

Male initiation ceremonies have several functions in a culture.
- They educate the youth about cultural values.
- They provide training in sexual issues.
- They unite the age group and families.
- They make men out of boys.
- They provide entertainment.
- They provide status to elders.
- They supply income for certain people.

Discuss the questions below for the issue you are working on. Give references that support your opinions.
1. Which beliefs and practices are in agreement with Scripture?
2. Which need to be modified?
3. Which need to be removed?
4. Analyse the functions of any belief or practice that you feel needs to be removed and propose functional substitutes that are acceptable for Christians.

Assignments

1. Continue working on the issue that you have identified as important for your community. Remember to do the following:
   - Study the problem without judging.
   - Determine what is true.
   - Determine an appropriate Christian response to the issue.
2. Make a list of topics for a series of Bible studies which address the root causes of your issue. Keep this to work on for the Bible studies in chapter 11.
3. Look up the word "fear" in a concordance. List three passages you would use to make a thematic Bible study on fear.
4. Discuss in your groups ways that believers can support each other during an important cultural event. Who can you share this workshop with to create more support among believers?
5. A Scripture engagement workshop that is very helpful in addressing these issues is called "Culture Meets Scripture" (https://scripture-engagement.org/content/culture-meets-scripture). The EMDC Online website hosts the online training (https://www.emdc.online). These workshops can be face to face with believers from several language groups, or online. Explore the possibilities of some of your leaders organizing or attending a workshop.

Readings

Beekman, John. "A Culturally Relevant Witness." In *Readings in Missionary Anthropology*, ed. W. A. Smalley, 132–35. Pasadena, CA: William Carey, 1974.

———. "Minimizing Religious Syncretism among the Chols." *Practical Anthropology* 6, no. 6 (1959): 241–50.

Burnett, David. "Exploring Other Worlds." In *Clash of Worlds*, 25–36. Eastbourne: Monarch, 1990.

Carpenter, Mary Yeo. "Familism and Ancestor Veneration: A Look at Chinese Funeral Rites." *Missiology* 24, no. 4 (1996): 503–17.

Grebe, Karl, and Wilfred Fon. *African Traditional Religions and Christian Counselling.* Yaoundé: CABTAL, 1995. Also available on *Tools of the Trade* CD. Nairobi, Kenya: SIL AFA.

Hiebert, Paul G. "Critical Contextualization." In *Anthropological Reflections on Missiological Issues*, 75–92. Grand Rapids, MI: Baker, 1994.

———. "The Flaw of the Excluded Middle." *Missiology* 10, no. 1 (1982): 35–47.

Hill, Harriet. *The Anthro Guide.* Nairobi: SIL Africa Area, 1995.

———. *Petit guide d'anthropologie.* Nairobi: SIL Africa Area, 1997.

———. "Witchcraft and the Gospel: Insights from Africa." *Missiology* 24, no. 3 (1996): 323–44.

Howell, Alan B. "Through the Kaleidoscope: Animism, Contextualization, and the Atonement." *International Journal of Frontier Missiology* 26, no. 3 (2009): 135–42. https://www.ijfm.org/PDFs_IJFM/26_3_PDFs/26_3_Howell.pdf.

Loewen, Jacob. "Religion, Drives, and the Place Where It Itches." *Practical Anthropology* 4 (1967): 49–72. Reprinted in Jacob Loewen, *Culture and Human Values: Christian Intervention in Anthropological Perspective.* Pasadena, CA: William Carey, 1975.

Ommani, John L. "Tharaka Female Circumcision: A Case Study in the Role of the Translation Organization." *Notes on Anthropology* 4 (2000): 45–52. https://scripture-engagement.org/wp-content/uploads/2020/09/Ommani-J-2000-Tharaka-Female-Circumcision.pdf.

Pike, Eunice. "The Concept of Limited Good and the Spread of the Gospel." *Notes on Scripture in Use* 2 (1982): 3–7.

Sauma, Rabban. "Ancestor Practices in the Muslim World: A Problem of Contextualization from Central Asia." *Missiology* 30, no. 3 (July 2002): 323–45.

Steele, Mary. "Witchcraft and Scripture Impact." *Scripture in Use Today* 6 (2003): 30–31.

West, Amy, and Jo Shetler. "Crisis Meets Culture, Culture Meets Scripture: A Workshop Report." 2010. https://scripture-engagement.org/wp-content/uploads/2020/09/West-Shetler-2010-Crisis-meets-Culture.pdf.

Zahniser, A. "Ritual Process and Christian Discipling: Contextualizing a Buddhist Rite of Passage." *Missiology* 19, no. 1 (1991): 3–19.

10

Providing Necessary Background Information

Introduction

People may have the Bible in their language, but they can still have trouble understanding Scripture if they don't know the background information the biblical author assumed his audience would know. For example, many readers wouldn't know why Jesus was upset when his host didn't wash his feet (Luke 7:44). In most places in the world today, guests wouldn't expect their feet to be washed. To understand why Jesus was upset, we need to know about the Jewish practice of foot washing and hospitality. Research carried out in Côte d'Ivoire shows that when background information is supplied, people's understanding of Scripture increases dramatically.[1] In this chapter, we discuss this issue of background information and suggest ways to provide it.

PASTOR SIMON REALIZES SOMETHING IS MISSING

Pastor Simon was pleased that using Palapala in the church services was helping his members. He remembered how he had given a written Bible quiz to some of them before he started teaching in Palapala. Now he felt sure they would do much better if he gave them another test. It was nearly Easter, so he prepared a test on the passages in John on the last supper that Jesus ate with his disciples. He had people read or listen to John 13 and then asked them questions such as "What feast were the Jews about to celebrate?" He also asked questions that required more thought, such as "How did Satan enter Judas?"

---

1. See Hill, *Bible at Cultural Crossroads*.

A good cross section of the congregation was willing to take the test. Pastor Simon wondered if their education would make a difference to their answers, so he had them record the number of years they had gone to school. Since women pass on what they learn to children, he wanted to be sure that they were understanding Scripture well, so he noted the gender of the person who took the test. Finally, he expected that church leaders would understand the passage well, but he was also interested in how much laypeople understood, so he kept their sheets in a separate pile.

Pastor Simon took a whole week to mark the answers and look at the results. By the end, he was concerned. If an answer was obvious in the passage that people were reading, the vast majority of them answered correctly. He was happy about that at least, as this showed a big improvement from the days when he did all his teaching in Kisanu. He found that the more education someone had, the better that person did on the test. He also discovered that church leaders had done better than other members of the church and that men had generally done better than women. None of this surprised him. His concern was that almost all the people did badly on questions that required knowing background information that was different from their culture. For example, many people had misunderstood the reference to the Jewish festival of Passover and thought that it was Easter or a harvest festival.

Pastor Simon explained all this to his wife as they ate supper together. He said, "I thought that once we had the Bible in Palapala, everyone would understand it well. What is wrong?" His wife thought about this for a while and then suggested he go and discuss it with the bishop in the nearest town. They had become friends during the previous seminar.

The next week Pastor Simon arranged to see Bishop John. He explained the problem at some length and then waited to see what the bishop would suggest. After a long silence, Bishop John said, "I think your basic problem is that your church members are not Jews living in the first century AD!" After a few minutes, Pastor Simon saw what the bishop was saying. As they discussed together, Pastor Simon realized that he needed to provide much more background information to help people understand the Scriptures. "But where do I find these things?" he wondered.

Are there passages of Scripture that you find difficult to understand, even in your mother tongue? Give examples.

1. Why Is Background Information Important?

In all communication, speakers guess the amount of background information their audiences have and say just enough to bring it to their minds. They don't say everything but expect their audience to understand what they mean from what they say. For example, when Jesus said to his host in Luke 7:44, "You did not give me any water for my feet," Luke's first audience would have known about Jewish hospitality and how Jews honoured guests by washing their feet. They would have understood that Jesus was insulted by this breach of etiquette.

The amount of background information that people need to understand a text is far greater than the amount of information contained in the text itself. It can be compared to the part of a water buffalo that is underwater.

When we read or hear communication addressed to us, the intended background information comes to our minds so quickly that we aren't even conscious that it wasn't stated. But the Bible was addressed to people who lived in very different cultures from ours. So when we read it, even if it's in our language, it's like reading a letter addressed to someone else. We can understand the words, but if we don't know the intended background information, we won't be able to understand what the author meant. If no background information comes to mind, we realize that we don't understand. For example, when reading Luke 7:44, audiences that don't know about Jewish foot washing may simply wonder why Jesus would want water for his feet. In other instances, we may use the wrong background information and think we have understood when, in fact, we've misunderstood the author's meaning. For example, when Jesus gave the bread to Judas at the Last Supper, people from cultures where witchcraft can be transmitted by enchanted food may think that Jesus made Judas a witch.

At other times, we may know a concept but by another name, and so we may not realize we know what the author is talking about. For example, at a workshop in Uganda, a speaker was talking about the "spirits" who rebelled against God at the beginning of creation. One participant didn't understand what the speaker was referring to. When someone whispered to her, "Spirits are like divinities," she suddenly understood. She knew all about spirits but called them by a different name. This can happen often in translation. In these cases, helping people understand Scripture can be as simple as using the term they are familiar with.

The table summarizes the ways background information can affect our understanding of Scripture.

	We think we know the intended background information	We don't think we know the intended background information
We know the intended background information	We use the intended background information and understand.	We don't realize that we know the background information. We don't understand when actually we could.
We don't know the intended background information	We use wrong (or unintended) background information and think we understand but actually we misunderstand.	No background information comes to mind, and we know we don't understand.

1. Imagine the church at Ephesus. They have just received a letter from Paul and very enthusiastically read it aloud for everyone to understand. What background information did Paul and the Ephesians share, which helped them understand the letter?

    (After taking suggestions, add the following if not already stated: Greek culture, including worship of many gods; Greek Olympic games, including the races and the crown of leaves; Roman culture, including the armour of a Roman soldier; and knowledge of the Old Testament.)

2. Read Luke 10:13–14. What is some of the background information that Luke's readers knew? If necessary, look in study Bibles to find this information. Remember that background information is information people know before they read or hear the text. It is not an explanation of what the text means.

    (After taking the group's suggestions, add the following if not already stated: Tyre and Sidon were Gentile cities, renowned for their wickedness; Chorazin and Bethsaida were Jewish cities; Jews felt the kingdom of God belonged to them and not to Gentiles; Jews thought God would punish Gentiles; and miracles show that a prophet is sent by God.)

> To understand Scripture, people need both the text and the intended background information.

2. Identifying Needed Background Information

Since the background information isn't in the text, how do we know what it is? We can use the same method we use in ordinary conversation. Since speakers and authors want to be understood, they make it as easy as possible for their audiences to understand them, so audiences can take the first background information that comes to mind as the information the author intended. We need to identify what that was for the first audience of Scripture and then see if our audience shares it.

A. Understanding Biblical Cultures

Although we can't know with certainty what came to mind as the first audience heard Scripture, we can learn many things from the Bible itself and from other documents.

Knowledge of the Bible

The story of God's plan of salvation for humankind does not start at Matthew 1:1. When Matthew wrote his gospel, he was mainly writing for Christians who were Jews. He expected them to know the Old Testament. Modern-day readers also need to know the Old Testament to be able to understand the New Testament, but many lack this knowledge.

Often people hear the Bible in bits and pieces. They may hear a psalm, then the story of Noah, followed by Balaam and his donkey, and David and Bathsheba. This is very confusing. People need to have an overview of the main events in the Bible in chronological order. An overview like this is often referred to as a panoramic Bible when it is in printed form, or chronological Bible storying when told orally. (See chapter 16.) It should include the key passages that are necessary for understanding God's plan of salvation.[2]

In your churches, do you have a way for people to get an overview of the Bible from Genesis to Revelation? If not, what can you do about this?

Knowledge of Daily Life in Bible Times

Biblical authors assumed that their audiences knew about the culture and society in which they lived, so they didn't tell them what they already knew.

---

2. People who are already familiar with the Bible but want to understand the order in which things occurred may benefit from a programme entitled Walk Thru the Bible. This goes through the Old Testament or the whole Bible in one day, and does so in a way that is fun and easy to follow. Visit http://www.walkthru.org.

For example, Matthew didn't have to explain who Herod was, what a synagogue was, or that the Romans oppressed the Jews. Although he didn't include this information in his gospel, it is necessary to know these things to understand it. For the passages studied in the Côte d'Ivoire research referred to at the beginning of the chapter, only 55 percent of the background information needed to understand the passages studied could be found in other parts of the Bible. The more we know of the biblical cultures, the better we can understand the Bible. Thankfully, study Bibles, Bible dictionaries, commentaries, and other resources tell us a lot about the cultures in the different periods of the Bible.

1. When Jesus ate at the Pharisee's house in Luke 7:36–50, why was he insulted that his host didn't wash his feet and kiss him (7:44–45)?
2. In Matthew 22:15–22, how is the Pharisees' question a trick question? What background information do you need to know to understand this? (For answers, see 4, p. 292.)

Cultures Change
Like all cultures, Jewish culture changed as their living situations changed.

What are some of the different periods in Jewish history?
List them on the board. (Add any from the list below that are not mentioned.)

The periods of Jewish history can be summarized as follows:
- The nomadic period of Abraham
- Slavery in Egypt
- 40 years in the desert and the conquest of the promised land
- The period of the judges
- The period of the kings
- The exile
- The post-exilic period, including the rebuilding of the temple
- The intertestamental period – including the Maccabees
- Under Roman rule: 63 BC to AD 70
- Under Roman rule after the destruction of the temple in AD 70

The laws that were given in the desert at Sinai had to be adjusted when Israel settled in Canaan. The temple replaced the tabernacle, and Jerusalem became the place of worship. In the exile, when people could not come to Jerusalem each year, synagogues replaced the temple, and the law had to be adapted again to this new situation. In addition, the Israelites were influenced by many ideas in the countries where they stayed. When we read about Old

Testament laws in the New Testament, we need to know how the Jews of the New Testament period interpreted these laws. We need to be sure that our audiences know this background information too.

1. What Jewish practices or beliefs do you find difficult to understand?
2. What Jewish practices or beliefs do you find similar to those in your culture?

B. Understanding the Receptor Culture

Once you have determined the background information the original audience used to understand the meaning of a passage, you need to find out what comes to mind for your audience. Compare these two sets of background information. Notice any differences. This is the information you need to tell your audience.

Each audience is different. Your culture may share certain beliefs or practices with biblical cultures that others do not. On the other hand, there may be information your people need that others do not. You don't need to tell people things they already know, but if you don't supply information people are lacking, they won't be able to understand the text. So it's very important to find out exactly what they are missing.

Look at Luke 10:13–14 again, think about the background information you identified, and ask these questions:

1. Do people lack any of the necessary background information?
2. Do people use other background information and so misunderstand the text?

3. Providing Needed Background Information

After identifying the background information your audience needs to understand a passage, the next step is to provide it for them.

A. The Kind of Background Information to Supply

For background information to be relevant, it needs to help people understand the passage better, and it must be true. For example, read the following passage:

> ⁹When considerable time had passed and the voyage was now dangerous, since even the fast was already over, Paul started admonishing them, ¹⁰saying to them, "Men, I perceive that the voyage will certainly be with damage and great loss, not only of

the cargo and the ship, but also of our lives." ¹¹But the centurion was more persuaded by the pilot and the captain of the ship than by what was being said by Paul. ¹²The harbor was not suitable for wintering, so the majority reached a decision to put out to sea from there, if somehow they could reach Phoenix, a harbor of Crete, facing southwest and northwest, and spend the winter there. (Acts 27:9–12 NASB)

Decide how relevant the following items of background information would be for your audience: very relevant, somewhat relevant, or not relevant at all.

- Verse 9: "the fast" refers to the Day of Atonement, when all Jews fasted. It happened in September or October, a time when the weather made sailing very dangerous.
- Verse 9: Paul was an expert sailor.
- Verse 12: "southwest" is between the compass points of South and West. "Northwest" is between the compass points of North and West.
- Verse 12: Phoenix is the name of a magical bird that comes back to life from death.
- Verse 12: the voyage would have been about 40 kilometres in total.

1. Read John 13:26–27 on Satan entering Judas.
   (a) How would your audience understand verse 27?
   (b) How would it affect your audience's understanding of the text if you supplied the following background information?

   In Jewish society, when a host gave a piece of food to a guest, it was a way of showing special affection to that person.

2. Read John 13:2–17 on foot washing.
   (a) What would your audience understand about why Jesus was washing the disciples' feet?
   (b) How would it affect your audience's understanding of the text if you supplied the following background information?

   In Jewish society, showing hospitality to guests started with washing their feet. This was a way of greeting them. The foot washing was done by a Gentile slave or, if there wasn't a slave, by the women or children. A Jewish male, even if he were a slave, would not be asked to do this very menial task.

B. Ways of Supplying Background Information

Background information can be provided in many ways in the ministry of the church: sermons, Bible studies, children's and youth ministries, films, books, and booklets.

Some Scripture products, such as Bible stories, can be written or told in a way that weaves the needed background information into the text. This can be important for evangelism or sharing with people who don't know much about the Bible. Background information can also be supplied alongside the biblical text in extra-textual helps, such as introductions and footnotes. These are not the inspired word of God but are provided to help us understand the Bible. Research has shown that both men and women of all educational levels and ages are able to use extra-textual helps to understand the Bible better.[3]

There are many websites and apps that help provide background information, such as BibleProject (https://bibleproject.com). Bible apps often include definitions of key words as well as other background helps.

What kinds of helps have you noticed in Bibles?
List responses on the board. (Add any from the list below that are missed.)

Bible helps from which you can get background information include the following:

- Introductions
- Section headings
- Footnotes or side notes
- Glossaries
- Concordances or topical indexes – for example, "If you are frightened read Matthew 10:26–31; Luke 12:22–31; . . ."
- Illustrations
- Maps

For these helps to be beneficial, people need to be taught how to use them. Here are some ideas of how to teach the use of these helps.

Introductions

Find a Bible that provides helps, and read the introduction to the Gospel of Mark.

How would this help someone understand this book better?

---

3. See Hill, *Bible at Cultural Crossroads*.

Section Headings

Read Mark 6:1–5 out loud to the group without reading the section heading.

1. What was the main point of this section?

Next, read the section heading.

2. How does the section heading help the audience?

Footnotes or Side Notes

Background information related to the interaction taking place in passages is best supplied in notes, either side notes (in the side margins) or footnotes (at the bottom of the page). One way to teach the use of notes is to read verses with several notes and show the group how to find the note each time. Then ask them to turn to a different passage and find the footnote associated with it. The first person to find it should read it out loud.

Glossaries

Prepare a worksheet for people to fill in the definitions of words using the glossary in a Bible, such as the Good News Bible. For example:

1. Who were the Epicureans? _____
2. What is a Sadducee? _____
3. How many different King Herods are there in the gospels? _____

Concordances and Topical Indexes

Prepare a worksheet to give practice in using a small concordance. For example, ask the group to find three references to the Feast of Unleavened Bread in the Bible.

A useful alternative to a concordance is a topical index, which classifies references according to situations, such as marriage, divorce, illness, and so forth. If one is included at the back of your translation, make up exercises along the following lines:

1. Give two references that tell us what Christians should do when they are ill.
2. Give three references that tell us how we can know that God will forgive our sins if we confess them.
3. Give two references that would help people who are being persecuted for their faith.

Illustrations

Often people need help to learn how to read illustrations because they may not be used to seeing things represented on paper. Encourage them to study an illustration and describe what they see in detail. For example, if there is a picture of Jerusalem in your Bible, you could ask: What can you see outside the main part of the city? Where is the temple? In Islamic areas, however, it might not be acceptable to have any illustrations in the Bible.

Maps

The best way to help people learn how to use maps is to begin by making a map of the local area. Help the participants learn that symbols represent things like roads or rivers. Then show a map of your country, and point out your local area. Then show a map of the world, and point out your country. Then find Israel on the world map, and show where it is in relation to your country. If it's possible to get a large map of Bible lands, put it up in front of the group. Point out certain places, and explain the symbols used. Invite people to come up and point to a town. Then discuss the biblical events that took place there.

> For Bible helps to be beneficial, people need to be taught how to use them.

1. Which one of these helps do you use the most? Why?
2. How can you encourage people in your church to use these helps more?

Assignments

1. Read John 4:1–26. Use study Bibles or other helps to find out what background information the text brought to mind for the original audience. Identify four biblical background facts your audience needs in order to understand the text.

2. In Acts 13:16–41 when Paul preached in Antioch, he started by talking about the history of the Jewish people. Compare this with how he started his sermon in Acts 17:22–31 when he preached in Athens. Why do you think he presented the same gospel in such different ways?

3. Use your mobile phone to search for information about specific Jewish holidays or practices, such as Passover, the Feast of Tabernacles, foot washing, etc.

Readings

Adeyemo, Tokunboh, ed. *Africa Bible Commentary: A One-Volume Commentary Written by 70 African Scholars*. Nairobi: WordAlive, 2006.

Barnwell, Katharine. "Training New Readers to Use Bible Helps." *Notes on Literature in Use and Language Programs* 17 (1988): 23–25.

Brown, Rick. "Selecting and Using Scripture Portions Effectively in Frontier Missions." *International Journal of Frontier Missions* 18, no. 4 (2002): 10–25. http://www.ijfm.org/PDFs_IJFM/19_2_PDFs/10%20Using_Scripture_Portions.pdf.

Fergie, Clayton. "Timelining Scripture Workshop." 2009. https://scripture-engagement.org/wp-content/uploads/2020/09/Fergie-C-2009-Timelining-Scripture-Workshop.pdf.

Gutt, Ernst-August. "Aspects of 'Cultural Literacy' Relevant to Bible Translation." *Journal of Translation* 2, no. 1 (2006): 1–16.

Hill, Harriet. *The Bible at Cultural Crossroads: From Translation to Communication*. Manchester: St Jerome, 2006, 27–32, 37–52, 72–82.

Keener, C. S. *The IVP Bible Background Commentary: New Testament*. Downers Grove, IL: InterVarsity Press, 1993.

The Learning Bible: Contemporary English Version. New York: American Bible Society, 2000.

Wright, Jennifer. "Bible Overview Workshop: An Interactive Journey through the Old Testament." 2014. https://scripture-engagement.org/content/bible-overview-workshop/.

Zinkuratire, Victor, and Angelo Colacrai, eds. *The African Bible*. Nairobi: Paulines Publications Africa, 1999.

Other Resources

https://www.internationalmediaservices.org/bible-backgrounds – Bible Backgrounds videos from International Media Services (IMS): Bible Backgrounds video templates use scripts with photo images to explore background information on a variety of cultural, historical, and geographical topics. Explore the topics available in this video template format.

https://bibleproject.com/languages/ – BibleProject produces free Bible videos, podcasts, blogs, classes, and educational Bible resources to help make the biblical story accessible. The BibleProject videos, which are quite popular in the US, have already been translated into eighteen major world languages and in many cases have been localized as well.

http://www.walkthru.org – The official Walk Thru the Bible website.

http://www.hebrew-streams.org – Explains the Hebrew background to the New Testament.

Providing Necessary Background Information 89

- https://www.logos.com/product/194909/logos-9-basic – Logos 9 Basic: This free version of Logos Bible Software provides insights from across all of Scripture and a collection of key biblical resources.
- https://www.olivetree.com/bible-study-apps/ – Olive Tree Bible App (for laptop and phone): The Resource Guide makes it easy to study by presenting all the relevant information in your library alongside your Bible passage.
- Biblegateway.com – This website has the Bible in hundreds of languages and versions as well as extensive Bible study tools.
- https://play.google.com/store/apps/details?id=systems.emmaus.zam&gl=DE – Emmaus Bible Courses: This app has a wide variety of Bible courses.
- https://play.google.com/store/apps/details?id=org.africanpastors.e_vitabu&gl=DE – eVitabu for those in Africa. This app has many resources and Bible study materials for African pastors.

11

Preparing Bible Studies

Introduction

One of the best ways to help Christians study the Bible in depth is by organizing groups within the church to do this. The term "Bible study" can mean very different things in different places. The type of Bible study recommended in this chapter involves group participation rather than the leader giving a sermon.

EVERYONE'S COMING TO BIBLE STUDY

When Pastor Simon was at Bible college, he had learned about how to lead a Bible study. He decided to organize one because even though members of his church understood Scripture better, they still didn't know the Bible very well. He announced that the next Wednesday literate people with Bibles should come for a Bible study. The time arrived, and ten people came. Some people came with an English Bible, some with the Palapala New Testament, and some with the Kisanu Bible.

Pastor Simon chose a passage from the New Testament. First, he read it aloud. Then he preached a sermon based on this passage for forty-five minutes. At the end of the time, he asked for questions. A few people asked questions, but they were about things not really connected with the passage. They ended in prayer and went home. The following week only three people came, and so Pastor Simon cancelled the Bible study because he decided people weren't interested.

A month later, Pastor Simon was invited to go to another seminar for pastors to learn more about using the New Testament in Palapala. As he learned so much at the first short seminar, he was very willing to go again. A major theme of this seminar was how to lead a Bible study.

On his return he decided to put what he had learned into practice. He announced in church that anyone who would like to understand the Bible better was welcome at a Bible study the next Wednesday. At the seminar, he had been able to buy some inexpensive copies of Mark's gospel in Palapala. He showed them to the congregation and encouraged them to buy copies after the service to bring to the Bible study. He also told them that everyone was invited, whether they could read or not. Then he found four mature leaders in his congregation and asked them if they would be willing to lead small groups. All agreed, and they set a time to come to his house and prepare the passage together.

Wednesday arrived, and thirty-five people came. Pastor Simon divided them into four groups according to how well they could read. They chose the passage on John the Baptist with the theme that repentance results in changed lives. Each group had a trained leader who had been given a list of questions on the passage.

Let's visit Mr. Yuh's group, made up of those who are able to read the majority language well. First he asks someone to pray. Since the group is not used to reading their own language, he reads the passage aloud and then helps the group to read it for themselves. Then he reads the first questions from the paper he has been given, which are about the content of the passage. The group members take turns to answer, always looking back at the text to find the answers. Then they come to a general question about the passage and discuss that for a while. Finally, they come to an application question about how the passage applies to their lives. At the end, a number of the group pray about what they have learned.

Mr. Thomas is leading a group of people who can't read. First, he takes the passage and reads it to them quite slowly three times. Then he reads just a couple of verses and asks for someone to tell what they have heard in his or her own words. The group members help each other do this. He continues to the end of the passage and then asks if anyone can tell the whole story in his or her own words. After two or three people have done this, Mr. Thomas takes the list of questions on the passage and helps the group to answer them. He also takes one verse of the passage and helps them to memorize it. At the end of their time, they pray together.

When all the groups have finished, they meet together briefly to sing and pray.

1. How is a Bible study different from a sermon?
2. Is studying the Bible commanded in Scripture? Where? (For answers, see 5. p. 292.)
3. Why might some pastors be afraid of Bible studies in which the church members participate?
4. Does your church have Bible studies? If so, do you consider them to be successful? Explain why or why not.

1. Two Kinds of Bible Study

Two basic kinds of Bible studies are those that are based on passages and those that are based on themes. When preparing a Bible study on a passage, select a passage that is relevant to people's daily lives. It should address root causes of problems and not just visible behaviours. For example, if people continue practising female excision because they are afraid of being punished by the ancestors or excommunicated by the community, you might focus the Bible studies on God's protection and doing what is right in God's eyes, regardless of what people may think. (See chapter 9.) The passage should be between ten and fifteen verses long.

A thematic Bible study explores one topic, such as humility or temptation. Instead of using just one passage of Scripture, a thematic Bible study uses verses from two or three passages. The total number of verses should not exceed fifteen, and they should be taken from no more than three passages. This type of study is more difficult to do than a Bible study on one passage, as there is a danger of taking passages out of context. There is also a temptation to use too many passages, which makes the Bible study difficult to follow and remember. When working with Christians from different kinds of churches, remember to avoid subjects that churches view differently which may cause controversy.

If the participants in either kind of Bible study are not used to reading in the language used for the Bible study, it is important to choose passages that are easy for them to read. Passages they are already familiar with, such as the Christmas story, are easier to read. Topics readers are familiar with are easier to understand than those that involve things they've never heard of, as they already know much of the background information. For example, the parable of the sower may be easy for farming people to understand; the story of Abraham and Lot may be easy for cattle herders. Generally, stories are easier to understand than passages like Romans or Ephesians where the author is trying to persuade people. As people progress in their Bible knowledge, you can choose passages that are not as well known.

If only part of the Bible is available in the language used for the Bible study, you may need to print out a supplementary sheet with extra verses from the parts of the Bible not yet published. You should ask trained translators to translate extra verses needed for a study. It is also perfectly possible to have a Bible study with no printed materials if the passage is available on an MP3 player or Scripture app, or there are other means of listening to the passage.

2. Understanding the Passage and Its Background

Once you have selected a passage, you need to understand it well. To understand a passage, you need to understand where it fits in the chapter and have an idea about how it fits in the book. Read it in different versions, if possible, and read any available commentaries, study Bible notes, or other helps. Find out who wrote the book and why it was written. As part of your preparation, read through the passage several times, as well as reading the whole chapter.

Prepare any needed background information your audience might be missing. It can be communicated in introductory remarks before people read the passage. Remember that background information is simply the things the original audience would have known from their situation before they heard the text – for example, beliefs about ritual purity, or marriage customs. It is not an explanation of the text. Bible study leaders must resist the temptation to preach a sermon!

3. Preparing Questions

After understanding a passage, Bible study leaders need to prepare good questions that help people discover what God is saying to them through the passage. Sometimes pastors feel that if they aren't going to be talking about the passage, they don't need to take much time to prepare, but just the opposite is true. It takes more preparation to think through how to help people to discover for themselves what the passage is teaching than to preach a sermon on it.

There are four types of questions:

A. Polar Questions

Polar questions have a yes or no answer. For example, "Did Jesus go to Jerusalem?" These are not a good type of question to use because participants can answer them without giving the passage much thought.

B. Content Questions

The answers to content questions are found in the passage. Content questions help people understand what the text says. For example, "What did Jesus do?" If you are preparing a handout sheet with all the questions, give the number of the verse where the answer is found in brackets after the question.

C. Reflection Questions

Reflection questions demand an answer that requires thinking about the passage as a whole rather than a particular verse. They make people think more deeply about the text as they search for an answer. For example, from the book of Jonah, you could ask, "Why do you think Jonah didn't want to go to Nineveh?" These questions often begin with "why."

D. Application Questions

Application questions do not have clear answers from the text but help people to apply the principles of the passage to their lives. For example, in a study on Jesus teaching his disciples to be servants in John 13, an application question could be, "After reading this passage, do you think pastors should change their behaviour towards church members in any way?"

Most of the questions in a Bible study should be *content* questions, with one or two reflection questions, and one or two application questions. In thematic Bible studies, be sure to put the questions in logical order, so each one builds on the previous one. Prepare these questions in advance and test them with a small group of people to make sure they are clear. Depending on the abilities of the group and the difficulty of the passage, participants can answer five to nine questions in thirty to forty-five minutes.

On a printed handout containing the questions, mark any non-content question with an asterisk so participants will know that they need to reflect on the text to find the answer.

Model a Bible study on Mark 1:21–28. Read the passage, having people take turns reading one verse each. Then ask the following questions and have the group answer.

1. What kind of place was Jesus in? (verse 21)
2. What did he do? (verse 21)
3. When the people there heard Jesus's teaching, what did they think? (verse 22)
4. What happened in the middle of his teaching? (verses 23–24)
5. What did Jesus say to the evil spirit? (verse 25)
6. What did the people say? (verse 27)
7. What does this passage tell us about Jesus's power?
8. If we meet someone with an evil spirit, what should we do?

Make a Bible study on Luke 12:13–21.

1. Read the passage in the large group and ask for an example of a content question and a reflection question.
2. Divide the participants into language groups and have them make up questions in their language on this passage. Have them write four content questions, one reflection question, and one application question.
3. Ask some of the language groups to share an English translation of their questions with the whole group.

4. Conducting a Bible Study

In the story, Pastor Simon divided the thirty-five people who came to his Bible study into four groups so that everyone had an opportunity to answer questions. Groups shouldn't have more than twelve people in them. Meeting somewhere other than the church building may help people feel more relaxed. Sitting in a circle encourages group discussion.

Each culture has norms for who can speak to whom and who can discuss things together. For example, a younger person may not be allowed to ask a question of an older person. Or older people may not be willing to discuss certain things with younger people. Or women may not be allowed to discuss things when men are present. The groups should be organized in such a way that everyone feels free to participate. Pastor Simon divided those who were literate from those who were not, but in some cultures, this may not be acceptable.

During a Bible study, leaders should listen much more than they talk. The group will remember much more if they can discuss the passage and discover its meaning and its application to their lives.

> We remember
> 20 percent of what we HEAR
> 30 percent of what we SEE
> 70 percent of what we DISCUSS with others
> 80 percent of what we EXPERIENCE
> 95 percent of what we TEACH others.[1]

If you are working with a group that has never done a Bible study of this sort before, prepare them for what will happen by giving them examples of questions and answers. This helps them understand that the answers are in the text, and there is no trick or mystery to the questions.

Some people may want to talk non-stop while others may not talk at all. Leaders need to encourage some to speak more and others to speak less so that everyone in the group has a chance to take part.

It is your job as leader to keep the Bible study focused on the topic. If participants ask questions or make comments that are not about the subject of the study, tell them you will address these things later. End the Bible study on time. Generally, it's better to finish a bit early than to drag on until the group is

---

1. Quoted from Edgar Dale, *Audio-Visual Methods in Teaching* (New York: Holt, Rinehart, & Winston, 1969).

bored or exhausted. People are much more likely to come back the next week if you respect the time agreed upon to finish.

1. What different types of people in your church need to meet separately for Bible studies?
2. What types of people in your church could you train as small-group leaders?
3. What types of people may cause problems for the leader of a Bible study? How would you advise leaders to deal with these people?
4. What time and day are best for your community? Where is the best place to meet?

5. Audio-Listening Bible Study

Many people do not read or do not like to read and prefer to listen to Scripture. In some groups, the majority of people fall into this category. They still need Bible studies, and audio-listening studies can be very successful. In fact, people are much more likely to engage with audio Scripture in a group than alone. Organizing people into audio-listening groups can greatly increase their engagement with Scripture. Here is one way to do an audio Bible study:

1. Provide any background information your audience might need to be able to understand the passage.
2. Play the passage through on a device such as a Proclaimer or a Bible app on a mobile phone two or three times.
3. Ask someone to tell back the whole passage. Have others help by filling in any missing details from the passage.
4. When you are sure the group knows the content of the passage, ask the Bible study questions you have prepared.
5. Select a memory verse and help the group to learn it.

Another way to do Bible studies orally is through Bible storying. We discuss this in chapter 16.

6. Using Multiple Languages in Bible Study Groups

Sometimes people in a Bible study group speak more than one language. They may want to use two of their languages during the Bible study. This can easily be done by reading or listening to the Bible passage in two languages. Then the discussion can happen in any language or mix of languages that the people in the group want. This works best if everyone in the group is multilingual. If some people cannot understand the different languages, it may be difficult for them. Groups can be organized by language just as they can be by gender or age.

Work through this thematic study on servant leadership together as an audio-listening Bible study. Start by giving the following background information:

In Jewish society, washing the feet of guests was a very important part of showing hospitality. This task was performed by Gentile slaves, or if there were none, by women or children. A Jewish man would never be expected to do it.

Play Matthew 20:25–28 and John 13:2–5, 12–17.

1. What is the normal behaviour of chiefs and leaders towards those under their authority? (Matthew 20:25)
2. How did Jesus tell the disciples to behave? (Matthew 20:26–27)
3. What service did Jesus perform for his disciples? (John 13:2–5)
4. Who normally would have done this?
5. By doing this, what lesson was Jesus trying to teach the disciples?
6. How can we apply this to the way we treat those we consider under us?

Assignments

1. The root issues you identified in chapter 9 may need to be addressed by a series of Bible studies. Develop one Bible study on a passage that responds to at least one part of the issue. Share this with the large group.
2. Conduct a workshop for group leaders on how to lead an audio-listening Bible study (see the article by Richard Margetts at the end of the chapter on how to do this).
3. Describe one Bible study you have attended, and say what you enjoyed or how it could have been improved.

Readings

Benn, Keith. "Bible Study Cassettes: A Tool Which Churches Perceive to Be of Value in Furthering Their Goals." *Notes on Literature in Use and Language Programs* 7 (1984): 8–13. https://scripture-engagement.org/wp-content/uploads/2008/10/Benn-K-1984-Bible-study-cassettes.pdf.

Fee, G. D., and D. Stuart. *How to Read the Bible Book by Book: A Guided Tour.* Grand Rapids, MI: Zondervan, 2014.

———. *How to Read the Bible for All Its Worth.* 4th ed. Grand Rapids, MI: Zondervan, 2014.

Gruenig, Hanni. "Bible Courses for Women." *Scripture in Use Today* 6 (2003): 29–31. https://scripture-engagement.org/wp-content/uploads/2009/02/Gruenig-H-2003-Bible-Courses-for-Women.pdf.

Konkomba Team. "Konkomba Faith Comes By Hearing Project: What We Have Learned – Team Report." *Scripture in Use Today* 5 (2002): 15–21. https://scripture-engagement.org/wp-content/uploads/2020/09/Konkomba-Team-2002-FCBH.pdf.

Margetts, Richard. "Bible Listening Groups: Training Guide." 2016. https://scripture-engagement.org/content/bible-listening-groups-training-guide. This is available in English and French.

Other Resources

https://www.faithcomesbyhearing.com – This is the website for Faith Comes By Hearing, and it has many good resources related to listening to Scripture by audio.

https://www.scriptureearth.org/00i-Scripture_Index.php – This website is a resource for text, audio, and video Scripture in many different languages. These materials can be used for Bible studies or individual use on mobile phones or other devices.

12

Preparing Sermons

Introduction

Church leaders invest a lot of time and energy in preparing sermons, but often, after the service, people can't even remember what the sermon was about. In churches that don't have Scripture in a language people can understand, sermons may mainly involve translating the text into the local language. When mother-tongue Scripture becomes available, that task is already done, and church leaders need to learn new ways of preaching. This chapter provides some basic ideas that can help church leaders prepare interesting sermons that communicate well.

LAMBO'S SHORT SERMONS

One day Lambo, the Catholic catechist from the next village, came to see Pastor Simon. After they had exchanged greetings and news of their families, Lambo said, "I have a real problem to discuss with you. As I think you know, since we went on the seminar, I have become convinced that my congregation needs to hear God's word in Palapala. In fact, we have been encouraged by the bishop to hold the whole service in Palapala now. But this is giving me a new problem. Up to last month, I used to read the three passages of Scripture set for each Sunday in Kisanu and many of the people didn't really understand what the readings were about. Because of this, most of my sermon was taken up with explaining in Palapala the meaning of one of the Kisanu readings. Now everyone understands the readings, so what do I talk about in the sermon? I remember learning about sermon preparation at catechist school, but that was fifteen years ago, and I've forgotten what they said! My sermons are very short now, and I don't think that is good!"

If Lambo came to you, how would you help him?

1. The Parts of a Sermon

The two main types of sermons are preaching from a passage and preaching on a theme. A good preacher uses both kinds, but preaching well on a theme requires much more preparation. In this chapter, we look at preaching from a passage.

A sermon should have three parts:

- *An introduction:* start by telling your congregation the subject of your sermon in a way that makes them want to listen.
- *A main part:* between one and three points. Explain and illustrate them.
- *A conclusion:* end by summarizing what you have said, and show the hearers how to apply what they have heard to their lives.

2. Steps in Preparing a Sermon

What steps are involved in preparing a sermon?
List responses on the board. (Mention any of the following points that are relevant but have not been listed.)

A. Study the Bible

As you study the Bible, you will get ideas for sermons. Make notes on your ideas as you may use them at a later date.

B. Pray for Guidance

Pray for God to guide you as you prepare. His words, not yours, are what will touch people's lives deeply. Although God can choose to speak through you if you haven't prepared, in general, the better you prepare, the better he can speak through you. Pray as though it is all up to the Holy Spirit and work as though it is all dependent on your preparation, and you will have a good sermon.

C. Choose a Passage

You can choose a passage in a number of ways. If your church uses set readings, you can use one of the passages for that Sunday. If you are preaching through a book, you can use a different section of the book each week. Or if you want to preach on a theme that is relevant for your church, you can look for the best passage on the theme. Your passage should be no longer than a chapter. It will usually be shorter.

D. Identify the Main Subject of the Passage

Read the passage carefully and decide on the main subject. Just as you don't eat all of the kinds of food that are available in a single day, so you don't need to cover everything in a passage in one sermon.

Read the passage in various versions, if possible. Think through the meaning of the key terms in your mother tongue, even if you're preaching in another language. It is good to use commentaries and other helps to be sure that you understand the passage well. Take notes on good ideas in case you want to use them later.

Notice how the writer explained the main subject. Although some passages have three or four clear points, others consist of a single subject followed by an application. Parables are often like this. To help yourself understand the meaning, ask yourself these questions:

- What did the passage mean to the original audience?
- What does the passage mean to us today?
- How should we respond?

E. Think of Ways to Illustrate the Main Point of the Passage

Think of illustrations to make the point clear. Use stories from your life, the lives of others, and the lives of people in the Bible. Many preachers use folk stories or proverbs. These can be very good and the congregation will listen very attentively, but be careful that they illustrate your main point and don't become the focus of the sermon. After the sermon, if people remember only the stories and not why you told them, the stories haven't served you very well.

F. Prepare the Conclusion

If you are preaching in a church where you think most people are Christians, about 70 percent of your conclusion should be addressed to Christians and about 30 percent to non-Christians. It might include an action you want them to take – for example, a decision to believe in Jesus or a decision to tell a non-Christian neighbour about Christ. It might also include an idea people can think about all week.

G. Prepare an Introduction for the Sermon

Introductions are very important. People will decide whether or not to listen to your sermon depending on your introduction. It should be brief, catchy, and clear. Many people prefer to prepare this as their last task after they know what the sermon will say. An introduction must do two things:

- Catch the congregation's attention. Remember that many people in the church will be thinking about all sorts of other things when you begin your sermon. You need to attract their attention with a question, a proverb, or a personal experience.
- Give them an idea of what you are going to talk about so that they can easily follow your ideas. Be sure to tell them clearly where you are going, and then go there. Don't get lost along the way.

> A sermon should have one main point, possibly with subpoints.

In groups of four or five, read Mark 4:35–41 through twice. Then fill out the following sheet, discussing each point together.

1. What is the main point of this passage?
2. How is this teaching expressed? List some points for the passage. Use as many or as few lines as you need. (a) _____ (b) _____ (c) _____ (d) _____

> 3. What is a good illustration of this main teaching?
>
> 4. Write notes for the conclusion. Include an application for both Christians and non-Christians.
>
> 5. Now think about the introduction. Write down your opening sentence.

1. Think about three sermons you have heard or preached in the last few months.
   - What language was each sermon preached in?
   - What language were the Scriptures read in?
   - What was the subject of each sermon?
2. Which kind of sermon is most frequently preached in your church?
   - A translation of the majority-language Scriptures with some extra explanations.
   - A sermon on a passage, going through it verse by verse.
   - A sermon on a theme.
3. What improvements would you like to see in the sermons in your church?

Assignment

Select a passage and make a sermon outline for it, as you did for Mark 4:35–41.

Readings

Chapell, Bryan. *Christ-Centered Preaching: Redeeming the Expository Sermon*. Grand Rapids, MI: Baker Academic, 2018.

Crowter, Phil, et al. Pray-Prepare-Preach Series. 6 vols. The Good Book Company, 2009–2015. https://www.logos.com/product/177640/pray-prepare-preach-series.

Keller, Timothy. *Preaching: Communicating Faith in an Age of Skepticism*. New York: Penguin, 2016.

Other Resources

http://www.langhampartnership.org – The Langham Partnership is dedicated to helping local pastors know how to preach. This site is full of resources, announcements of seminars, and other helps.

There are many websites and apps that have free materials to help pastors prepare sermons.

13

Meditating on God's Word

Introduction

In the Christian context, meditation has been defined as a prayerful reading and pondering of the Scriptures. It is a time when we let God speak to us through his word. In this chapter, we will explore how Christians can engage with Scripture and grow closer to God through meditation.

PASTOR SIMON GETS QUIET

Pastor Simon was invited to another Scripture engagement seminar in a town some distance to the north. He was somewhat worried about the travel arrangements, so the first thing he did was to find out which other church leaders were going from his area. He found out that he would be travelling with three other church leaders: Lambo, the catechist from the local Catholic church; John, a pastor of a Pentecostal church; and a Lutheran pastor who lived a bit further to the south. They all met as planned and went together in a minibus to the place where the seminar was being held.

That evening, they arrived safely at their destination and settled in. The next morning, the seminar began. After the opening, one of the first sessions was about meditation. The participants heard about the need to listen to God as well as to talk to him. The next morning, instead of the usual devotional time of singing, Bible reading, and a short talk, one of the church leaders led them in a meditation on a Bible passage. The following morning, everyone was given a passage for meditation, John chapter 10, and told to find a quiet place and to be still and listen to God for twenty-five minutes while they thought about the passage. This seemed like a long time to Pastor Simon, longer than he had ever waited in silence before God. Part of him became impatient, but he sat quietly. As he did so, he sensed the wonder of God's love in a new and real way. When the group came back together, some people shared what they had learned.

In the minibus going home, the four church leaders were squeezed together on the back seat. They discussed the seminar for most of the journey. John, the Pentecostal pastor, said, "For me, the most extraordinary thing about this seminar was being told to sit in silence and meditate on a Bible passage. I'd never tried anything like that before. To start with, I thought it was a strange idea, but once I really experienced it for myself, I knew this was something people in my church need to learn. Now I see that there are many different ways of listening to God, and it doesn't always have to involve preaching!" They agreed this was something to teach people when they got home.

1. Have you ever tried to get quiet inside and let God speak to you through a passage of Scripture? If so, how was this experience for you?
2. Do you find it easier to hear God speak when you are alone or when you are with a group of Christians? Why do you think that is?

1. What Is Biblical Meditation?

Think of someone who is a good friend of yours. Will you get to know your friend if all you do is talk and never listen to what he or she wants to say to you?

Bible studies give us a foundation of Bible knowledge which can keep us from being led astray. We also need to let God speak to us personally through his word. Meditation involves reading a short passage of Scripture slowly or repeatedly, thinking about it deeply, and listening to what God has to say. Often, people meditate alone, but meditation can also be done in a group. Meditation and study are both essential to understanding the word of God and applying it to our lives.

> We need to be silent and let God speak to us personally through his word.

2. What Does the Bible Say about Meditation?

Read the following passages aloud, and then discuss what each verse says about meditation.

Psalm 77:12	I will think about all that you have done; I will meditate on all your mighty acts. (GNT)
Psalm 119:99	I understand more than all my teachers, because I meditate on your instructions. (GNT)
Joshua 1:8	Keep this Book of the Law always on your lips; meditate on it day and night, so that you may be careful to do everything written in it. Then you will be prosperous and successful. (NIV)
Philippians 4:8	In conclusion, my friends, fill your minds with those things that are good and that deserve praise: things that are true, noble, right, pure, lovely, and honorable. (GNT) ("Fill your minds" here has the same sense as meditate.)

In many non-Western societies, activities are normally done by groups of people. Because of this, people may find it a strange idea to meditate alone on God's word. Can you think of ways to make meditation easier for them?

3. Practical Suggestions for Meditating on Scripture

Before beginning to read a passage, tell God all the things that are worrying you, and imagine putting them into his hands and leaving them there. Get quiet on the inside as well as on the outside. You may need to confess sins before beginning and know that he has forgiven you.

If you are reading a passage that tells the story of an event, imagine that you are there watching the action or are one of the characters. For example, in the story of the prodigal son (Luke 15), you could imagine you are the prodigal son, his brother, his father, his mother, or someone observing.

One phrase or sentence in the passage may stand out for you. Stay with that thought, and let God speak to you through it. Don't be in a hurry to move on. Linger in God's presence. You may want to memorize it so that you can go on thinking about it during the day. Our minds are quick to absorb a lot of information, but our hearts take time to let even one simple idea sink in deeply. It's when an idea sinks in deeply that it changes our lives.

Don't get discouraged if you don't sense God's presence or voice. The discipline of getting quiet and waiting on God will have an effect even though you might not recognize it until later. You may simply enjoy a time of being with God reflecting on his word, or he may speak to you through the passage either then or later in the day.

People who can't read can still meditate on God's word, by listening to recordings, mobile phone apps, or the public reading of Scripture. If a leader reads a passage aloud, especially two or three times, then the members of the group who cannot read will be able to think about the passage well and let God speak to them through it.

1. Set the scene for the story of the calling of Matthew.

    Matthew was a tax collector, and no one liked tax collectors. The Jews considered them traitors, and the Romans saw them as cheats. One day Matthew left his house to go to his office. As he went down the street, not even the children would greet him. They ran away as they saw him coming. He arrived in his office and settled down to arrange his papers and count his money. As you hear this story, imagine yourself in the scene, either as Matthew or as someone watching this happen.

2. Invite the participants to shut their eyes to prepare for the Bible story. Read Mark 2:13–17 sentence by sentence, leaving a long pause after each sentence so that the participants can imagine themselves in the scene.

3. When you have finished reading the passage, ask people to reflect on what they have heard and allow a few minutes of silence.

4. Ask anyone who wishes to share with the group what he or she experienced or what he or she recognized.

5. Ask someone, perhaps a different reader, to read the same passage again, perhaps in a different translation. Ask the group what they believe God would like us to do in the light of this story.

6. Pray together, either with open prayer or facilitated by a group leader. Ask for God's help to put into practice what he has shown the participants.

4. Sacred Reading and Listening

For over a thousand years, individuals and groups of people have practised a way of meditating called Lectio Divina, meaning "Sacred Reading." Both readers and listeners can participate. There are four steps: reading, meditation, prayer, and contemplation.

A leader assigns one to four readers to read aloud, letting them know what to prepare either in advance or at the beginning of a meeting, so they can get ready. Readers practise reading expressively. Alternatively, if all participants can read, the leader may ask them to gather in groups of four people, so that each group member has a turn reading.

The leader may take a little time to introduce the topic at the beginning and provide some historical context. Then in the first step, reading, someone reads the passage aloud to the group without commentary and without preaching. We listen carefully and think in silence for a few minutes about what we have heard.

In the second step, meditation, we listen to the passage read again, perhaps by a different reader or from a different translation. We pay attention to parts of the reading such as words, phrases, or ideas that stand out to us. After a few minutes of reflection, we may share briefly with one another about what we are observing. We may want to write down or draw key words or ideas.

The third step is to first listen to the passage again, perhaps in a different translation or read by a different person in the group, and then all pray in response to the passage, either silently or out loud. We may ask the Holy Spirit for understanding of what he would like us to learn from this today. We may ask what he would like us to do in response to this passage. We may ask him for his help to respond.

In the last step, contemplate, we read or listen to the passage a fourth time, and enjoy God's presence with us. A leader may ask questions such as, "How would you like to respond to the Lord? Do you have unspoken fears, questions, or feelings that you would like to express to him? Have you experienced a new freedom in Christ or realized something new for which you would like to thank him?" Then, anyone who would like to may pray. We make requests and thank God, either silently or aloud, for what he has shown us.

Assignments

1. In what ways is leading biblical meditation different from leading a Bible study? How is leading meditation different from preaching?
2. Meditate on a passage alone. If God speaks to you during this time, write down what he has shown you. Sometimes your meditation will lead you to create a new song, poem, drama, visual art, or other Scripture-infused work to share.
3. Decide on a passage that you would like to use for meditation with a group you know. Decide on four people you will ask to read the passage for the four steps of Lectio Divina, or plan whom you would like to ask to read each part of a long reading. Let these people know what to read in advance so they can practise reading aloud expressively. You could consider asking different people to read various translations. Lead a meditation in a group.
4. Write down or discuss your reflections on how meditation has helped you and how you find it challenging.

Readings

Demarest, Bruce. *Satisfy Your Soul: Restoring the Heart of Christian Spirituality.* Colorado Springs, CO: NavPress, 1999.

Dysinger, Luke. "Accepting the Embrace of God: The Ancient Art of Lectio Devina." 1989. http://www.valyermo.com/ld-art.html.

Foster, Richard. "Meditation." Chapter 2 of *Celebration of Discipline: The Path to Spiritual Growth – Special Anniversary Edition.* San Francisco: HarperOne, 2018.

Manneh, Elizabeth. "Lectio Divina: A Beginner's Guide." Busted Halo, 1 March 2020. https://bustedhalo.com/ministry-resources/lectio-divina-beginners-guide.

Nouwen, Henri. *The Return of the Prodigal Son: A Story of Homecoming.* New York: Image, 1993.

Silf, Margaret. *Inner Compass: An Invitation to Ignatian Spirituality.* Chicago: Jesuit Way, 1999.

Taylor University Center for Scripture Engagement. "Lectio Divina." Forum of Bible Agencies International, 2014. http://www.scripture-engagement.org/content/lectio-divina.

Other Resources

Lectio 365 – Apple App Store or Google Play Store.

There are many Lectio Divina, Christian mediation, and prayer apps available on both the Apple App Store and Google Play Store for free. These can be wonderful resources to explore.

14

Trauma Healing

Introduction

One way to show people that the Bible is relevant to their lives is to do what is called an "integrated Bible study" to address their human concerns. This type of study combines material from Scripture with information from another field to help meet a need in the community.

This chapter gives an example of such a study on trauma healing. When widespread trauma strikes a community through war, natural disaster, criminal activities, or a pandemic, biblical truths and practical counselling principles can help bring healing to those who are suffering pain in their hearts.[1]

TROUBLES IN SANATU

The country of Sanatu had been stable for many years, but when the head of state died, it began to experience political troubles. As a result, violent crime increased significantly. The police and army seemed unable or unwilling to do much about the situation. As Pastor Simon looked to the future, he could see that the troubles were likely to increase rather than decrease, and he was afraid it might lead to war. "Is there any way I can prepare my Christian brothers and sisters for this?" he wondered.

One day the local school director, Mr. Randa, came to him. Mr. Randa was very distressed as he told how his family had been tied up on the road while coming back from visiting relatives. They had then been beaten and robbed of everything they possessed. Worst of all, his wife had been raped in front of their whole family. With bitterness in his voice, Mr. Randa asked, "If God loves us as you say, why did he allow this to happen to

---

1. An entire seminar could be devoted to this topic. An excellent resource is *Healing the Wounds of Trauma: How the Church Can Help*. It is listed in the readings at the end of this chapter. Also see the Trauma Healing Institute website for information about materials and courses, traumahealinginstitute.org, or email support@traumahealinginstitute.org.

us? Was he asleep? Was he punishing us for some wrong we had done?" Pastor Simon tried to read passages from the Bible to help him, but nothing seemed to help, and Mr. Randa went away even more angry.

The next week, Pastor Simon heard that the catechist, Lambo, had been involved in a car accident, and went to visit him. Pastor Simon was shocked and saddened to hear that Lambo's wife and two of his children had been killed. A drunk driver had rammed his truck into the back of the taxi they had been travelling in. Pastor Simon came to sit with Lambo in his grief, but he found that Lambo was very busy arranging the funeral and helping other family members. When Pastor Simon asked him how he was feeling, Lambo said, "I'm a Christian, so I shouldn't grieve. I know I will see them again in heaven." Other family members were expressing their anger with the drunk driver, but Lambo said, "I'm a Christian so I have to forgive him." Pastor Simon went away thinking that something was not quite right. He also wondered how he could learn to help people in these situations.

Have you ever tried to help people who have experienced trauma?

1. If so, what seemed to help them?
2. What didn't help them?
3. What do you think of Lambo's reaction to the tragedy?

1. Why Is There Suffering in the World?

Why do you think there is suffering in the world?
Discuss the group's responses, and then bring out any of the following points that have not already been mentioned.

The following is what the Bible tells us about the reasons for suffering:

1. Sin entered the world when Adam and Eve disobeyed God. Because of this, everyone, whether Christian or not, experiences the effects of this disobedience (Gen 3:1–23; Rom 5:12).

2. Satan has rebelled against God and tries to get us to rebel as well. Satan is a liar and a murderer, and he tries to get people to do his evil work in the world today (John 8:44; 1 Pet 5:8–9).

3. God gives us freedom to choose whether we will obey him or not. He made all people with the freedom to choose to do good or evil (Matt 7:13). We can suffer because of our own bad choices or because of bad choices others have made (1 Pet 3:17–18).

2. What Happens When Someone Is Grieving?

Grieving takes time and energy. As Christians, we do not grieve like those who have no hope, but it is still normal for us to be very sad or angry when someone we love dies or when we lose something important to us, such as our job, our house, or an arm or leg. The Psalms show us what to do with these feelings. When the psalmist experienced feelings of anger, abandonment, and sadness, he expressed how he felt to God in a lament (for example, Pss 3, 4, 5, 6, or 13). He cried out honestly to God and at the same time praised him for his faithfulness and love. We, too, can find healing by expressing our feelings honestly to God. If we pretend we are not affected by the loss, it will be much more difficult for us to recover.

We can think of grief as a journey that leads us through three villages.

A. Village of Anger and Denial

Immediately after the death of a loved one, people often feel as if their emotions are numb. They may find it hard to believe the person is really dead. They may also be angry with the person who has died for leaving them, or with God for taking the person away, or with other people who they think have caused the death. This stage often lasts about a month.

B. Village of No Hope

In the second village, people often feel sad and depressed for some months. They may feel that life is not worth living, and have little interest in the ordinary things of life. They may feel very lonely and guilty, thinking that it was their fault that the person died. After losing a job, for instance, people may feel as if they have lost their identity.

C. Village of New Beginnings

If people take time to be sad, to cry, and to feel their loss, gradually their pain becomes less acute, and eventually they are ready to begin life anew. When people get to this village, they show signs of new life. For example, they may be interested in finding a new husband or wife, or in having another child. If someone very close has died, the first two stages may take a year or more. This is normal.

D. The False Bridge

Sometimes Christians feel that, because they have the promises of God, they shouldn't feel pain or grief when a loved one dies or they suffer other losses. This is not biblical, and it will not bring healing. People call this "the false bridge" because it seems to provide a straight path from the moment of loss directly to the village of new beginnings without passing through the first two villages. God made us with the need to grieve our losses. Even Jesus cried when his friend Lazarus died, and he expressed painful emotions on the cross when he said, "My God, my God, why have you forsaken me?" (Matt 27:46).

Church leaders need to take special care to grieve their losses. Since they are busy helping others, they may feel it is inappropriate to be angry or sad. This will lead to serious problems in the long run. Going through grief honestly, as the psalmist did, will not only bring them healing, but it will also give their church members a healthy model to follow.

Have the group divide into pairs for this discussion.

1. Think of a time when someone you loved died or you lost something important to you, such as your job or your house. Did you go through these villages?
2. What helped you during your time in the first two villages?
3. When a major catastrophe affects a whole community or nation, like a pandemic, how may this make people go through the three stages?

3. How Can We Help People Who Are Grieving?

Sometimes we avoid people who are grieving because we don't know what to say or do. Here are some suggestions that may help:

- Help them to know that it is normal to feel sad and that they need to express their grief. If people do not allow themselves to grieve, the loss stays like an unhealed wound inside them. Eventually it will cause problems. These problems could be nightmares, unresolved anger towards people, or physical problems such as ulcers or headaches.
- Eventually they need to be able to bring their pain to God and ask for his healing, but this will not usually happen right away.
- Help them to write their own laments. This should include a statement of trust in God as well as expressing their pain.

1. Make up two drama scenes of a church leader visiting a woman who has just lost her husband. In one scene, the leader does everything wrong: he goes to visit her alone, preaches to her, tells her not to cry, and talks too much. In the other scene, the church leader goes with his wife or another woman, listens to the widow, helps her to grieve, and offers practical help.
2. Compose a personal lament about a pain you have experienced. It may be a written text, a song, or a song with dance.

4. Trauma Leading to Addictions

People may develop alcohol or drug addictions, pornography or sexual addictions, or gambling or other addictions for many reasons. One significant reason is trauma. People sometimes turn to addictions to deal with their pain. Addictions become deeply rooted in people's lives, so it takes a deep change for them to be able to stop their addictive behaviours.

Addicts need supportive groups that help them talk about and deal with the pain in their lives as well as learn healthy thinking habits. Because addicts use their addiction to deal with their pain, they need to develop new ways of thinking so that they can stop depending on their addiction to cope. Learning to apply the truths of the Bible to the struggles they have is an important part of this process. You can find out if there are addiction recovery groups in your area that can help. Also, Freedom Ascent trains leaders to hold Bible-story-based Christian addiction recovery groups in their community. Recovering from an addiction is a long-term process to establish a new identity and lifestyle that replaces old dysfunctional beliefs and behaviours. It is a lot of work and requires the support of the family, church, and community.

Assignments

1. List three principles in this study about grieving that were taken from Scripture and three principles that were taken from general knowledge about mental health.
2. What other kinds of integrated studies would be helpful in your context? Where would you find reliable information that you need, other than biblical information? What are the main points you would like to develop?

Readings

Finifrock, Jacob. "What Can a Pastor Learn from a Donkey?" *Scripture in Use Today* 9 (2004): 27–34. https://scripture-engagement.org/wp-content/uploads/2020/09/Finifrock-J-2004-What-can-a-pastor-learn-from-a-donkey.pdf.

Hill, Harriet, Margaret Hill, et al. *Healing the Wounds of Trauma: How the Church Can Help.* Nairobi: Paulines Press, 2016.

Other Resources

https://traumahealinginstitute.org/ – This website has extensive resources related to trauma healing.

"Hope Rising: Stories of Trauma and Healing." American Bible Society, 2014. https://scripture-engagement.org/content/hope-rising/. This is a video documentary that shows the "transformed lives of trauma survivors who have found hope and healing through the Bible's message of forgiveness and restoration."

https://www.storyweaversglobal.org/freedom-ascent – Freedom Ascent Addiction Recovery: this is a ministry that conducts online and in-person trainings for Christian leaders to begin Bible-based addiction recovery groups in their own communities.

15

HIV/AIDS and the Church

Introduction

Approximately 76 million people have become infected with HIV since the start of the epidemic. As of 2020, there were about 38 million people living with HIV, and tens of millions of people had died of AIDS-related causes. Progress in education about AIDS as well as testing and treatment for HIV have all helped to decrease the numbers of new infections, but access to these services is limited in some contexts.

AIDS STRIKES AZI AND SAM

"This isn't a death sentence!" Pastor Simon was talking to two young men in his church who had just found out they were HIV-positive. Azi was a young university student who had come back for the summer break and decided to go to the local clinic because he hadn't been feeling well for some time. His friend Sam was working for his uncle, making bricks in the nearest big town. He and Azi had talked together about how they both felt tired and had stomach upsets from time to time, but they thought the clinic would just give them some medicine and they would feel better. They were both totally shocked when the blood tests showed they were HIV-positive. They both were feeling frightened and went off to talk to Pastor Simon.

The clinic nurse had already explained to them that there was very good medicine called antiretroviral drugs, or ARVs, and if they took this every day, they would soon be feeling better and could get on with their normal lives. The nurse said that it was very good that they had had the blood tests now and could start taking the medicine before they became really sick. She warned Sam that he might have infected his wife and that she should come in to be tested. She also explained that when they first started taking the medicine, they might feel unwell, but after a few weeks their bodies would get used to the medicine, and they would feel all right again. But above all she said they must take the medicine every single day for the rest of their lives.

Pastor Simon talked and prayed with them, and they began to calm down. Azi was also feeling very guilty and talked to the pastor on his own to confess that he had slept with prostitutes. Sam had probably been infected when he was taken to a clinic after a bike accident and had a lot of injections. Even at the time he had been worried because they were using the same needle for a number of people and just washing it in between.

One year later, both the men were back in the village, but Pastor Simon was shocked to see how thin and sick Azi was. Sam looked fine, but he was worried about his friend. Pastor Simon sat outside his house with the two men, and as they drank tea together, he asked them how they were getting on. Sam said he was feeling normal and was glad to report that his wife's test was negative. He had not infected her, so she had not passed HIV on to their new baby either. The clinic doctor had told Sam that as long as he faithfully took his ARVs, he couldn't infect his wife.

Azi just sat looking down at the ground. Finally he burst out, "You said this disease wasn't a death sentence, Pastor, but I am getting very sick!" As they talked, it came out that Azi had not been taking his medicine. He had taken it for a month, but then, when he felt well, he had stopped taking it. "I wanted to forget I had HIV! Besides, I was so ashamed at the thought of anyone seeing me go to the AIDS clinic to collect my meds," he said. Gradually he became sick again, this time with a bad cough. The clinic had just told him that the medicine he had been given wasn't working any more because he hadn't taken it regularly. The nurse said that now he needed a different ARV medicine, one which was much more expensive and harder to get. He also needed to be treated for TB. Pastor Simon shook his head. "We'll have to see if we can find people to help you. I have some contacts and will try to get the medicine for you. Now let's pray about it."

1. How did the two men contract HIV/AIDS?
2. Why was Sam living a normal life while Azi was very sick?
3. What had stopped Azi from taking his medicine? How could the church have helped?

1. Facts about HIV/AIDS

The first step to overcoming HIV/AIDS is to know the facts about it. Give the quiz below to the participants. When you have finished, go over the answers provided at the end of this book (see 6. p. 292). Make sure everyone understands the medical facts connected with the transmission of the HIV virus.

1. What do the letters in the word AIDS stand for?
2. What does it mean to be HIV-positive?
3. How do most people get HIV/AIDS?
4. What is the second most common way?
5. Is there a medical cure for this disease?
6. Is there treatment for HIV/AIDS?

7. If a person starts taking ARVs before he or she gets seriously sick, and continues to take them every day, how long might that person live for?
8. Can you get HIV/AIDS in the following ways:

    (a) Hugging a person with HIV/AIDS?

    (b) Sharing the same razor blade with a person who has HIV/AIDS?

    (c) Using the same toilet as a person who has HIV/AIDS?

    (d) Having sex with a person who has HIV/AIDS?

    (e) Through an injection using a used needle?

    (f) Sharing food with a person with HIV/AIDS?

    (g) Through receiving a blood transfusion?

    (h) Kissing a person with HIV/AIDS on the cheek?

    (i) Drinking out of the same cup at Holy Communion?

    (j) Treating the open sores of a person with HIV/AIDS?

    (k) Through insect bites?

9. How can you tell if you have HIV/AIDS?
10. If a person takes the ARV medicine regularly and blood tests show the virus is not active, can that person give HIV to others? Why or why not?
11. If an infected person cannot get ARVs, what else can that person do to protect his or her spouse who is not infected?
12. What are the church's responsibilities in connection with HIV/AIDS? Name at least three.

> HIV/AIDS is only transmitted through body fluids:
> - Men and women's sexual fluids
> - Blood
> - Breast milk
>
> The virus can live outside the body only for a few minutes.

2. The Church's Role in Fighting HIV/AIDS

Local churches can play a key role in addressing HIV/AIDS. International organizations can provide medical and nutritional resources, but the local churches can provide equally important resources. They can bring people into communities of caring relationships. They can also give people moral guidance and hope for the future. They can teach the basic facts about HIV and AIDS, especially if there are no professional organizations in the community doing so. And if churches partner with international organizations in fighting HIV/AIDS, both groups can increase their effectiveness.

Three important areas in which churches can make a real difference are education and prevention, encouraging people to get blood tests, and encouraging HIV-positive people to take their medicine every day.

A. Education and Prevention

The most likely way for a young person to get HIV is through sexual activity, so churches need to educate young people about sex and HIV/AIDS. They need to help young people understand and accept the biblical pattern of abstinence before marriage and faithfulness within marriage. This education should be given before a child becomes sexually active, which can be as young as ten years old in some societies. Many Bible-based programmes that address these issues are available.[1]

It is very important that young people go to a clinic or hospital for blood tests if there is any possibility that they have contracted AIDS. If this is discovered before a person gets sick, there is a very high chance that that person can lead a normal life and not die young if he or she takes ARVs every day.

1. In your community, are there already programmes teaching about HIV/AIDS and its prevention? Are your local churches involved in this?
2. Do you have a programme of HIV/AIDS prevention education for ten- to twelve-year-olds in your church? If not, what could you do to start one?
3. Do the young people in your church know why they should get tested for AIDS? Sometimes the church can arrange for a group of people to go together for testing.

B. Care for AIDS Patients and Others Who Have Serious Illnesses

It is not easy to care for someone who is very ill. It is even more difficult in the case of AIDS because of the social stigma associated with the disease. Yet caring for the sick is an important ministry of the church, both to help and comfort Christians and to lead others to a real faith in Christ before they die. Even where ARVs are available, there will still be some people who will die from AIDS for a variety of reasons.

---

1. An entire workshop could be devoted to this topic. An excellent resource is *Kande's Story* by Kathie Watters and Margaret Hill. It is listed in the readings at the end of this chapter.

Help Them Prepare for Heaven

If the people who are ill are Christians, they will receive comfort from hearing about heaven. If they are not Christians, often they will be open to hearing about how their sins can be forgiven and how they can be sure of going to heaven. Either way, we should read Scripture, pray, and sing with them and their families. Let them know that they can tell God exactly how they feel. Psalm 38 shows how David expressed his feelings to God. Psalm 69 describes how we can cry out to God in our suffering.

Help People Understand HIV/AIDS and Talk about the Illness

Everyone needs to understand how HIV/AIDS is spread so as to avoid getting or spreading it. People who care for AIDS patients also need to be very clear about the things that do not lead to HIV/AIDS. For example, they need to know that they will not catch it by touching, eating with, or taking care of the needs of a person with HIV/AIDS.

Often people who have HIV/AIDS want to hide the fact that they have it. They feel ashamed and may be rejected by their friends and family. This does not help them or their community. President Museveni of Uganda said that Africans should deal with HIV/AIDS in the same way they deal with a lion that is stalking their village: no one would keep quiet about that! They would warn other villagers about the danger. It takes brave people to be the first to say publicly that they have HIV/AIDS, but this is the first step in "trapping the lion." Their courage can help others with the virus to speak openly.

Help Them to Continue to Be Part of the Community

People need other people! One of the worst aspects of having HIV/AIDS is the fear of being rejected by family and friends. Churches can work to help people accept those with HIV/AIDS rather than be afraid of them or reject them. Churches can help those who have HIV/AIDS by arranging times for them to meet together and talk openly about their experiences and feelings. In some areas, a group of people will meet once a month to receive their medicine, support each other, and sometimes learn other useful things such as how to start up a small business.

Help Them Work through Their Grief

It comes as a tremendous shock to people to find out that they are HIV-positive. They often go through various stages of grief such as anger, denial, depression, and finally acceptance. It may take months before they can accept their situation. Good helpers will be patient with such people and help them understand the grieving process. (See chapter 14.) Accepting that they will be HIV-positive for life is an important step. Once they accept this, they are more likely to take their medicine regularly.

1. Do people in your church admit that they have HIV/AIDS? What makes it hard for them to do so?
2. Does your church have a way to train people to visit those who are ill with any sickness, not just AIDS?

C. Helping Widows and Orphans

> Religion that God our Father accepts as pure and faultless is this: to look after orphans and widows in their distress and to keep oneself from being polluted by the world. (Jas 1:27)

The church has a clear responsibility to look after the poor and needy who do not have others to care for them. As well as giving food, clothing, and shelter, a local church can help orphans and widows learn to support themselves. In many areas, churches can work with organizations to help widows and orphans with the following types of projects:

- Make land available to small groups of widows or orphans, and give them the necessary tools and seeds to get started planting crops.
- Set up vocational schools where older children can learn trades such as carpentry, building, or sewing.
- Give a small group of three to six widows an interest-free loan to start a small business. For example, they could make clothes, furniture, jam, or snack food. They might cultivate land, set up a bakery, or breed animals. They pay back the loan after one or two years.
- Help orphans go to school by giving scholarships for tuition fees and providing textbooks and clothes.
- Look at some of the cultural practices that make it very hard for widows – for example, the in-laws taking away all a woman's belongings when her husband dies. Church leaders should look seriously at these practices and decide if they are what the Bible teaches or if they need changing.

1. How does your church help widows and orphans?
2. Can you think of any new ways of helping them?

D. Other Diseases

HIV/AIDS is not the only problem facing communities. Increasingly, there are new viruses spreading across countries and sometimes the whole world, like COVID-19. One of the reasons for this is that as the population of the world grows, people start farming and building houses where wild animals live. Because of this, there is a danger of more diseases jumping from animals to humans. Examples of this are Ebola, SARS, MERS, and COVID-19. In general, it is wise to avoid bush meat and particularly bats as they are known to transmit a number of diseases.

When a new disease or epidemic comes to a community, it is important to follow the guidelines of the local, national, and international health organizations, such as the World Health Organization (WHO). It is easy to pretend that an epidemic won't affect our community even though it has hurt other communities. Proverbs 27:12 says, "The prudent see danger and take refuge, but the simple keep going and pay the penalty." We want to use wisdom in helping our communities prevent and overcome sickness. Therefore, if vaccines are available to protect us from these diseases, as with Ebola or COVID-19, we should accept them. This is both for our own sake and for the sake of other people we might infect. This is a way to care for our families and communities.

Assignments

1. Find the most recent statistics available for the percentage of people who are HIV-positive in your country.
2. Make a list of at least five organizations in your country or region that you know are working to prevent the spread of HIV/AIDS. Describe how your church denomination can work more closely with at least one of these.
3. Find any statements made by your government about HIV/AIDS. What is their policy towards making antiretroviral drugs, or ARVs, available?

Readings

Carter, Isobel. *Responding More Effectively to HIV and AIDS*. Teddington: Tearfund, 2004.

Dixon, Patrick. *AIDS and You*. Secunderabad: OM Books, 2004.

Hill, Margaret, Harriet Hill, Dick Bagge, and Pat Miersma. *Healing the Wounds of Trauma: How the Church Can Help*. Nairobi: Paulines Publications, 2016, 60–68. Print-on-demand available under "Store" at https://traumahealinginstitute.org.

Madangatye, Tembinkosi. *AIDS: You Don't Have to Get It!* Pretoria: OM Books, 2002.

Raen, Konstanse. *Where Is the Good Samaritan Today?* United Bible Societies & Norwegian Church Aid, 1993.

Watters, Kathie, and Margaret Hill. *Kande's Story*. Learner's Book and Facilitator's Manual. Nairobi: Paulines Publications, 2009. In English and French. Revised 2012. https://scripture-engagement.org/content/kandes-story/.

Yamamori, Tetsunao, ed. *The Hope Factor: Engaging the Church in the HIV/AIDS Crisis.* Monrovia, CA: World Vision, 2003.

Yamamori, Tetsunao, Bryant L. Myers, Kwame Bediako, and Larry Reed. *Serving with the Poor in Africa*. Monrovia, CA: MARC, 1996.

16

Bible Storying

Introduction

People don't have to learn to read before they can understand the Bible and grow in their faith. In this chapter, we discuss an oral method of engaging with Scripture: Bible storying. This involves telling a series of key Bible stories starting with creation and going through to the resurrection and sometimes the start of the church. This method is particularly helpful in reaching unevangelized people, but it also helps Christians have a clearer understanding of God's plan of salvation and how to grow in their faith.[1]

THE KATAKARI WANT TO KNOW MORE!

Ngiri Baya was an evangelist sent by his denomination to work among the Katakari people. Traditionally, they followed another world religion and had been very resistant to Christianity, but since the Katakari Bible became available, a small number of people had become Christians. Ngiri found one small Protestant church and one small Catholic church in a region of about 500,000 people. As soon as he could, Ngiri settled down to learn the language.

Ngiri got to know the two groups of Christians. They told him how they had tried to persuade Katakari people to join literacy classes, but with very little success. They also told him how previous attempts at evangelism had been unsuccessful. Ngiri was very discouraged and wondered how in the world to start his work. Just then he received an invitation to attend a seminar on Bible storying, which he happily accepted though he had little idea what he was going to learn.

---

1. This chapter is a brief introduction to storying. If you feel it would be an important means for engaging with Scripture in your area, you may want to hold an entire workshop or series of workshops on this subject.

At the seminar, the leaders started by explaining that Bible storying was an oral approach that involved telling Bible stories in chronological order to a group of people over a period of time. He learned a set of stories in the national language and how to help a small group learn a story and apply it to their lives. He also learned how to select and develop new stories. He learned how to ask the group questions about stories that helped them discover lessons from them. He had lots of fun preparing dramas and songs based on these stories. When he played Noah in a drama, he built his boat with great enthusiasm!

At the end of the seminar, Ngiri had learned to tell four stories really well. He was ready to choose a set of stories that he thought would help the Katakari understand the overall plan of the Bible from the creation of the world to the beginnings of the early church. The Katakari traditionally bred animals, so he included stories from the Bible about sheep and goats. Since he had the Bible in Katakari, he was confident he could prepare the rest of the stories with the help of a Katakari speaker.

When Ngiri returned home, both the Protestant and the Catholic churches asked him to tell them what he had learned. He decided that the best way to do this was to tell a story in Katakari and then help them to learn it. He also had the group discuss what they liked about the story and what they found hard to understand. The Christians were very enthusiastic about Bible storying, and soon Ngiri had a small group of people who wanted to go with him to tell stories in a village that didn't have a church.

They set off the following week, and after getting permission from the chief of the village, they gathered together a group of men, women, children, and even all the village dogs! Ngiri told the story of how God created man and woman, and then he asked some questions to help his audience understand what they had heard. Then his group sang a song they had composed, using traditional Katakari music, about how God created Adam and Eve. By the end, the audience was joining in the chorus and a couple of the women were dancing! The villagers told Ngiri and others to come back soon and tell the next story.

Ngiri and the members of his group settled into a pattern. Each Monday, Ngiri spent most of the day preparing the next two stories. He read them a number of times in the Bible and then, because his mother tongue was not Katakari, he worked with a group of mother-tongue Katakari speakers to develop the best way of telling the stories. On Tuesday, he went over the stories again with his group. Then they prepared either a drama or a song for each story. On Wednesday afternoon and Saturday morning they went out to the village to tell the stories. After the first few weeks, Ngiri had Katakari members of his team tell the stories. He always asked the audience to repeat the stories they had already heard, and he asked them questions to bring out the important parts of the story.

After about six weeks, Ngiri's group had told twelve stories and were approaching the stories about Jesus that showed God was planning to send a Messiah. The week they planned to tell about the death and resurrection of Jesus, all the Christians met to pray that the Katakari would accept Jesus. As they came to the end of the account of how Jesus rose from the dead, many of the village people did just that.

1. How is Bible storying different from preaching?
2. Why do you think this approach would be successful among unreached people groups?

1. Preparing an Individual Story to Tell

It takes time to prepare a story. It is much easier to prepare if the passage is already translated into the language you are using. If the passage has already been translated, here are some steps to follow.

A. Familiarize Yourself with the Story

1. Choose a section of Scripture that is the appropriate length so that people in the community can learn the story and tell the story to others. If it is a long section of Scripture (for example, the story of Noah), you can tell it as short, separate stories.

2. Read through or listen to the story at least twice. Use different versions or languages, if possible.

B. Make Use of Aids for Learning the Story

Part of preparation involves finding ways to bring the story alive, so the audience can experience what happens. There are a number of methods that can be used to help a storyteller learn and teach a new story:

- *Dramatization:* Act out the story. This can be with one person reading the passage while the characters act it out without speaking. Alternatively, the characters can begin learning their parts and saying their lines.
- *Storyboarding:* Draw simple stick figures showing the sequence of the story.
- *Sensory walk-through:* Imagine you are in the story. Is the story taking place in a house or by a lake? Use all your senses. Smell the smells of the scene. See the sights in your mind. Hear the sounds. Taste the flavours, and so forth.
- *Hand motions:* Begin developing a series of hand motions that go with the sequence of the story. This can be particularly helpful for non-narrative sections of stories such as that of the suffering servant or the Sermon on the Mount.
- *Objects 1:* Have everyone empty his or her pockets, then grab all the objects in the room and put them in the middle of the crafting group. Then begin picking one object to represent each line or section of the story. So for the suffering servant story, "My servant will be lifted up and given a place of great honour" is represented by the tallest

object. "But he's also a lot like a tender shoot, pushing his way up through the ground" is represented by a leaf someone went outside and plucked.
- *Objects 2:* Similar to Objects 1 except that each object becomes a character, prop, or setting in the story. For the story of the calming of the storm, Jesus (a flashlight) gets in the boat (a cardboard box) with his disciples (a group of small sticks) and starts across the lake (a coffee table).

C. Identify Any Background Information Your Audience Will Need

Look in study Bibles or other helps to be sure you understand the background information that would have come to mind for the original audience. Then think of your audience and the background information that might come to mind for them. They may be missing some of the intended background information or use some from their culture that leads them to misunderstand the author's meaning. For example, in the story of the Passover, you may need to explain unleavened bread, or the sacrificial system, or the relationship between the Egyptians and the Israelites. In the story about the four men taking their paralytic friend to Jesus, people may need to be told that Jewish houses had flat roofs with tiles that could be removed. Some of this information can be given before starting the story, some may be woven into the story, and other things may be addressed in the discussion afterwards. Illustrations can be helpful to show things people have never seen before. (See chapter 10.)

D. Practise Telling the Story

Now it's time to practise telling the story so you are comfortable with it. Close your Bible, put away any notes you may have made, and try telling the story in your own words. Decide what details to include in the story. A story with no details is not very interesting, but too many details can make it very hard to tell. For example, in the story of blind Bartimaeus, you don't need to say that he is the son of Timaeus unless genealogies are important in your culture. In the story of Noah, the exact size of the boat is not important, but it is important that people understand that it was large. Be sure you don't leave out any details that are needed to bring out the main teaching of the story. Don't add extra details simply to embellish a story, such as exactly how drunk the prodigal son became. Let the story speak for itself.

Bible Storying

Every language has different ways of telling different kinds of stories. True stories may be told one way, folk stories another, and parables yet another. For example, if you hear a story in English that begins "Once upon a time" and ends "and they lived happily ever after," you know that it is a fairy story and not true. Find the correct way of telling each story from the Bible. It might not be the same for the story of Noah and for a parable.

Keep telling the story to your family and friends until you are confident you can tell it well. Watch their reactions to see if they are able to understand and find it interesting. Then record it in some way, for example on a computer, MP3 player, mobile phone, or voice recorder.

Finally, before the story becomes part of a set for general use, play the recording of your story for a person who has been trained to check Bible stories (often called a consultant). That person will check it for accuracy and style. If the consultant doesn't speak the language, translate the story back into a language your consultant does speak. If the consultant suggests making changes in the story, record a new version of the story. Always keep a good recorded version of each story to refer back to and to share with others.

Divide into small language groups and prepare to tell a story using the process just described. Each person should try telling the story. If you have Genesis in your language, tell the story of the fall in Genesis 3. If Genesis is not yet available, prepare to tell another story, for example the calming of the storm in Mark 4:35–41.

2. Preparing to Discuss the Story with the Audience

After the story has been told, the next step is to help the audience learn the story and then to ask them questions about the story. One good way to begin is to ask the audience to retell the story. You could go around the circle and ask each person to add a couple of sentences to the story. Another way to begin the discussion is to ask the group to act out the story.

When everyone has learned the story and can retell it well, then you can spend time discussing the story. You want the group to participate, so try asking some reflective questions. The questions below usually work well. You can also use some questions that help you achieve your purpose in telling the story. For example, if the story is part of a story set with a sacrifice theme (see below), then the overall aim is that people realize that sin separates us from God and that they accept Christ's death as the sacrifice for their sin. Here are some questions that help the audience think about these issues:

- What did you like about this story?

- Was there anything you found difficult or troubling about this story?
- What does this story tell us about God?
- What does this story tell us about human beings?
- What are some things you see God saying to us through this story?

The discussion period is not a time to preach or teach but rather a time to lead the group to reflect on the story themselves. This can be more difficult than it may seem, and you may need practice, especially if you are used to preaching or lecturing.

Allow the group to answer freely without correction. However, only observations from the story are valid, so ask those who give answers to say which part of the story supports their answer. If the group doesn't understand everything at first, don't worry. As they hear more stories, they will gradually understand more.

Use culturally appropriate means of conducting the discussion. In some cultures, questions may be used mainly to insult, scold, and mock a person, and commands may be more appropriate in the discussion time. For example, rather than asking a question, it may be more appropriate to say, "Tell me what Adam and Eve were not allowed to do in the garden."

For each story, think of local beliefs that might come to people's minds. Some parts of the story may be similar to local beliefs and reaffirm them. For example, a story might reinforce the idea that sacrifices are necessary. Other parts of the story may challenge local beliefs. For example, the story of Jesus healing the Gadarene demoniac may challenge the local belief that a mad person can never be cured by anyone.

Some local beliefs may cause people to misunderstand the story. For example, in the story of the storm on the lake, local beliefs may cause people to think that the disciples had sinned in some way and so were responsible for the storm. Some stories may seem to reaffirm local beliefs at first but then challenge them. For example, a group whose highest divinity was the serpent found the story of the fall similar to stories in their culture at first, but then had their belief challenged when the serpent was punished by God. Bring out in the discussion local beliefs that affect how people might understand the story.

> Let people discover what the stories teach!

Practise discussing the story of the fall in small groups. Have one person lead for five minutes, and then switch roles. If the leaders begin to preach or teach, the rest of the group should correct them.

3. Choosing the Story Set

Storytellers select a set of stories that are appropriate for their situation. They consider four main things when choosing their story set: the cultural background and needs of the audience, the main message of the Bible, the chronological link between stories, and the aim of the storytelling.

A. The Cultural Background and Needs of the Audience

No two people groups are identical. Each group has natural bridges that serve as points of contact between their worldview and the Bible. Each group also has barriers that may prevent them coming to Christ. For example, for many non-Christians in North America or the UK, you might find the following bridges and barriers:

Bridges
- People are open to new ideas.
- The Judeo-Christian heritage still has influence on the culture.
- Because of the lack of community, many people are lonely and unsatisfied with life.

Barriers
- People are mainly interested in material prosperity.
- There is very little sense of a spiritual world.
- Many people are independent and feel they are self-sufficient.

1. Draw up lists of bridges and barriers for your ethnic group.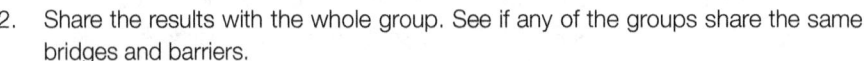
2. Share the results with the whole group. See if any of the groups share the same bridges and barriers.

Take one bridge and one barrier that have been chosen by most of the groups. Find a Bible story that addresses them. For example, the story of the tower of Babel would address the issue of people thinking they are in control of their destiny.

B. The Main Message of the Bible

Every story set must have the five essential stories listed below. All the other stories chosen should be fitted in around these five in chronological fashion.

- The creation of man and woman
- The fall
- The birth of Jesus
- The crucifixion of Jesus
- The resurrection of Jesus

After deciding on a series of stories, check to see that it covers the main beliefs of the Christian faith. One way to do this is to compare your story set with the Apostles' Creed (see box), since it expresses these beliefs.

> I believe in God, the Father almighty, creator of heaven and earth.
> I believe in Jesus Christ, God's only Son, our Lord, who was conceived by the Holy Spirit, born of the Virgin Mary, suffered under Pontius Pilate, was crucified, died, and was buried; he descended to the dead.
> On the third day he rose again; he ascended into heaven, he is seated at the right hand of the Father, and he will come again to judge the living and the dead.
> I believe in the Holy Spirit, the holy catholic church, the communion of saints, the forgiveness of sins, the resurrection of the body, and the life everlasting.

C. The Chronological Link between Stories

Stories should flow from one to the next. Where there is an obvious gap in time between stories or a change of focus, a transition is needed. For example, if the story after the fall is the story of Elijah on Mount Carmel, the storyteller needs to say something like this at the beginning of the Elijah story:

> Adam and Eve had children, and they in turn had children, until there were many people in the world. Some of these people obeyed God; some were disobedient. God sent prophets (those who spoke his word) to warn people about the wrong things they were doing. One of these prophets was a man named Elijah, and one day . . .

D. The Aim of the Storytelling

The aim of the storytelling may be to share the good news, to disciple new Christians, or to help new church leaders grow. An evangelistic story set helps people understand what went wrong in the garden of Eden and the need for sacrifice, so they understand their need for Christ's sacrifice. A discipleship story set shows how God has worked with his people over time. A topical story set addresses a relevant issue. For example, a set of stories might be developed to help new Christians who are facing persecution from their community.

Below are a couple of examples of story sets of twelve to fifteen stories that you can use to explore which stories and themes might work well in your community. These are only examples, and each language group will need to make up their own set. More stories can be added until you have a more complete panorama of the Bible. The new stories should be inserted in chronological order.

Sacrifice Theme	Jesus as Victor over Satan Theme
Creation (Gen 1:1 – 2:3)	Creation of people (Gen 2)
Fall (Gen 3)	Fall (Gen 3)
Cain and Abel (Gen 4:1–16)	Elijah and the prophets of Baal (or Balaam)
Abraham and the sacrifice of Isaac (Gen 22)	Zechariah (Zech 1:1; 2:10–11; 3:1–9; 11:4–13)
Passover (Exod 12)	Birth of Jesus (Matt 1:18–25)
Day of Atonement (Lev 16)	Parable of the weeds (Matt 13:24–30)
Suffering servant (Isa 52–53)	Healing of demon-possessed boy (Mark 9; or some other relevant story of Jesus casting out a demon)
Birth of Jesus (Matt 1:18–25)	Parable of the strong man (Luke 11:14–22, 37–40, 53–54)
Baptism of Jesus (Behold the Lamb of God) (Matt 3:13–17; Mark 1:9–11; Luke 3:21–22; John 1:29–34)	Jesus's betrayal (Luke 19:47–48; John 12:27–31; Luke 22:2–6; Matt 26:15; Luke 22:39, 47, 52–54, 71; Matt 27:1–7)
Two or three stories of the ministry of Jesus, his teaching, and conflict with religious leaders	Jesus's crucifixion (Luke 23:1–3, 13–24; Matt 27:27–31; Luke 23:32–53)
Jesus's crucifixion (Luke 23:1–3, 13–24; Matt 27:27–31; Luke 23:32–53)	Jesus's resurrection and ascension (Luke 24:1–12, 36–53; Acts 1:8–11; Mark 16:19; Eph 1:20–21; Col 1:13; Heb 2:14–15)

Jesus's resurrection (Matt 28; Mark 16; Luke 24; John 20)	Simon the sorcerer (Acts 8:4–25; or some other relevant story of spirit-world interaction in Acts, for example the Jewish sorcerer, Acts 13:4–12; the slave girl fortune teller, Acts 16; sons of Sceva, Acts 19:8–20)
Paul in Corinth and Ephesus (including 1 Cor 5:7)	
A better sacrifice (Heb 9:6–14)	

Design a set of twelve to fifteen stories for your ethnic group. Start with the five essential ones, and build around them. State why you have added each one.

4. Conducting the Storying Session

Here is the usual way to have a storying session:

1. Review the previous story you told the group by asking questions about it or by asking a couple of people to tell the story.
2. Tell the new story.
3. Help the audience to learn the story (see section 1B above).
4. Lead a process of discussion and application (see section 2 above).
5. Prepare a song or drama based on the story and perform it for the group. (See chapters 24 and 25.)

Reread the story at the beginning of this chapter, noting how Ngiri moved through this process.

5. If the Scripture Passages Have Not Been Translated

Providing Scripture in oral form to people who prefer oral communication puts the Bible within their reach. But it is equally important to give the Scriptures to them in the language they know best. If there is no mother-tongue translation of the particular Scripture passages, try to arrange for a trained translation team to translate them, or ask people with expertise in storying in languages without a translation of Scripture to help you craft the stories.

If there is only a New Testament in the language, it will contain many terms needed for Old Testament stories – terms for sin, spirit, angel, and so forth. Find and use them in your stories.

Translating stories is easier than translating Scripture passages because storytellers can leave out details that don't contribute to the main point. Often the most difficult challenges of translation are in these details. For example, finding a way to express "gopher wood" in a local language may be quite difficult, but in a story, you can simply say "wood." Another factor that makes translating stories easier than translating Scripture passages is that the stories often begin with the Old Testament, which has fewer abstract terms than the New Testament. Regardless of the number of difficult terms, however, each one needs to be worked through carefully so that the correct meaning is expressed in a way that people can understand. (See chapter 2.)

Make a list of all the terms in the story of the fall in Genesis 3:1–9 that would be difficult to express in your language. Put brackets around terms that it will not be necessary to include in the story, such as "fig" leaves.

6. Stories in Other Media

Stories can be told live, but they can also be recorded and distributed in many different ways. This is especially useful in situations where people are not free to come to a story group due to social pressure or illness but are very interested in hearing recordings of the stories. If stories are recorded with actors taking different parts, it makes them livelier than having one person do all the parts. Groups can listen to the stories and then discuss them. Bible stories can also be distributed in printed form. These are especially useful in family devotions, Sunday schools, and as reading material in literacy programmes. Some church leaders may use a series of Bible stories as a series of sermons over a two- or three-month period.

Assignments

1. Can you think of ways in which you could use storying in your church?
2. Why is it that all denominations and churches can use Bible storying?
3. If you have Internet access or a mobile phone, go to http://www.orality.net (International Orality Network) and make notes on one article you choose from that site.
4. In addition to telling stories orally in small groups, what other ways of delivering the stories would be appropriate in your context?

Readings

Brown, Rick. "How to Make Oral Communication More Effective." *International Journal of Frontier Missions* 21, no. 4 (2004): 173–78. Also at http://www.ijfm.org.

Bull, Celia. "Chronological Storying: A Case History." *Scripture in Use Today* 6 (2003): 2–7. https://scripture-engagement.org/content/chronological-storying-case-history/.

Koehler, Paul F. *Telling God's Stories with Power: Biblical Storytelling in Oral Cultures.* Pasadena, CA: William Carey Library, 2010.

Other Resources

http://www.onestory.org – Read about OneStory, a multi-agency partnership that trains people to craft stories across languages and cultures.

http://www.faithcomesbyhearing.com – Faith Comes By Hearing records Scripture and organizes listening groups in language groups of all sizes around the world.

http://globalrecordings.net – Gospel Recordings Network, also known as Global Recordings Network, has free downloads of Bible stories and basic Bible teaching in many languages.

http://www.orality.net – There are many helpful articles about Bible storying on this International Orality Network site.

17

Preparing for Good News Encounters

Introduction

One of the reasons we read and study the Bible is so that we can apply biblical principles to problems in our lives and also help others. Discovering and experiencing great truths that we find in the Bible is often called a "good news encounter."

A common path to a good news encounter is through a personal conversation, either spontaneous or planned, in which a Christian helps a fellow believer or an unbeliever to discover how Scripture helps with a specific concern in his or her life. This usually happens between two people or in a small group. It is much more personal than a general presentation because it involves just a few people in close conversation. Unfortunately, many Christians feel very unprepared for such a conversation.

Preparing for good news encounters with others begins with experiencing them ourselves. This happens through meditating on Scripture with an open heart and applying it to our life. The next step is for us to engage others in conversations about Scripture. Having a realistic, flexible, and practical approach to that is the subject of this chapter. Finally, learning to train others for good news encounters helps them to experience this process.

This chapter will build on the concepts of Bible storying in chapter 16, and will help you to be prepared for chapter 18 on Scripture-based evangelism.

HELPING FRIENDS DISCOVER GOOD NEWS

People frequently came to Pastor Simon's house to ask for help with many different kinds of problems. One day Mr. Mba and his wife Grace came to talk with him. Grace had obviously been crying. After they had greeted one another, Pastor Simon invited them to sit down and tell him how they were doing. Mr. Mba said, "When our teenage son ran away two months ago, you were so kind to help us even though we don't attend church and don't really believe what you believe. The way you listened to us, your support, and the story you told about Jesus coming to seek and to save those who are lost meant, and still means, so much to us in our time of great sadness. However, since our son ran away, our sorrow has not gone away, and we have struggled with shame in addition to all our grief."

Pastor Simon said, "Thank you for coming to talk with me about your struggle. A broken relationship with a child can be so painful. My wife and I know that because one of our daughters decided to cut ties with us and doesn't speak to us any more. However, we have also experienced God's help to have true and lasting peace in the midst of uncertainty and brokenness. But I'm curious as to why you say you are feeling shame about your son running away?"

The Mbas talked about this for a long time. Pastor Simon would occasionally nod his head with understanding or ask a question to help them elaborate some aspect of their story.

After the Mbas had finished sharing all this, Pastor Simon said, "Thank you for telling me that. I appreciate your being willing to share how you feel. It reminds me of when I was in the worst part of my worry and sadness after our daughter decided to stop speaking to us. Sometimes I felt like I was in a raging flood of anxiety that was carrying me away, and I couldn't see that it would ever end. But then my wife and I discovered something that changed things for us." He waited to see if the Mbas would respond.

"What was that?" asked Mr. Mba.

Pastor Simon continued, "I rediscovered that the Bible, which is God's holy word to us, contains many stories about parents who one way or another lost their children and were overwhelmed with sorrow just like I was. In those stories I came to realize that God is not far away and uncaring as I had begun to think, but rather that he is very near and is filled with love for us. These are amazing stories that changed everything for us. Have you ever heard one of these stories?" The Mbas said they had not. "Would you like to hear one of them?" asked Pastor Simon.

"You know we have said that we did not believe in God and at other times we haven't wanted to listen to what you have shared with us. But now we don't know where else to go or how to deal with this situation. I think we would like to listen now," said Mr. and Mrs. Mba.

Pastor Simon then told the story of the prodigal son. As they talked about the story together, Mr. and Mrs. Mba realized that the story was about a father loving his son even though the son had sinned, as well as about God's love for people. Mr. and Mrs. Mba related to loving their child even though he was doing wrong. They also saw the way God loved them even though they hadn't been following him. The Mbas were tremendously encouraged that God loved them and wanted to help them through their painful situation with their son. Throughout the discussion, Pastor Simon helped them to feel comfortable sharing their questions and insights.

After they had discussed the story and had reflected on what they had learned from it, Pastor Simon asked quietly, "Would you like to know God in a way that will give you true and lasting peace?"

The Mbas looked at each other, and then back at Simon. Then Mr. Mba looked down at the floor and said, "We have not always been good people. There are things we have done . . ."

Grace added, "Maybe we are like the prodigal son too. We have been the kinds of people who are not acceptable to God."

Pastor Simon looked at them both with a big smile on his face. "Then I have very good news for you! You actually fill the qualifications for being the kinds of people that God loves to help! I want to tell you a story about that which will make you smile."

1. The Big Picture: Biblical Story-Weaving

Biblical story-weaving helps us to speak with immediate relevance to where people are at in their spiritual journey, and to bring Scripture to the centre of the conversation in a timely way to address a specific concern of those who are talking together. This approach can be adapted to one conversation or many conversations, as needed. Biblical story-weaving encourages us to enjoy Scripture, enjoy people, and enjoy helping people engage with God through Scripture.

The basic flow of a biblical story-weaving conversation is known by the acronym TOGA:

- **T**heir story – the other person's life experiences and concerns, and especially his or her spiritual experiences and a concern that is particularly in focus for that person at the present time.
- **O**ur story – one of our own experiences which is relevant to the other person's story, and which shows that we have truly experienced the love and power of God in a life-changing way. But keep this part short and don't let most of the conversation be about your problems!
- **G**od's story – a passage from the Bible that is highly relevant to the person with whom you are conversing.
- **A** new story – beginning a new story in our relationship with God, whether as a new believer or as one who is in the discipleship process and wanting to grow in some way.

The most important concept in TOGA is connecting. Connecting begins with personal preparation in which we connect with God each day, listening to him through Scripture and continuing to develop our experience of living out what we learn from the Bible. We connect to the other person's story in ways that are meaningful to that person and which demonstrate understanding and our genuine concern, respect, trust, and friendship. We connect that person's experience and concerns to our experience with God in a way that is relevant and understandable to the other person. We then connect to God's greater story in a way that makes sense to the other person in a highly relevant way. Finally, we help people to connect with God to begin a new relationship with him.

2. "But We Are So Different!"

Sometimes people have very different life experiences from ours. We therefore need prayerfully to seek God's help to understand our underlying connection with the other person's experience. We have all experienced shame, fear, guilt, disappointment, sadness, loneliness, and loss, in one way or another, and we have all had hopes and dreams. These experiences take place in countless different ways in people's lives, but the underlying issues are basic to the challenges we all face. It is from the underlying experiences we have in common that we can show others the difference that God has made in our life by his power and love.

To prepare for conversations with people who are very different from us, we can do the following:

- *Whenever we read or listen to Scripture*, we should ask ourselves, "In what way does this Scripture speak to a basic underlying concern in my life and in other people's lives?" When a verse or passage of Scripture clearly speaks to these concerns, then we should take time to learn that Scripture well in order to apply it to our life and to be able to share it with others as the Lord gives us opportunity.
- *Whenever we are in a conversation*, we should listen thoughtfully to the other person to understand what he or she is saying, and why. Our purpose is not to argue or criticize but rather to help the other person think through the concerns he or she faces and to consider how Scripture speaks to them. When appropriate, take time to go deeper – to explore in depth what is troubling the other person. This will help us to understand how to talk to the other person from a point of underlying connection between his or her story and our story or experience. It will also help us to know what Scriptures to bring into focus.

3. Let's Get Prepared!

The following exercises will help you to become a wise and skilful practitioner of this approach to good news encounters.

A. Get Prepared

1. Make a ranked list of people's concerns in your community.
2. Choose one major concern in your community as a starting point, and identify Bible passages that speak powerfully to that concern. The topic you choose should be one with which you can identify from your personal experience of how the power and love of God have helped you.
3. Meditate on one Bible story that addresses the major concern in your community. Think about how that story impacts you, and learn to tell the story well. The Bible story you select should have a clear connection to the issue of concern that you chose. Spend time, perhaps over the course of a week, meditating on the Bible story. Envision it over and over in your mind, and ask God how he wants to speak to you from this Scripture passage.

B. Put into Practice the Preparation Activities Listed Above

1. *Role playing* a conversation with a friend is a helpful way to test your ability to enter into a conversation without knowing where that conversation will go. For the purpose of the role play, however, agree with your friend that your conversation will focus on the topic that you have chosen.
2. After the role play, *debrief* on how it went. Each of you should say what you think went well and also what could have been improved.
3. Finally, *pray* for opportunities to share this story with unbelievers or with believers, however the Lord might lead.

C. Prepare Bible Stories

Think of how each of the following Bible stories could be used to discuss at least three different issues of concern in your community. If you are doing this as a group, challenge each other to see who (or which group) can come up with the most applications for each of the passages listed. (You could lengthen this list to include many more Scripture references, but try to keep it to effective "Ah ha!" moments of realization so that people can genuinely learn from it.)

- Genesis 1–2
- Genesis 3
- Genesis 4

- Matthew 4:1–11
- Mark 4:35 – 5:20
- John 18:1–27

4. Consider More Topics for Bible Stories

Further expand your ability to make relevant connections by starting with a topic of concern.

For each of the following topics that are common concerns worldwide, see how many Bible stories you can think of that could be used to speak to them:

- Abuse
- Alcoholism
- Broken relationships
- Death of a loved one
- Deception
- Discouragement
- Fear
- Poverty
- Shame
- Suffering
- Witchcraft

Be willing to have more than one conversation in order to get to the goal of life-changing Scripture engagement. If the most effective way to connect with someone is talking through a difficult life situation, it may take "forty cups of tea" (this means many conversations) before that person feels that he or she has been heard and is ready to hear you share God's word.

Caution: avoid "verse-bombing." Verse-bombing is when a person tells one Bible verse after another in a short time in such a way that listeners feel as if they have been attacked and bombarded with an overwhelming barrage of verses. This will usually ruin a conversation, either by leaving listeners feeling discouraged, or bewildered by more information than they can handle, or by prompting them to become defensive and closed to the truth.

Now try this exercise:

1. Select individual Bible verses that speak directly to each of the community concerns that you listed earlier in the preparation exercises in this chapter. Then choose one of those concerns and memorize a key verse for it.
2. Now pair up with a friend to have a practice conversation on that topic of concern. Listen to your friend talk about that concern and then discuss it using a key Bible verse. Afterwards, discuss together what went well and what could have been improved in this kind of conversation.

Readings

Brown, Rick. "Choosing Relevant Scriptures." *Scripture in Use Today* 8 (2004): 7–9. http://scripture-engagement.org/content/choosing-relevant-scriptures.

Dye, Wayne. *The Bible Translation Strategy: An Analysis of Its Spiritual Impact*. Dallas: Wycliffe Bible Translators, 1985, 39–61.

Willis, Avery, and Steve Evans. *Making Disciples of Oral Learners*. N.p.: International Orality Network, 2007.

Other Resources

Media for Learning or Teaching Bible Stories

https://www.lumoproject.com/ or https://www.youtube.com/thelumoproject – Lumo is also available through apps such as Bible.is and YouVersion.

Topical Concordances

OpenBible.info/topics/
StudyLight.org/concordances/

Bible Memory Verse Sets

www.navigators.org/resource/topical-memory-system/ – The Topical Memory System consists of sixty Bible passages organized into thirty topics which are divided among five categories. You can prepare yourself by memorizing key verses so that they are instantly available to you for your personal reminders and mediation, or for sharing with others in a moment of need.

For further information about practical and locally reproducible training for biblical story-weaving, email info@StoryweaversGlobal.org.

18

Engaging People with Scripture in Evangelism

Introduction

When we share Scripture with Christians, our aim is to help them grow in their faith. When we share Scripture with non-Christians, our aim is to lead them to accept Jesus as their saviour. As the evangelist John said at the end of his gospel, "These [things] are written that you may believe that Jesus is the Messiah, the Son of God, and that by believing you may have life in his name" (20:31). Evangelism involves communicating the message of the Bible to those we want to reach for Christ, and this is best done in the heart language of the hearer. This chapter focuses on developing skills in leading non-believers to Christ.

CATCHING FISH

In the area around Pastor Simon's village, there were five other small villages that had very few Christians. For some time, Pastor Simon had been thinking and praying about the people in those villages who didn't come to church, and wondering how to lead them to faith in Christ.

Like many places, there had been an evangelistic campaign a couple of years earlier, but it had reached only a certain part of the population. Some people were completely uninterested in the meetings. Others had come forward to receive Christ, and the evangelist had gone home feeling satisfied, but not much changed in their lives.

Pastor Simon was thinking about Ngiri Baya's success using Bible stories among the Katakari when another evangelist from his denomination came from the capital to visit the area. Pastor Simon thought the evangelist would want to run an evangelistic campaign as he had done before, so it was surprising when he asked, "When you go hunting or fishing, you know what animal or fish you are trying to catch. We first need to know more about the non-Christians in this area. Who are they? What do they believe? What is important to them?"

The evangelist and Pastor Simon prepared some questions and then visited people in the five villages to see how they would answer the question. Some of their questions were as follows:

- What do you know about Jesus?
- When we pass from this life, as we all will one day, where do you think we will go?
- What do you worry about?
- Are you afraid of anything?

After they had listened to people in many different compounds, they sat down to put all the results together. They found there were basically two different beliefs about God. There were the people who believed in the divinities and a God who was far away. These people did not consider themselves Christian. They consulted the traditional healer every time anything went wrong. They felt the church had nothing to do with them except occasionally they might go there for a funeral or a wedding service.

The second group of people considered themselves to be Christians. They went to church, especially at times of festivals like Christmas, and might have gone forward once at an evangelistic campaign to receive Christ into their lives. But their Christianity was very much on the surface and didn't change much in their lifestyle or worldview. If there was real trouble in the family or serious illness, they went quietly to the traditional healer to find out who had cursed them. Pastor Simon and the evangelist didn't find any followers of other major world religions in the area.

The people in these groups had similar fears and worries. These included fear of poverty, AIDS, COVID-19, and spiritual attack, worry about family members, and concern about what would happen after they died. Pastor Simon and the evangelist prayed together for a long time and then began to discuss the best way to reach these people. Since most people were affected by HIV/AIDS in some way, they decided to start by addressing that. They prepared a booklet in Palapala that explained the disease from both a Christian and a medical point of view. It also taught people how to share the good news of salvation in Jesus Christ with those who have HIV/AIDS. They went to the chiefs of the villages and offered to hold seminars using the booklet. Four of the five chiefs accepted their offer with great interest, and dates were set.

1. What are some advantages to finding out what people think and need before beginning to evangelize them?
2. In your own home area, would you find the same two groups of people Pastor Simon found in these villages? Would you also find other categories of people?

1. Using the Mother Tongue in Evangelism

In 1932, a man named Cameron Townsend was evangelizing in Guatemala, a country in Central America. As part of his ministry, he sold Bibles in Spanish to the people. One day an Indian from the hills asked him for a Bible in his local language. Cameron didn't have one. The man asked, "If your God is so great, why doesn't he speak my language?" Cameron took up the challenge of translating the New Testament into this man's language and went on to found Wycliffe Bible Translators and SIL. The aim of these organizations is to make God's word available to all people in a language they understand well so that they can know Christ and grow in their faith in him.

Why do you think people may be more open to Christ when they hear about him in their mother tongue?

2. Connecting Felt Needs to Salvation

To help people understand the way of salvation, we need to be able to connect it with people's felt needs. The same basic information about salvation can be presented in different ways for different situations.

You have the chance to explain the gospel to the following people from your culture. After listening to them, which Bible stories would you use?

- A man who has never been to church and thinks God is far away and uninterested in people.
- A woman who goes to church occasionally and thinks she will go to heaven because she does more good things than bad.
- A woman who wishes to become a Christian after an evangelistic meeting.
- A follower of traditional religion who is in great fear of the spirits.
- A man who has just come out of prison after committing a crime and feels very ashamed.

3. Explaining How to Know Christ as Saviour

As we engage in good news encounters, we need to recognize that people's most basic need is to know Christ as their saviour, regardless of their immediate problem. We can't assume that if someone goes to church, even for many years, he or she has this new life in Christ. Even church leaders can know all about Christ without ever knowing him personally. If we have any doubt about whether people know Christ, we can look for appropriate ways to offer them the opportunity to take this step.

We need to be able to explain the way of salvation in a way that is relevant to people in their cultural context. Explanations of salvation developed in the West often focus on whether people will go to heaven or hell when they die. This may not be the most pressing concern for people of other cultures. For example, missionary John Beekman found that the Chol Indians of Mexico were much more concerned about this present life and protecting themselves from the attack of malicious spirit beings. He presented the gospel by stressing Christ's power over evil spirits and nature here and now. This was good news for the Chol, and they responded in great numbers.

1. The Yanamamo of Venezuela believe that God exists and that he is powerful and good, but they believe that he does not like them. They believe they are under the power of spirits, which provoke them to attack and kill one another, making life very difficult. What story from the Bible could you share with a Yanamamo?

2. Below is the way one group from a traditional religion in Democratic Republic of Congo (DRC) began their explanation of God's plan of salvation. What things have they brought out that might be important for their audience?

    In the beginning of the world, God made people to be like him. He put them in the garden of Eden that had all good things in it. God loved the man and woman he had made very much. God came to the people, he talked with them, and he walked with them in the garden. So you can see how much God loved them (Gen 1–3). But although God showed his love to these people, they disobeyed his words and did wrong. Even though they turned away from God, God didn't turn away from them. God made a way so that people could return to him.

3. The verses listed below are often considered basic for leading someone to give his or her life to Christ. Decide if they would be the most appropriate verses to share with people from your culture. If not, suggest other verses and explain the main point you want to communicate by each one. At the end of your discussion you should have a list with no more than ten of the most important Scripture verses for people from your culture that bring out four or five main points. The list should be short enough for people to memorize.

    - God loves us – John 3:16.
    - People are separated from God by sin – Romans 3:23.
    - Jesus is the only bridge that people can pass over to get to God – Romans 5:8; 1 Corinthians 15:3–5; John 14:6.
    - Trust that Jesus can save you – John 1:12; Revelation 3:20.

4. Some evangelists prefer to use Bible stories to explain the road to salvation. They listen to a person's story ("their story"), then share a related personal story ("our story"), and then share a relevant story from the Bible that points them towards salvation through Jesus ("God's story"). The following is one set of Bible stories that can be shared over five conversations to lead people to a salvation decision:

- *Creation* (Gen 1–2) – God made a good world with a close relationship with people.
- *The fall* (Gen 3) – Human disobedience brought all the world's trouble and separated people from relationship with God.
- *The prodigal son* (Luke 15:11–24) – God desires us to be with him even though we don't deserve it.
- *Jesus's sacrifice* (John 1:1–14; John 19–20; Matt 28:1–19; John 14:2; Rom 5:8) – Jesus paid for our sins so we could have peace with him now and for ever. *Weave these into one story.*
- *Believe!* (based on Luke 24:36–44; John 20:19–31; John 3:16) – Jesus urges us to stop doubting and to believe.

Be sure to tell these as stories using the pattern described in chapter 16 about Bible storying and in conversations as described in chapter 17 about good news encounters.

5. People who don't know Christ may not feel comfortable praying to receive him as their saviour. You can encourage them to talk to God in exactly the same way they talk to other people, but it is often helpful to have a prayer of confession ready that people can say. Here's an example of one from the Democratic Republic of Congo (DRC):

> *Lord Jesus, I thank you because you died on the cross because I am a sinner. I trust you, and I ask you to come into my life and be the chief over all I do. Thank you because you forgive all my sins, and you give me life that never ends. Please direct my life, and help me so that all I do will please you.*

Now compose a prayer in your language that would be meaningful for people from your culture to say if they were ready to accept Christ into their lives.

Assignments

1. Think of an average village pastor, catechist, or church member of your denomination. What sorts of non-Christians does that person meet day by day? Mainly Muslims? Pagans? Nominal Christians? If you are not sure, ask a selection of church leaders in the area.

2. What kind of training would be most appropriate in your church to teach people how to lead non-Christians to Christ?

Readings

Beekman, John. "A Culturally Relevant Witness." In *Readings in Missionary Anthropology*, ed. W. A. Smalley, 132–35. Pasadena, CA: William Carey, 1974.

Brown, Rick. "Working Together to Advance the Kingdom of God: An Integrated Strategy for the Total Team." *Scripture in Use Today* 5 (2002): 3–9. https://scripture-engagement.org/wp-content/uploads/2020/09/Brown-R-2002-Working-Together.pdf.

Colgate, Jack. "Relational Bible Storying and Scripture Use in Oral Muslim Contexts, Part 1." *International Journal of Frontier Missiology* 25, no. 3 (Fall 2008): 135–42. https://www.ijfm.org/PDFs_IJFM/25_3_PDFs/colgate.pdf.

Dillon, Christine. *Telling the Gospel through Story: Evangelism That Keeps Hearers Wanting More*. Downers Grove, IL: IVP Books, 2012.

Other Resources

https://www.storyweaversglobal.org – Storyweavers Global trains Christians to do conversational evangelism and discipleship using Bible stories.

19

How Muslims Use the Bible

Introduction

To translate the Bible into action in Muslim communities, Christians need to understand how Muslims think and especially how they view the Bible. This can help Christians to interact with Muslims in a respectful and relevant way. This chapter explores these issues.

YUSUFU'S STORY: PART 1

In the far north-east of Sanatu, there is an area where many people are followers of Islam. One young man there, Yusuf, is twenty years old. After the third year of secondary school, he left school and now works as a guard at a bank. All of Yusuf's friends and family belong to a Muslim community that considers Christianity to be a corrupt religion. Yusuf had read a little about Christianity at school, but the only thing he remembered were the descriptions of the Crusades.

Yusuf works with a small group of men who know each other well. One day Yusuf heard that his mother was very ill in their home village, and he wanted to go home and see her. He worried about it all day, but only one of the other guards listened to his worries. His name was Ali, and he was a follower of Jesus. Ali even lent Yusuf a little money to help him pay for the transport to his village. Yusuf went home, and soon after he arrived, his mother died. All the family mourned together.

When Yusuf returned to work, he began to spend time with Ali. Whenever he told Ali about a problem, Ali responded with a relevant story from the Bible that he had learned.

Yusuf found Ali to be a kind man who truly loved God, and this attracted him to hear more. But he was concerned that the Bible might be corrupted and teach the worship of multiple gods. So one day Ali opened a Bible app on his phone while they were eating lunch together at work. He showed Yusuf a short video with Mark 12:28–30. There Jesus said that the greatest commandment was to remember that "the Lord our God, the Lord is one," and that we should "love the Lord your God with all your heart and with all your soul and with all your mind and with all your strength." Yusuf was relieved that the Bible clearly taught the worship of one God. He asked Ali how he could watch and listen to Scripture videos and recordings at home. Ali showed him how to download the Bible app onto his mobile phone.

Ali encouraged Yusuf to share this story from Mark with someone else that week. Yusuf invited his brother, Ahmed, to listen to the recordings with him. As they listened to the Old Testament passages about various prophets, they realized that all people are sinful, even the prophets. They discussed how God is so good and holy that he cannot put up with sin at all. They also saw that God loves people and provided sacrifices to cleanse them from their sins.

Ali showed Yusuf and Ahmed a passage in the Qur'an, 3:45–55, that describes how unique and important Jesus is. They were surprised and wanted to learn more about Jesus. So Ali showed them where to find the Gospel of Matthew on the Bible app. Yusuf and Ahmed began listening to it with their close family and discussing it.

Yusuf was shocked when he listened to Matthew 11:20–26, where Jesus said that the people who saw his miracles and didn't repent and believe in him would be condemned on the day of judgement. This frightened Yusuf. He had always said that he believed in the Prophet Jesus, but did he really believe? Did he need to repent and become a follower of Jesus like Ali? He knew he deserved to be rejected from paradise and sent to hell because of his sins, but now he thought that if he believed in Jesus, he might be saved from this.

When Ali told them that God revealed himself to ordinary people who had childlike faith, they were even more shocked. They had always thought you needed to be very educated to hear from God. Then they listened to Matthew 11:27: "My Father has entrusted everything to me. No one truly knows the Son except the Father, and no one truly knows the Father except the Son and those to whom the Son chooses to reveal him" (NLT). In their culture, rich families made the eldest son responsible for the servants and for allowing visitors to see the father, so all this made sense to them. As they discussed this verse, Yusuf realized that Jesus was claiming to be the only mediator between God and human beings, and that Jesus had the authority to reveal the truth about God. Yusuf had known from the Qur'an that Jesus had done wonderful miracles that no other prophet had ever done and that Jesus had never sinned, but now he realized that Jesus is Lord of all and the way to God. He is more powerful than any prophet.

One day the group listened to Matthew 11:28–29: "Come to me, all of you who are weary and carry heavy burdens, and I will give you rest. Take my yoke upon you. Let me teach you, because I am humble and gentle at heart, and you will find rest for your souls" (NLT). As they thought about this, Ahmed said. "Rest for your souls! This is what people pray for at funerals! Peace! This is what people wish on each other in their greetings." Yusuf said that all his life he had been afraid of many things: punishment in hell, shame, curses, the Evil Eye, and Jinn. Jesus was offering him rest from all these fears.

They continued for some months to listen to Scripture recordings and discuss them. The group noticed that the Old Testament prophets had told about Jesus's coming. The stories showed that Jesus had died in their place as punishment for their sins and had risen from death and ascended to heaven where he reigns as Lord of all and as saviour of those who believe in him.

Yusuf prayed that God would show him what to do. Then one night he had a dream. In this dream, Jesus stood by his bed and said, "I love you. Why don't you follow me?" When Yusuf woke up, he knew that he wanted to follow Jesus. He and Ahmed went to find Ali, and they prayed together. Yusuf gave his life to Jesus Christ, and his heart was filled with joy. Ahmed was not yet ready to give his life to Jesus, but he supported Yusuf in his decision.

Yusuf didn't tell his extended family or all of his friends about this right away. He wanted to prepare them first. He started by being kind to them, just as Ali had been to him. He told them about the dream he had received from God. This impressed many of his friends and family members. Yusuf continued to share deeply with his close family. Gradually, he was able to listen to the Scripture app with his extended family and other friends and discuss the passages. They had already downloaded the app onto their phones. Ahmed soon prayed and gave his life to Jesus. The family discussed it and agreed that Yusuf and Ahmed should obey the call of Jesus to follow him. They said they would support them, as long as they didn't shame them by ignoring their customs and dishonouring their prophet.

Eventually Yusuf and Ahmed became part of a group of Muslims who met in Ali's home to pray and to study the Scriptures together. Yusuf also began mentoring a larger group of friends and family members in his village who had begun studying the Bible together.

1. Why do you think Yusuf began listening to portions of the Bible?
2. What were the main factors that led Yusuf to believe in Jesus Christ as his saviour?
3. Why do you think Ali encouraged Yusuf to begin discussing some of the Bible passages with his relatives right away?
4. Yusuf's family accepted his testimony about Jesus the Messiah, but they asked him to honour their customs and their prophet. What might this look like practically?
5. Do you know people like Yusuf? What things were most important for them in their journey to Christ?

1. Muslims and the Bible

Muslims are taught to believe in God, the day of judgement, angels, prophets, and Scriptures. The four main books of their Scriptures are the first five books of the Bible (which they call the Taurat), the Psalms (Zabûr), the New Testament (Injîl), and the Qur'an. In practice, most Muslims have only ever read the Qur'an, but many of the people in the Bible are mentioned in the Qur'an as prophets, and Muslims want to know more about them. The main prophets are Adam, Enoch, Noah, Job, Lot, Abraham, Ishmael, Isaac, Jacob, Joseph, Moses, Aaron, David, Solomon, Elijah, Elisha, Jonah, Ezekiel, Zechariah, John the Baptist, and especially Jesus the Messiah. So unlike most non-Christians,

Muslims know about prophets and divinely inspired Scriptures, and they believe that they are important.

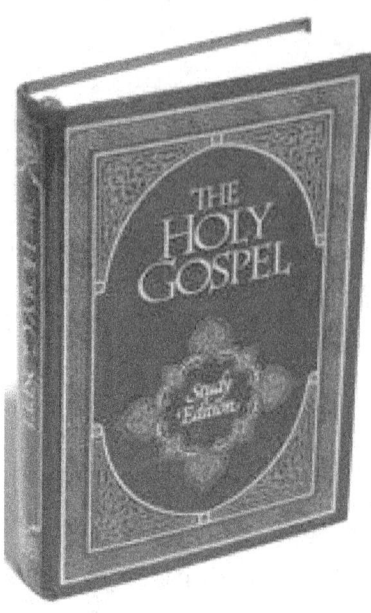

Several things discourage Muslims from reading the Bible, however. One is the Muslim belief that Jews and Christians have distorted these books. They fear that the Injîl has been altered to teach people to worship many gods: Allah, Mary, and Jesus.

If translations use names and terms different from those used by Muslims, this can cause further problems. For example, some translations use "Yezu Kristo" for Jesus where the Muslims in that language community have always used the form "Isa al Masih" (Jesus the Messiah). Some translations use a form like "Yuhannes" for John the Baptist where the Muslims know him by the name "Yahya." Although Muslims call Jesus "the Messiah" and "the Word of God," they don't know what these terms mean in the New Testament. There are many other terms in Scripture they might misunderstand, so they need help from a tutor or friend or an explanation in the introduction or glossary of Scripture publications.

Another problem Muslims have with Christians is that they are suspicious of people who distribute Scripture. Many Muslims feel more comfortable when Scripture is available in more Islamic or more neutral places, such as book fairs, ordinary bookshops, market stalls, or on websites that are respectful towards Muslims. Many Muslims also prefer to study Scripture with others, either other Muslims or a Christian who is able to answer questions about it.

Finally, Muslims feel that since Scripture is holy, it shouldn't have illustrations on the cover or inside. The cover itself should be elegant, not black, and not made of paper. The text of Scripture should be on off-white paper surrounded by a frame, and the introductions, footnotes, section headings, and cross-references should be outside the frame.[1] For digital materials, special care needs to be taken regarding other items on the website or social media page, such as illustrations, advertisements, and links to other sites. Memes and videos need to be respectful, especially with regard to showing the faces of prophets and, depending on the community, human representation of any kind.

2. Studying the Scriptures Together

Muslim believers around the world live out their faith in Jesus Christ in different ways. Many stay within their culture and community. Continue reading Yusuf's story.

YUSUF'S STORY: PART 2

One day Yusuf met a Christian named John, who was from a different part of the country. Yusuf invited him to his house for tea. Unlike the Christians who ran the bars in Yusuf's town, John was a deeply religious man who knew the Bible well. They talked about the

---

1. See *The Holy Gospel* published by the Australian Bible Society and other Bible societies as a good example of a Muslim-friendly format.

Pharisees, Sadducees, Herodians, and Zealots, what these groups believed, and why they rejected the saviour whom God sent to them. Then they tried to think of similar characteristics in their own lives that might be hindering their walk with God. John told Yusuf that if he continued to observe the fasts and feasts, as his family had asked, he would be like the Pharisees. Then John said, "A group of people come to my house every Sunday to study the Bible. Would you like to join us?" Yusuf smiled.

On Sunday, Yusuf went to John's house. When he walked inside, he immediately felt uncomfortable because he was the only one wearing a long robe and cap. The women were sitting with men, and that made him uncomfortable too, especially since these women weren't wearing clothes that covered their arms, legs, and hair. He tried to be very careful to avoid defiling himself by looking at them. They were preparing to pray and read the Bible, but Yusuf was surprised that he was the only one who had removed his shoes. Worse yet, some of them had set their Bibles on the ground. Some had even set them near their feet! On the wall there was an image of Jesus, and Yusuf wondered if this was the idol his friends had told him Christians worshipped. The whole atmosphere didn't seem reverent to him. The group sang one song in English and another in his mother tongue, but the melodies were foreign and sounded odd to Yusuf. Then John read a short passage of Scripture and talked for a while. At the end of the meeting, Yusuf said to himself, "I'm never coming back here."

On Wednesday, Yusuf and his brother, Ahmed, went to Ali's house to study the Scriptures with a group of men who gathered there once a week. The women met on different days and were led by Ali's wife, Maryam. Ali welcomed Yusuf and Ahmed. They removed their shoes at the door, washed their hands and feet, and sat cross-legged in a circle with the others on clean mats. After they prayed, Ali opened the Scripture chest, took out the Injîl, and set it on a special stand. He read two chapters aloud, and prayed that God would give them light. Then they meditated quietly for a few minutes on what they had heard, looking to the Holy Spirit to help them understand its application to their lives and thoughts. Different people talked about the passage in turn, saying what it taught them about God, about their duty to one another, and about how they should live.

Ali read a key verse from the passage several times and everyone repeated it until they had memorized it. After that, they talked about other passages that they had read during the week, difficulties that they had faced, victories that they had won, and things that they wanted prayer for. Then they prayed together about their problems and gave thanks to God for his blessings and love. Then they drank tea and talked with one another as friends. Yusuf and Ahmed felt that they were among the family of God.

1. How did Ali show respect for Yusuf and his culture?
2. What could John have done to show more courtesy and respect?
3. How did the two meetings differ in the way they treated and studied the Scriptures?
4. What are some Muslim customs about handling Scripture that it is important to respect?
5. If a Muslim asked you why he or she should study the Bible, what would you say?
6. If a Muslim asked you how to study the Bible, what would you say?

3. Accepting Cultural Differences

The apostle Paul said, "I have become all things to all people so that by all possible means I might save some" (1 Cor 9:19–23). Sometimes we do things as Christians that make it likely that Muslims will reject our message. As far as possible, we should adopt the cultural practices of those with whom we work. Many cultural practices are neither good nor bad – for instance, wearing a cap – but are simply an expression of the identity of a group.

Many things about the way traditional Christians worship God are offensive to Muslims or make them feel uncomfortable. To experience how this feels, do the following exercise as a large group (it is not meant to be a model for a new church!):

1. Sing a well-known Christian chorus together.
2. Then change the mood by asking everyone to remove their shoes and line up in a row, with each person about 4 feet away from the person next to them. The women should line up in a separate row at the back, at a bit of a distance from the men. Find out which direction Jerusalem is and make everyone face that direction.
3. Now have everyone sit cross-legged in a circle and pray the Lord's Prayer with their palms facing upwards as if to receive the Lord's blessings.
4. Have them pray in the same fashion for the seminar or for any current requests.
5. Then ask the group:
   (a) How did you feel when we sang the Christian chorus?
   (b) How did you feel when we prayed?
   (c) Was it all right to pray in this way?

> As far as possible, we should adopt the cultural practices of those with whom we work.

Below are some questions that a Muslim who is following Christ might ask. Have each small group discuss one of them. Then have them share their response with the large group, giving Scripture verses to support their views.

1. I'm used to wearing my long robes and my embroidered caps. Does the Injīl (the New Testament) allow this?
2. I don't want to eat pork or drink alcoholic beverages. It would make me feel polluted, and my witness would be compromised. Does the Injīl allow me to abstain?
3. Ramadan is coming. I would like to use this as an opportunity to fast and pray in Jesus's name. Does the Injīl allow this?
4. I would like to continue saying my prayers, confessing that Jesus is the Lord and saviour. Does the Injīl allow this?

5. In the evenings, I like to go to the mosque to pray and to talk to others about the Lord Jesus, the Taurat, and the Injîl. Does the Injîl allow this?

Assignments

> But in your hearts revere Christ as Lord. Always be prepared to give an answer to everyone who asks you to give the reason for the hope that you have. But do this with gentleness and respect. (1 Pet 3:15)

1. If a Muslim asks you about the Bible or Jesus, how can you use Scripture and testimonies to "give the reason for the hope that you have"?
2. How does giving "the reason for the hope that you have" differ from arguing or trying to convince someone?
3. How can you show gentleness and respect for the customs and religion of another person?
4. If you have contact with Muslims, think of two questions they've asked you and Scripture references that would be appropriate to share with them.

Readings

(All articles in the *International Journal of Frontier Missions* are available at http://www.ijfm.org.)

Brown, Rick. "Presenting the Deity of Christ from the Bible." *International Journal of Frontier Missions* 19, no. 1 (2002): 20–27.

———. "Selecting and Using Scripture Portions Effectively in Frontier Missions." *International Journal of Frontier Missions* 19, no. 2 (2002): 10–25.

Garrison, David. *Wind in the House of Islam*. Monument, CO: WIGTake, 2014.

Hays, Jeffrey C., and Philippe Accad. *Fouad Accad's Building Bridges*. Independently published, 2020.

Massey, Joshua. "God's Amazing Diversity in Drawing Muslims to Christ." *International Journal of Frontier Missions* 17, no. 1 (2000): 5–14.

Nealson, J. *Baghdad Believer*. Minneapolis, MN: Mill City Press, 2007.

Williams, Brad. "The Emmaus-Medina Intertextual Connection: Contextualizing the Presentation of God's Word." *International Journal of Frontier Missions* 23, no. 2 (2006): 67–72.

Woodberry, Dudley. "To the Muslim I Became a Muslim?" *International Journal of Frontier Missions* 24, no. 1 (2007): 23–28.

20

Engaging Hindus with the Bible

Introduction

To translate the Bible into action in Hindu communities, Christians need to understand something about the Hindu belief system. Unlike Islam, Hinduism is not a Monotheistic religion and Christians can sometimes find it hard to understand their beliefs and practices. This chapter starts with a true life story.

LALIT'S STORY: A REAL ACCOUNT OF A HINDU MAN COMING TO FAITH IN CHRIST

My name is Lalit, and I come from a very strong Hindu family from the state of West Bengal in India. It was at school that I first read of Jesus Christ and knew he was a god of a foreign land. I didn't have any opportunity to learn about Jesus, though, and never thought about him.

One day a Muslim neighbour, who was like a mother to me, came to Christ. That was my first encounter with somebody converting to Christ. She soon shared the gospel with me, and the transformation that I saw in her was so obvious and true. I could not believe what had happened, and that led to many questions, for example: Can God really speak to us? What is salvation? Why do I have to repent of my sins? Who among the 33 million Hindu gods can give me salvation? Why have I not heard any Hindu priest telling me that my god loves me? Why am I living, and what is my purpose in life? What is the real truth? I had many other questions as well.

I had to go on a long journey to get the answers to these questions. I started reading the Bible, watching videos, and reading books about Jesus and Hinduism. I started attending daily evening devotions in an evangelist's home for some years before going to church. Eventually, I wanted to go to a church service. It was not easy for me to attend the church service as my parents were noticing my desire to follow Christ, and they were not at all pleased about it. Because it was difficult for me to go to church regularly without them knowing, I started going to guitar lessons and at the same time going to church secretly, so my parents thought I had simply gone for my guitar lessons. This carried on for some years, and I have to accept that I lied hundreds of times to go to church.

After some time, I was convinced that Jesus was the true God and I needed to accept him, but I lacked the courage to tell people. One thing that struck me about Jesus was that he loves me, and he cares for me. I had never before experienced love from God or even heard that my gods loved me and had sacrificed themselves for me. This love was alien to me, but the love of Christ felt so real that still today I cannot describe it. My eyes fill with tears when I think about how much he loves me.

Twelve years ago, I had an encounter when I was praying with a group. Suddenly, a circular beam of light scanned me from head to toe. I started crying and repenting of all my sins; I remembered all the bad things I had done. As I was praying, I started speaking in tongues. I was not able to control myself but went on speaking and speaking. After a while, I felt incredibly light, as if I could float in the air. The following Sunday, in front of the church, I made the declaration that I had accepted Christ as my personal saviour. However, I didn't tell my family, as I knew they would not like it. Meanwhile, I continued to secretly attend church services, read the Bible, and pray after everyone had gone off to sleep. I spent a lot of my time reading the word of God. When sleeping, I had some experiences in which I felt someone or something was trying to choke me. But when I spoke the name of Jesus, it would leave my room and go. My family was not at all happy, but they thought it was just a phase I was going through. They valued being respected in the community more than anything else. My conversion would bring shame on my family, and the community might even ostracize all of them.

Meanwhile, I was continuing my studies, and a few years later I surrendered my life to serve God. I also opened up to my family that I had been baptized. In my community, Christians are the ones who follow a religion that they call a "below-water religion." You become untouchable when you follow Christ.

When I returned from my advanced studies, my dad asked me to leave the house. I have a verse as my motto – Matthew 6:33: "But seek first his kingdom and his righteousness, and all these things will be given to you as well." God also spoke to me before I left, telling me that I would have to hand over all the money and cards I had, which I did. So I didn't have a penny in my pocket when I left my father's house. I moved out of my father's house in faith, and God provided me with a job within fifteen days. My life had been turned upside down. I had a job interview and was selected to join a Christian organization, and I am still there today, serving God.

1. What were the main factors that led Lalit to believe in Christ as his personal saviour?
2. What should Lalit have done about his new faith in Jesus: should he have shared it earlier with his family? Discuss the factors and implications for Lalit's life for either decision.
3. In what ways can we encourage Hindu seekers to safely listen to and engage with the Scriptures and, where possible, attend church or Christian fellowship groups?

1. Introduction to Hinduism

Hinduism is about practices and the way of life rather than about beliefs or doctrines. It would be a mistake to approach a Hindu and expect to have a conversation about what he or she believes about Hinduism. The way to engage a Hindu devotee is to approach that person as an individual with his or her own set of beliefs and understanding of what constitutes his or her own Hindu faith system. Try to understand how and what your friend practises, why, and what he or she gets out of it. It could be said that each Hindu picks up what he or she thinks is important for belief in Hinduism, and that Hinduism is a religious system that values practice and conduct more than a particular set of beliefs or doctrines.

Having said that, there are some basic beliefs in Hinduism. The following list describes what many Hindus believe, but it is not a set of beliefs that one must have in order to be considered Hindu. This is different from the Christian faith because there are beliefs that are considered essential for a person to have in order to be a Christian.

1. There is a spectrum of beliefs about God in Hinduism. But essentially, Hindus believe in one God, who is called Brahman, the supreme God and the creator, and all the other gods and goddesses are representations of the various forms of Brahman.

2. Each Hindu and household may choose to perform *puja* or worship in accordance with their choice of god (clan deity) to worship. In India, villages worship local gods, who are seen as guardians of that location, and these gods

are representatives of the major gods. So, in a nutshell, Hindus are free to choose on which god or goddess (from 33 million gods) they will focus their devotion. Each state and area will have different ways to worship and different gods that are worshipped by the household.

3. Hindus also believe in reincarnation, which is the belief that the soul is eternal and lives many lifetimes through birth, death, and rebirth. The soul is sometimes born into a human body, sometimes into an animal body, and sometimes into a plant body. Hindus further believe that the process is governed by the concept of karma.

4. Karma is determined by how one lived one's previous life, and that determines how one is reborn. The aim is to be reborn into a better life than before. After several cycles of rebirth, death, and rebirth, the desire is to achieve freedom from this reincarnation cycle of life and to become one with Brahman. This state of being where the soul becomes one with Brahman (who along with being the creator is also considered a universal soul) is called Moksha. So, the goal in a Hindu's life is to achieve Moksha, that is, to become one with Brahman.

5. Hindus differ on whether the Brahman is a personal or impersonal god. He could be regarded as either a being or a non-being, which is a universal principle or ultimate reality.

6. There is no single text or creed that forms the basis of all Hindu beliefs. The multitude of Hindu texts can be divided into two categories, the "revealed text" and those based on what humanity has learned and documented. The Vedas are in the first category, and the Mahabharata and the Ramayana are in the second category. The Puranas are stories about Hindu deities, and the Tantras are texts that explain ritual practices and observances.

7. Caste is a system of relationships within Hindu society, and at its core is the value of your relationship with your extended family. The caste system determines where your family grouping is within the community, what occupation you are to engage in, and whom you can marry. There are four accepted caste categories and one category for people who fall out of these four categories. There are the Brahmins (priestly), the Kshatriyas (warriors or administrators), the Vaishyas (tradesmen, farmers, merchants), and the Shudras (labourers). Those who fall out of these categories of caste are the outcastes, or Dalits (the untouchables).

2. Ways to Share Our Faith with Hindus

1. The first thing to do is to pray for your Hindu friend that God might open up his or her heart and mind to the gospel.

2. Remember that relationships are very important to Hindus, so listen sincerely to your Hindu friend, and try to understand where he or she is coming from in terms of his or her way of life. You can have open discussions about your friend's beliefs, traditions, and practices.

3. You can also share from the Bible and share your testimony, but don't contrast your friend's beliefs with yours or try to prove that yours are better. Show interest and respect. Don't try to argue with your friend, as this is likely to create hostility.

4. Live out your faith before your Hindu friend. What matters at this stage is not so much the belief system or doctrines as the practice of our faith. Tell your friend about what Jesus did and how he demonstrated his love for all people. Because Hindus put a strong emphasis on being devoted to a particular god, you can demonstrate your devotion to God and share with your Hindu friend about Jesus as well as reading from the Bible about who Jesus is, what he is like, and what he has done.

5. The concept of community is very significant for Hindus. Therefore, never ask a Hindu to leave his or her community to join yours. Instead, encourage your friend to explore the teachings and life of Jesus through the gospels. Later, you can share with your friend that you would like him or her to become a devotee or follower of Jesus as well.

6. It may be difficult for a Hindu to go to a church. Hindus will not be comfortable with a lot of things in church at first, so initially, going to church may not be the best thing for them to do. Instead, we should regularly do house visits and ask a new believer to join Bible study groups, retreats, and so forth. Where possible, reach out to the family as a whole unit, as opposed to just one member. This is because if an individual becomes a Christian, he or she would need to leave the family.

7. The following Bible passages may be helpful to use when reaching out to a Hindu:
    - *Psalm 131:* Affirm and live out a settled life and that a still and quiet soul is what is desired in a relationship with God. Humility and contentment of spirit, in simplicity, renunciation, spirituality, and

sacrificial service, are also values that Hindus can understand and accept, and are attracted to.
- *1 Corinthians 7:17-24:* Affirm that separation from family and culture is not necessary in becoming a disciple of Christ.
- *Luke 10:42; John 3:16-17; Romans 5:8; John 15:9-17:* Centre on the life and person of Christ Jesus and his love and sacrifice for all people, rather than on the church or Christianity. Picture Jesus as the ideal man who demonstrated love and care for all, whether poor and marginalized or rich and educated. He mixed with both men and women, the religious and "sinners." He healed people by answering prayers and liberated people who were oppressed physically, socially, or spiritually. He cared more for people's inner attitudes than ritual practices. These pictures of Jesus easily resonate with Hindus and attract them to Jesus.
- *Matthew 5:21-22, 27-28; Romans 6; Matthew 11:28:* Talk about sin (not just the act of sin but the inner attitude and thoughts as well) – the debt of sin that Christ Jesus has paid, taking up the full load of the debt. Sin need not be a burden that Hindus need to carry on their own in the way they understand karmic debt.

Assignments

1. Write out two questions that your Hindu friends might ask you about Christianity. Then give Scripture references that you could use to share with them a response to those questions.
2. When the translation of the Scriptures is ready in the mother tongue, in what ways could you make these available to help Hindus engage with the Scriptures?
3. How can you help the women in your church learn to use the Scriptures in sharing the gospel with their Hindu women neighbours?

Readings

Braden, Charles S. "Hindu Interpretations of the Bible and Jesus." *Journal of Bible and Religion* 12, no. 1 (Feb. 1944): 42–47.

Garrison, David. *Church Planting Movements: How God Is Redeeming a Lost World.* 6th ed. Midlothian, VA: WIGTake Resources LLC, 2004.

Klostermaier, Klaus K. *A Survey of Hinduism.* Albany, NY: State University of New York Press, 2007.

Thomson, Robin. *Engaging with Hindus.* New Malden: Good Book Company, 2014.

Other Resources

Carter, Joe. "9 Things You Should Know about Hinduism." The Gospel Coalition, 30 October 2019. https://www.thegospelcoalition.org/article/9-things-you-should-know-about-hinduism/.

"Caste System in India." Wikipedia. https://en.wikipedia.org/wiki/Caste_system_in_India.

Halverson, Dean C., and Natun Bhattacharya. "Witnessing to Hindus." CRI, 22 April 2009. https://www.equip.org/article/witnessing-to-hindus/.

"How to Share the Gospel with a Hindu." Dare 2 Share Ministries. https://www.dare2share.org/worldviews/hindus/.

Judson, William. "Engaging Hindus with the Gospel." Southwestern Seminary. Disciple6 resources, Lessons, Yellow Year no. 22. http://disciple6.com/lessons/.

Lawrence, Chris. "From Hinduism to Christianity." Cru.org. https://www.cru.org/us/en/how-to-know-god/hinduism-to-christianity.html.

Pickett, Mark. "Sharing Jesus with Hindu Friends." Bethinking.org. https://www.bethinking.org/eastern-religions/sharing-jesus-with-hindu-friends.

Richard, H. L. "Ten Tips for Ministering to Hindus." Mission Frontiers, 1 December 2001. https://www.missionfrontiers.org/issue/article/ten-tips-for-ministering-to-hindus.

21

Engaging Children and Youth with Scripture

Introduction

At a Scripture engagement seminar in West Africa, participants were asked to compare the amount of effort that was put into different ministries of the church. The ministry that received the least attention was working with children. This is often the case in spite of the fact that in sub-Saharan Africa more than 35 percent of the population is under the age of fifteen (compared with less than 18 percent of the population in most Western countries).[1] This chapter shows the importance of children's ministries and how to develop appropriate materials and programmes.

NO ROOM FOR CHILDREN

Pastor Simon's church congregation was growing larger! Each Sunday morning more and more people seemed to crowd into the building. Many came because they appreciated worshipping God in their own language. One day Pastor Simon called a meeting of the deacons, and one of the main items to discuss was what to do about the lack of space in the church on Sunday mornings. They discussed the possibilities of building a larger church, adding another section to the existing church, or starting daughter churches in outlying areas where people came from. They agreed to think and pray about all these possible solutions, but they knew they would not solve the immediate problem for the coming Sunday.

---

1. These statistics come from the World Bank and are correct for the year 2018. Available at https://data.worldbank.org/.

Then Mr. Yuh said, "There is a simple solution which we can carry out right away. We need to ask someone to look after the children during the service, and then we can clear all the children under the age of about fourteen years out of the church. Then we'll have lots of room for the adults." Everyone agreed that this was a brilliant idea. Pastor Simon didn't think about it again until Saturday. Then he quickly found a couple of women and asked them to take charge of the children during the service and to teach them something.

So on Sunday, as the families arrived, all the children were told to go outside. By the time the service began, about a hundred children and teenagers were waiting outside the church. One of the deacons came out and told the two women to take them further away from the church where they wouldn't disturb the service. The women did this and then started the children singing a simple repetitive chorus in English. They sung this over and over again, and then chose another easy song. After a while, one of the women tried to read a Bible story in English to them all, but the small children cried and wandered around, and the teenagers chatted to one another, so after a while they went back to singing again until the main service was over.

1. What was the attitude of Pastor Simon and the deacons towards the children in their church? How do we know this?
2. What could have been done to help the children learn something during the church service, either in the church or outside?

1. The Importance of Children's and Youth Ministries

Why is it important to help children come to Christ and grow as Christians? (Bring out any of the following points if they have not been mentioned.)

Children are small persons, but they are important for the church.

- Children are the leaders and members of the church of the future.
- Children come to Christ more easily than adults who already have their ideas fixed.
- Children can have Scripture influence during their formative years. This will affect them all their lives.
- Children are part of the family of God, and no part of the family should be ignored.
- Children can often reach other children for Christ.
- Parents may be brought to Christ through their children.

What types of children's ministries are active in your churches now? Have the small groups report back to the large group.
Add meetings from the following list that have not been mentioned.

The following are typical meetings that a church may run to cater specifically for the needs of children:

- Sunday school
- Children's weekday clubs
- Camps
- Youth meetings
- Youth choirs

2. Running Children's Meetings

Several things could help Pastor Simon improve his children's and youth ministry.

A. Use Appropriate Language

Sometimes people use Sunday school and other children's meetings to teach children the majority language. Additionally, they may use the majority language to teach because this is the language used in church or the language of education in schools. However, these approaches will not help the children to grow spiritually if the majority language is not a language the children use on a daily basis.

The main aim of these meetings should be to bring children to Christ and help them grow as Christians. Because of this, the language chosen should be the one the children understand the best. An easy way to find out which language is the best for communication is to listen to the language children use when they are playing outside. That is the language that should be used in children's meetings. In the case of small children, this is almost always their mother tongue. If different children speak different mother tongues, it may be possible to divide them up into language groups for the main teaching time, and then join together for other activities when a common language is used. Alternatively, two languages can be used together for teaching, both the local language and the majority language, with the key teaching points being expressed in both languages.

B. Divide into Age Groups

It is unrealistic to expect one person to teach anything meaningful to a group ranging in age from three years to fourteen! Children of different ages have different needs and varied capacities to listen. All the children could meet together to sing or watch a drama, but they should be divided into age groups when they are being taught a Bible story. If possible, the children should be divided by age into at least three groups: those from three to six years old (that is, those in pre-school and first grade who can't read much yet), those from seven to eleven years old (primary school age), and those who are over eleven. If there are a lot of children involved, more age divisions may be helpful. With older children, it may also be helpful to have groups for those who can read and those who cannot. Often older children can benefit from helping the groups of younger children – it can be a way to disciple these older children and help them learn to take on new responsibilities.

C. Use Scripture

Since the Bible is the foundation of our faith, children should hear Bible stories and memorize verses from a very early age while they are still eager to listen. The best way to do this varies with the age of the child. When the children are young, the best approach is for teachers to tell them Bible stories using their own words, but explaining first that the story they will tell comes from the Bible. In the case of older children (eleven years of age or older), teachers can read the Scripture passage, explain it, and ask the children questions. If a number of the children can read, they can take turns reading the Bible aloud.

Children of all ages can memorize Bible verses. Once they learn a verse, it will stay with them all their life, and God may well use it to speak to them years later. Children often enjoy competitions to see who can say the most memory verses or can answer the most questions on Bible knowledge correctly. Churches can hold these competitions, first within their church, and then with other churches.

In some youth organizations, young people win badges or certificates for learning certain practical skills, such as caring for small children. If the organization does not already have a Bible knowledge badge, it could introduce one that involves knowing the books of the Bible in order and memorizing certain verses. Another badge could be given for knowing how to read and write the mother tongue properly.

Children also enjoy singing, so sing with them, especially Scripture songs. A youth choir may be the only meeting that young people attend apart from the Sunday service. If that is the case, introduce a short Bible study for choir members before they begin practising. Choirs can make up new Scripture songs and publish the best in a songbook or record them (see chapter 24).

Even if a children's or youth meeting is primarily for games, singing, or fellowship, it is still good to include a Scripture reading, a short meditation, and a prayer.

D. Make It Interactive

Children cannot sit still and listen to a long sermon! When we teach the Bible to children, we need to make our teaching interactive. This will help the children to listen and learn. Children need to be given the chance to speak, see, and do as well as listen. Make sure your lesson includes a range of activities that all reinforce the lesson you are teaching.[2]

E. Train the Teachers

Would you ask someone to build a piece of furniture without any previous experience? Certainly not. Teaching children is a skill that needs to be learned like any other skill. Some people have more natural ability in this than others,

---

2. Some sections of this chapter, including this paragraph, are based on or taken directly from Katherine O'Donnell, *Sunday School Curriculum: Based on the Gospel of Mark* (n.p.: Wycliffe Bible Translators, 2018).

and the church should begin with them and help them improve their skills. Experienced teachers should be used to train new teachers.

Churches can also arrange periodic teacher training seminars for Sunday school teachers on a Saturday or for several sessions in the evening, or they can arrange a workshop lasting several days. To provide this training they could use a suitable book or video or invite an expert to come and help the church. At the end, they can give a certificate to those who pass a final test. If the certificates are presented to the teachers publicly in church and are accompanied by prayer for them in their important work, it will help them feel valued by the church members.

F. Protect the Children

Children are vulnerable. When they are in our care, we need to make sure they are kept safe. Teachers should think about what activities are suitable for the children so that they won't get hurt. They should also think about whether the environment they are in is safe. Churches should think about protecting children from abuse and protecting teachers from being falsely accused. A simple policy that says a teacher and child should never be alone together in a lonely place (such as a room with the door shut or a car) is one way to help address this issue. In addition, there should always be two adults with a group of children in case there is a problem or an accident.

1. In your church, do people consider working with children to be important? What shows this? If not, how could this be changed?
2. In the existing meetings for children and youth, do the leaders read Scripture or tell Bible stories? If so, in what languages? Are there areas that you would like to change?
3. Is there any sort of training for those who teach children? If not, what could be done about it?

3. Designing Sunday School Lessons

The first thing to do when planning your lesson is to decide which Bible passage you will use. It is always best to follow a particular theme or book of the Bible for several weeks. Then, decide what the main point of the story is and how you can apply it to the children in your class. You should choose one main point of application so that the children can remember it well.

If you are able to use a Sunday school curriculum, this will be very helpful – many Sunday school curriculums in major languages are available in good Christian bookshops and also online. If teachers use one of these to teach lessons in a local language, they will need to prepare beforehand how they will express things clearly in that language. They should read through the lesson a number of times, practise reading the Scripture passage in the local language, and prepare any visual aids the book suggests. As they do this, they should think about how to say things in their language. If only the New Testament is available in a local language, they should use books of lessons based on it.

If teachers don't have a book of Sunday school lessons, they can learn how to prepare lessons themselves. It's easy to take a theme from the Bible and choose a series of Scripture passages to use over a two- or three-month period. A good lesson is always based on a Scripture passage. The following are some possible themes:

- Miracles that Jesus did
- People whom Jesus met
- Parables that Jesus told
- Things that happened on Paul's missionary journeys
- The story of Joseph
- The story of Daniel
- The beginning of all things (creation and the fall)

> A good lesson is always based on a Scripture passage.

It is important that a teacher prepares the lesson carefully and prayerfully so that he or she can teach effectively. When planning a lesson for children, it is helpful to follow a simple structure. Below is a template that can be used for planning a Sunday school lesson, appropriate for children younger than twelve (primary school-aged children). A sample lesson, using this template, can be found in appendix 3.

> Title of lesson series:
> Title of this lesson:
> Bible passage:
> Main teaching point:
>
> ---
>
> Opening activity (e.g. colouring, game, song):
>
> Review last week's lesson:
>
> Introduction to today's lesson:
>
> Pray: *For God to help the children to understand his word.*
>
> Tell the Bible story:
>
> Teach and apply the Bible story:
>
> Memory verse:
>
> A review activity to help them remember what they learned (e.g. quiz, craft, colouring):
>
> Prayer:
>
> Closing activity (e.g. colouring, game, song):

The following are some guidelines for how to prepare each part of the lesson.

A. Opening Activity

A fun activity at the beginning of the class will encourage children to attend and to be on time! This could be a game, some songs, or some colouring. If possible, choose activities that relate to the lesson's theme.

B. Review Previous Lessons

Make sure the children can remember what they learned last week and even in previous weeks before you start teaching something new. You can do this by asking questions. This is very important when you do a series of lessons that follow a theme or book of the Bible as each lesson builds on the previous lesson. It is necessary to remind the children of where you have got to and to build a bridge between the previous lesson and the new lesson.

C. Introduction

Try to begin the lesson with something that will attract the attention of the children and make them want to listen. You might bring an object to show them. For example, if you were teaching about the miracle when Jesus stilled the storm, you might show them a pillow and ask, "Do you think Jesus ever used one of these?"

D. Tell the Bible Story

When you are teaching little children, tell the story in your own words, simplifying as needed. When you are teaching older children, you can read the story aloud a few verses at a time and explain it as you go along, or invite them to read it.

E. Explain and Apply the Bible Story

After telling the story, you need to help the children to understand what it means and how it applies to their life. Find out if the children really understand the story by asking questions. Some questions may have a one-word answer the children can find in the story – for example, "Where did Jesus go?" Others, such as "Why did the disciples wake Jesus up?," may require longer answers. Still others, such as "Why do you think the disciples had so little trust in Jesus?," may require the children to reflect on the answer. Avoid questions that have an answer of yes or no, because these kinds of questions don't make the children think about the story very much.

It is also important that the children know what the story has to do with their lives. For example, the storm on the lake teaches us to trust Jesus when we are afraid. Discuss real-life situations with the class and pray with the children. Encourage children to pray; they can pray aloud as well as adults.

F. Memory Verse

Each week have the children learn a memory verse, and review the verse from the previous week. Sometimes it is good to use the same verse for two or three weeks to make sure they have really grasped it. At the end of each month, review with them all the verses learned that month without adding any new ones. Help the children to remember each verse by using actions or putting it to music.

G. Review Activity

Make sure the children have understood and will remember the lesson by doing a review activity. A good way to do this is to have a quiz: split the class into teams and have a competition to see which team can answer the most questions about the lesson. Other activities you could use include drawing or colouring a picture from the story, or doing a craft, a drama, or even a game. Doing this will help the children to learn better.

Another fun way to review the Bible story is to use puppets. Simple puppets can be made out of cloth. The children can use the puppets to act out the story. Actors stand or kneel behind a high table with a cloth over it to hide them.

Dramas of any sort help children understand a story. If you don't use puppets, you can ask the children to act out the story themselves after they have heard it, or you can have an older group present a drama to younger children (see chapter 25).

H. Closing Activity

If there is time, there can be a final fun activity to close before the children return to their parents or go home.

1. Divide into groups of six. Have each group pretend to teach a different age of children.
2. Read the story of the storm on the lake (Mark 4:35–41). Give everyone fifteen minutes to prepare to teach their story. (They should just prepare to tell the story, explain it, and apply it. They do not need to include games or review activities.)
3. One person in each group starts to teach. After ten minutes, tell the groups to change teachers. The people in the group who are not teaching should behave like children of the age of their group. For example, if the group is supposed to be six-year-olds, and the teacher talks for a long time, they should wriggle and play around!
4. After two or three people in each group have had a chance to teach, discuss in groups how the teaching went and how it could be improved.

5. At the end, discuss as a large group what other activities would be suitable for the lesson (that relate to the theme of the lesson). What game could they play? What songs could they sing? What memory verse would they choose? What other activities could they use to reinforce the lesson?

4. Using Scriptures in Schools

Church leaders may be able to teach Scripture in local schools, or churches may have teachers in their congregations who would like to do so. If your local schools allow pastors to do this, the pastor should use Scripture in the appropriate language(s). The pastor's example will encourage the teachers and students to learn to read Scripture for themselves.

Some organizations prepare children's materials that can be used in schools. Contact a local Bible agency or a mission working specifically among children, or use the Internet to find out what is possible in your area.

1. How do you think the Scriptures could be used more in children's and youth meetings during the week? What about clubs or camps in the holidays?
2. Is the Christian faith taught in your local primary and/or secondary schools? If so, what is taught? Do church leaders have any input into what is taught?
3. Do you think that the most appropriate language(s) is being used in all these situations where children are being taught? If not, who could change the situation?

Assignments

1. Imagine that a deacon in your home church says to you, "Why are you wasting time teaching children? You have to wait until they are about fifteen years of age before they will understand anything." Write down what you would say to that deacon.
2. Make an outline for a lesson on Genesis 3 for seven- to eleven-year-olds.

Other Resources

www.scripture-engagement.org – This website contains links to useful resources under "Children" and "Young People."

www.scriptureunion.global – Scripture Union has a variety of ministries worldwide, all with the goal of making God's good news known to children, young people, and families, and encouraging people of all ages to meet God daily through the Bible and prayer.

www.cefonline.com – Child Evangelism Fellowship aims to reach boys and girls with the good news of the Lord Jesus Christ and to disciple them in the word of God and in a local church for Christian living. CEF has many different ministries for children, but the primary ones are the Good News Club and the 5-Day Club, which take place all over the world.

www.max7.org – Max7 is a library of free ministry resources for children, youth, and families.

www.globalrecordings.net/en/teaching – Global Recordings Network has multiple resources in different languages, including Sunday school materials, available for download.

www.ministry-to-children.com – Ministry to Children provides free resources for helping to tell children about Jesus.

www.openbiblestories.com – Open Bible Stories is fifty key stories of the Bible (including pictures), from creation to revelation, "for evangelism and discipleship, provided freely for translation and multi-media sharing in any language."

www.lausanne.org/networks/issues/children-and-evangelism – "The Lausanne Children and Family Network is committed to connecting children's leaders and influencers with ideas, resources, and each other in order to see *children everywhere walk with Jesus*."

https://www.globalyouthculture.net – This site provides information that OneHope researched about teenagers and trends.

www.deditos.org – Deditos is a children's video series of Bible stories that is translated into many languages and can be translated into more languages.

22

Family Prayers

Introduction

This chapter explores the importance of family prayers and shows how all the members of the family can benefit from them. It also discusses the language to use for family prayers. "Family" in this chapter means all the people who are living in the same house or compound.

FALLING ASLEEP IN FAMILY PRAYERS

One day Pastor Simon travelled to another town to see some of his extended family. While he was there, he stayed with one of his cousins, Josiah, and his wife, Caroline. Josiah and Caroline had six children, ranging in age from three to sixteen. One of Caroline's sisters and two children of Josiah's brother were also living with them.

The first evening Pastor Simon was there, he was very happy to see Josiah calling his family together to pray before they went to bed. But one hour later, he was not so sure he was glad they had family prayers! First they sang a song together, and then Josiah read part of Ephesians from a very literal and difficult-to-understand English Bible. Then he preached a sermon in Palapala about how children should obey their parents. He talked and talked, and soon the younger children were asleep and the older children were whispering to each other. Finally he stopped talking, and they all went to bed. His wife, Caroline, had not said a word, and the children had been involved only in singing a short song at the beginning.

1. If you were one of the children in Josiah's home, do you think you would look forward to family prayers? Why or why not?
2. What do you think Josiah could do differently to involve all of his family?

1. The Importance of Family Prayers

Why are family prayers important?
(After taking feedback, add any of the points below which have not been mentioned.)

Family prayers are important in Christian homes.

- It is the responsibility of Christian parents to teach their children about God (Eph 6:4; Deut 6:4–7).
- Family prayers show children that their parents care about them and are interested in their spiritual life. This is especially important for children of pastors, who may feel their parents are only interested in the people in the church.
- Family prayers teach children to pray aloud.
- Family prayers teach children that the Bible is important and true.
- Family prayers help the family to live together in peace. If there are problems between family members, it may provide a time to discuss them and find solutions.

2. Content of Family Prayers

What activities might be included in family prayers?
Family prayers are for the whole family! Discuss together possible activities that involve different members of the family. Add any of the points mentioned below that have not been stated.

A. Bible Reading and Reflection

All members of the family who can read should take turns reading the passage for the day. Children as young as eight can read a short section if they have help preparing to read it aloud. After the passage has been read, the father or mother can ask questions to find out if the children have understood the passage. Then parents should share only one thought about the passage. If there are small children in the family, the whole Bible teaching time should not be longer than ten minutes.

Children under eight have difficulty understanding passages directly from the Bible. They sometimes find Bible stories designed for children or a children's Bible a great help. If these are not available, it is better to tell a Bible story rather than read it aloud. If you have both younger and older children, tell the Bible story freely for the little ones, then read it from the Bible for the older ones.

Bible reading should be in the language the family understands best and normally uses to talk to each other. This is a time to help your children really believe and understand about God deep down in their hearts.

B. Singing Together

Singing Christian songs together can be fun, but don't let this take up a large part of the family prayer time. Families that are musical could create new songs or practise a song to sing for the congregation during a church service.

C. Praying

Sometimes people think that small children cannot pray. This is not true! As soon as children can talk to people, they can talk to God. They may have a simple trust in God that is good for adults to copy! Have a time when everyone in the family prays a very short prayer, thanking God for something that has happened that day or asking God about something that is going to happen.

D. Sharing Joys and Worries

Family prayers are a good time for everyone to share what they are feeling about things that are going on. For example, an eight-year-old boy may say he is scared of a big child at school who hit him, while an older girl may tell how happy she is to have received a good mark on her school test. The mother may tell about a friend who is ill and needs their prayers, and the father may tell them about his concern that the rain hasn't come yet. After sharing, they can pray together.

Family prayers are particularly important if there are problems in the family or in the area, such as robberies, riots, or war. It is much healthier for children to have the chance to share their worries at the end of the day than for them to go to bed and worry about them in silence. Parents need to listen to their children rather than just telling them what to do or what to believe.

E. Special Activities

Include some special activities once a week or month to help make your family prayers more interesting. The following are some possibilities:

- Learn memory verses as a family. One per week is enough. Large families can have competitions to see who can remember the most at the end of the year. Older children can write out the memory verses on cards and put them up on walls.
- Have older children write down things the family has prayed for, such as a new house, a friend for a lonely child, and books for school. When the request has been answered, they can write down the date.
- Let an older child lead the family prayers once a week.
- Act out the story you have read. Each person in the family should be a character. This can be fun to do, and it helps the children to learn the story well (see chapter 25).

1. Describe your own family prayers. Does everyone in the family take part?
2. Which of the ideas described here would be good to try with your family?
3. When and where are best for your family to meet for family prayers?
4. How can you continue to have your family prayer time when you have visitors staying with you?

> Family prayers should interest everyone in the family.

3. Selecting the Scripture Passage

Have a system for selecting the Scripture passage to read each night. You can do this in several ways.

- Use a list of readings prepared by your church or another organization, or one that is available in a local Christian bookstore. If your church selects passages that have not yet been translated into your mother tongue, encourage your church to use those that have been translated.
- Read one of the gospels, a paragraph at a time, from beginning to end. Leave out parts that may be too hard for the children to understand or that would not interest them, such as lists of names.
- Choose a relevant topic, and make a list of Scriptures that address it. A topical index can help in making a list like this. Read one or two references each day. Some topics may last a whole week.
- Choose some of the Bible stories listed in chapter 16.

1. Choose one Bible passage that would be good to use in family prayers – for example, Matthew 7:24–29 or Luke 15:3–7.
2. Give participants fifteen minutes to prepare a family prayer session based on the passage.
3. Then in small groups, discuss what you have planned.
4. Afterwards, have the groups share their best ideas with the whole group.

4. Overcoming Barriers to Family Prayers

What are some barriers to family prayers?

1. List the responses on the board in a column.
2. Then in a second column, list possible solutions, as shown in the table.

The table lists possible solutions to some of the common barriers to family prayers.

Barrier	Possible Solutions
Many visitors are present.	Involve the visitors in the family prayers. Ask the visitors to wait until the prayer time is over.
The parents don't feel capable of leading the family prayers.	The church can provide resources and training. Parents can work together.
The children of the family are still very small.	Keep the family prayers short. Use Bible stories rather than the Bible.
Family members are too busy.	Keep family prayers short. Make it a discipline to have them. Find a different time in the day to meet together.

Assignments

1. Do you think it is important to have family prayers? Why or why not?
2. Do you think that most families in your church pray together each day? If so, do they use Scriptures in the language they use normally in their homes?
3. How can you encourage church members to have family prayers regularly?
4. Does a book of Bible stories exist in your language? If not, how could one be made?
5. Do you have any lists of Scripture readings that could be used for family prayers? If so, what are they?

23

Using the Bible in Our Digital World

Introduction

The way we access God's word has changed over the centuries. The Ten Commandments were written on tablets of stone (Exod 24:12). The books of the Bible were written on papyrus or parchment. Jesus unrolled a scroll to read from the book of Isaiah (Luke 4:16–19). Early translations of the Scriptures were handwritten in the form of books (called codices).

Then, in the fifteenth century, Johannes Gutenberg invented something that would revolutionize the distribution of God's word: the printing press. This made it possible to make copies of the Bible available to many people much more quickly and cheaply than copying by hand.

In our twenty-first-century world, we are experiencing another publishing revolution that is changing the way people receive the Bible: the digital revolution. This chapter looks at ways in which we can encourage people to engage with God's word in our increasingly digital world.

PASTOR SIMON WANTS TO USE THE BIBLE WELL IN OUR DIGITAL AGE

Pastor Simon looked down at his phone, tapped the Bible icon, and began to read from John's gospel in Palapala. He was excited about all the possibilities that digital technology could bring.

"Look!" he said to his friend Pastor Daniel who had just come round to visit. "I can tap this button and listen to the audio recording too! All the translated Scripture in Palapala, both text and audio, in my pocket!

"And that's not all," he continued. "I can tap here and see the Palapala text next to the English text, or I can choose Kisanu too if I want."

"Indeed, the world has changed! And it continues to change fast!" said Pastor Daniel.

"And there's something else I am doing now," said Pastor Simon, keen to tell his friend all about what he was learning. "When I see a verse that is connected to the topic I am preaching about on Sunday, I tap on it and share it on WhatsApp or Facebook. That can sometimes start off a really good discussion between the members of my church, and it is a way of sharing God's word with them during the week."

"That's a good idea!" said Pastor Daniel. "I've not really started doing anything like that. I don't think so many people in my church are on social media . . . And I must admit that I am much more comfortable sitting down with my printed Bible."

"Yes, I still use my printed Bible," said Pastor Simon. "Having the Bible on my phone is so convenient, and it lets me do lots of things . . . but I agree, there are still times when I want to escape from everything digital. It can be so distracting!"

"You're right there about it being distracting," acknowledged Pastor Daniel. "I sometimes wonder when I am preaching whether some of the young people are really following along with what I am saying, or whether they are doing something completely different on their phones!"

"Yes, digital technology is changing our world – and changing us – often without our realizing it," said Pastor Simon. "I think we need to spend more time talking together in our churches about how we can use the Bible well in our digital age."

"Amen to that!" said Pastor Daniel. "Maybe you could come to my church next month and lead a workshop on the topic. We would really appreciate that."

"I would be happy to!" said Pastor Simon.

1. What changes in digital technology have you seen in your community and church over the past ten years?
2. Which digital media do you use yourself on a regular basis?
3. If you had a training workshop in your church on the topic of using the Bible well in our digital age, what issues would you want to include?

1. Understanding Digital Use in Your Community

There are many types of digital Bible resources, many ways of making them available, and many ways of encouraging digital Scripture engagement. In order to make good choices, we need to have an understanding of the different kinds of people in our communities.

Here are some questions we can ask:

- What are the digital media people already use and are familiar with?
- Where are they available and at what cost?
- Which are the most popular media? Which are the most popular apps?

- What types of phones do people have: feature phones? Android smartphones? iPhones?
- How much access do they have to the Internet?
- Which social media platforms, if any, do they use?
- What capacity do people already have to create digital media?
- What changes are you seeing in digital media use, and what might be happening in the coming years?

In your community, it is likely that use of digital technology will vary between people. Some might have the latest phones and reliable Internet access, and be regular users of social media. Others might have more basic phones and will be online less frequently or perhaps not at all. As you think about how to encourage the use of the Bible in our digital age, it is good to think about how to address the needs of these different groups of people. Not everyone will use the Bible in the same way.

2. Knowing Which Digital Resources Are Available

Some people will be up to date with how the Bible is already available digitally in their language. Others will not have much idea. It is good to spend some time making a list of the resources you know about already.

In what ways is the Bible already available in digital forms in the different languages that people speak in your community? Make a list of the audio resources, videos, apps, and websites that you know about. Don't look at the list below until you have made your own list.

Your list could include the following:

- Audio recordings of the Scriptures (single-voice narration and multi-voice recordings).
- Bible videos, such as the *Jesus* film.
- Bible apps for smartphones containing text and audio (this could include apps with multiple languages such as the Bible App from YouVersion and the Bible.is app from Faith Comes By Hearing, and apps that have been built specifically for your language with a tool, such as Scripture App Builder).
- Websites with Scripture to read, listen to, and/or download.
- Songs based on Scripture.
- Audio and video dramas illustrating the relevance of the Scriptures in daily life.

- Pages on social media that are dedicated to sharing Scripture in your language.

If you do not know what is available, the following are some good places to start:

- Contact the Bible translation organizations working in your country.
- Contact Christian media organizations in your region.
- Look at websites that contain links to digital resources in the world's languages, such as Scripture Earth (www.ScriptureEarth.org) and Find A Bible (find.bible).
- Look at the Bible.is app and website from Faith Comes By Hearing.
- Search for your language in the Bible App from YouVersion (www.bible.com).

Once you have your list of currently available resources, ask the following questions:

1. Given the ways in which people are using digital media today in your context, what additional kinds of digital Bible resources would it be helpful to develop? What is missing that would be really useful to have?
2. What steps could you take to turn these ideas into reality? Who in your community could be involved? Who could you contact for help? What kind of training would be useful?

3. Distributing the Bible Online and Offline

It is not enough to have a list of interesting digital Bible products. Somehow they need to get onto people's devices! Just as we do not want to see printed Bibles sitting in boxes and gathering dust, so we do not want to see digital resources failing to reach their intended audiences.

There are two main categories of digital distribution: online and offline.

A. Online Distribution

This is when people use an Internet connection to access and download the Bible. It could mean reading or listening to the Scriptures on a website, downloading Bible resources, or installing a Bible app from an app store. You could also share God's word on social media.

What specific examples of online Bible distribution do you know about?

B. Offline Distribution

This is when people obtain the digital Scriptures without connecting to the Internet. It could be by sharing content through a memory card or USB stick, or between phones by Bluetooth or a Wi-Fi transfer app. Resources could also be shared using a Wi-Fi media box. A common method of distributing audio Scriptures is to use digital audio players (portable solar-powered devices containing the Bible in audio).

What specific examples of offline Bible distribution do you know about?
   As you think about the needs and opportunities for digital distribution of the Scriptures in your community – and beyond – consider the following questions:
1. What are the advantages and disadvantages of these different types of digital distribution?
2. Which distribution methods would work well in your context?
3. Who do you know who could be encouraged to be actively involved in digital distribution of God's word?

4. Promoting the Scriptures in Digital Form

Creating appropriate digital products and making them accessible to people are important steps, but we must not stop there. We need to think about how people will find out about them. There needs to be an effective promotion and marketing strategy.

Imagine there is a new smartphone app that contains a selection of translated books of the Bible in your language. What kinds of things could you do to let people know about it? What could you do to persuade them to download the app to their phones, install it, and use it?

Here are some ideas:

- Print a brochure advertising the app, and send it to all the churches in the region.
- Post a link to the app on social media, and ask people to share it with their friends.
- Make a publicity video, and post that on social media.
- Make announcements in church conferences, youth conferences, and gatherings of church leaders.
- Announce it on local radio stations or television channels.

- Use paid publicity such as Facebook Ads or Google Ads (just a small investment in online advertising will often reach many people across your country and those in the diaspora abroad).
- Train a small group of young people who will visit churches in your region to show the app and help people to download and install it.

5. Engaging with the Digital Scriptures

The Scriptures in digital form open up new possibilities of engaging with God's word. Here are some examples:

- A group of friends studies the Bible together on WhatsApp. The group leader shares the passage as text or as an audio clip, and the group members talk together about it, typing or recording their comments.
- After preaching the weekly sermon, the pastor posts some follow-up questions on social media for members of the congregation to continue to discuss and think about how to respond to God's word.
- A Christian student downloads clips from the *Jesus* film onto her phone in different languages. When she meets a fellow student, she asks whether he or she would like to see a film clip about Jesus in the student's language. They watch it together and talk about it.

What other ideas do you have for how people can use digital Scripture resources to engage with God's word?

6. Appreciating Both Print and Digital

It can be interesting to do a survey of people in your church to find out which format they prefer to use for the Bible (reading a printed book, listening to audio, using an app on their phone, etc.).

Many people today like to use both print and digital but often in different situations. For example, they might like to sit down with a printed Bible at home but use their phone to read or listen to the Bible while travelling on public transport.

Fill in the table with what you see are the advantages of print and digital for engaging with God's word.

Advantages of Print	Advantages of Digital

The following chart shows some suggestions of the advantages of print and the advantages of digital.

Advantages of Print	Advantages of Digital
• Fewer distractions. • The printed Bible has no other function, so when you open it, you are reminded that you are in the presence of God's holy word. • You do not need to own a smartphone or keep the battery charged. • You can keep the same Bible for decades and write notes in the margins, and you get to know it very well, learning how to navigate within it. • You see a lot of text on the page at the same time, making it easier to see a passage in its context. • It can give you a better idea of the structure of the Bible and where you are in the overall outline of Scripture. • It is clear for others to see that you are reading from the Bible (e.g. when you are preaching or when you want to look for opportunities to engage others in conversation about God's word).	• You have access to the Bible in your pocket at all times, wherever you go. • You can carry several versions and translations of the Bible with you (no need to carry a set of heavy books). • You can have access to both text and audio. • You can share the Scriptures easily with others, via social media or by transferring content between phones. • You can have access to Bible study helps, commentaries, glossaries, and multimedia content for helping you understand the Bible. • Apps can contain daily verse notifications, Bible reading plans, and reminders to read. • It is easy to search for verses. • Digital Scripture resources are often free to distribute. • It is easy to use at night without needing a light. • People all over the world can get access to God's word in their language, including those who would not normally step inside a church or visit a Christian bookshop. • You can enlarge the size of the text for people with eyesight problems.

If someone asked you, "Which is best, print or digital for the Bible?," what would you advise that person?

7. Understanding the Effects of Using Digital Technology

As we use new technologies, they change us. They change the way we think, the way we handle information, and the way we relate to those around us. Many of these changes take place whether we are using technology for good or for unholy purposes. So, as we encourage people to use the Bible in digital forms, it is important for us to be aware of the effects that technology is having on our lives. There are many positive effects, but there are many negative effects too.

We have already looked at some of the *positive aspects* in the list of advantages of digital as compared with print in the previous section.

What *negative effects* or problems can you see?

The following are some examples:

- It is easy to get distracted with all the other things on our phone, and we can waste a lot of time.
- There is a tendency to skim-read (because we do this with social media) and not take the time to concentrate deeply on what we are reading.
- People are becoming more attached to interacting with others on their phones and can neglect the people around them.
- It is easier to look at unwholesome images and videos (violence, pornography, etc.) without anyone else seeing, which can become an addiction.
- People have more access to false teaching, gossip, and lies than ever before, and it can be hard to discern what is true and what is not.
- Social media can tempt us to look for praise from others and can encourage vanity and pride.
- Feeling we need to be online all the time can lead to tiredness and burnout as we fear missing out.

Read the following passages: Romans 12:1–2; Galatians 5:22–26; Colossians 3:12–15.

1. What do these verses teach us about how we should live as disciples of Jesus in our digital age?
2. What can you do in your church to help people better grasp the positive and negative effects of digital technology and respond with discernment to these realities?

Assignments

1. How could you better use digital Scripture resources in your personal life, family, and ministry?
2. If you could organize a training workshop in your church on the subject of using the Bible well in our digital age, what topics would you want to include?

Readings

Dyer, John. *From the Garden to the City: The Redeeming and Corrupting Power of Technology*. Grand Rapids, MI: Kregel, 2011.
Mobile Ministry Forum. "Mobile Ministry Made Easy: A Simple Guide to Begin or Advance Your Use of Mobiles." 2014. https://mobileministryforum.org/mobile-ministry-made-easy/.
———. "Social Media for Missions: An Introductory Guide." 2018. http://mobileministryforum.org/social-media-for-missions-an-introductory-guide/.
Reinke, Tony. *12 Ways Your Phone Is Changing You*. Wheaton, IL: Crossway, 2017.
Williams, Keith, and Leith Gray. "The Little Phone That Could: Mobile-Empowered Ministry." *International Journal of Frontier Missions* 27, no. 3 (July–Sept. 2010): 139–45.

The following articles are available to download at www.scripture-engagement.org:
Digital Strategy Guides. 2021. https://scripture-engagement.org/content/digital-strategy-guides.
Graham, Eric. "Digital Publishing – A Different Paradigm: Publish Early, Publish Small, Publish Often." 2019.
Lange, Martin. "Digital Distribution Strategy for Bible Dedication Celebrations: A Step-by-Step Guide for Using Wi-Fi Media Boxes at Your Event." 2020.
———. "Using Your Wi-Fi Media Box: 28 Ideas for Digital Distribution." 2020.
———. "Which Wi-Fi Media Box?" 2020.
Margetts, Richard. "Which Audio Player?" 2019.
Trotter, Cynthia. "Using Feature Phones to Promote Literacy and Scripture Engagement." 2020.

Other Resources

http://mobmin.org/ – Mobile Ministry Forum.
https://youtube.com/c/missionmediacoach – Mission Media Coach.
https://digitalacademy.cru.org/ – Cru Digital Academy.
https://software.sil.org/scriptureappbuilder/ – Software for building Bible apps for Android and iOS.
https://www.bible.com/ – Bible App and website from YouVersion

https://www.jesusfilm.org/ – *Jesus* film project app and website

https://www.scriptureearth.org/ – Scripture Earth: Scripture resources in thousands of languages

https://pray-as-you-go.org/home/ – Daily devotions with Scripture readings

24

Engaging People with Scripture through Music and Dance

Introduction

Music plays an important role in Christian life, and in many places, movement or dance is also an important part. It gives us a way to express our emotions and our thoughts in praise and worship. People of all ages enjoy singing, dancing, playing a musical instrument, or just listening to their favourite music. This chapter looks at the role of music and dance in connection with Scripture and how Christians can use many different forms including their own local styles.

SINGING FROM THE HEART

One Saturday, Pastor Simon needed to go to Retali for a meeting with people at the denominational office. While he was there, he decided to visit a friend he had met at the last seminar for church leaders. His friend, Pastor Zoki, was very happy to see him, and they talked nearly all night. On Sunday morning, Pastor Simon was happy to go to his friend's church. As this was a big church with people from at least three different language groups, Pastor Simon found it interesting to see how they managed to have some things in Kisanu but also readings from the Bible in the three local languages.

The part of the service that struck him the most, though, was the music. He'd never heard anything like it! The congregational singing was animated, and people really seemed to be worshipping God. The choir songs fascinated him. They were in a great variety of styles, some with local traditional instruments and some with electric guitars!

Later on that Sunday afternoon, as Pastor Zoki and Pastor Simon sat outside the house chatting, they compared their two churches, both the positive things and the problems. Then they talked about music. Pastor Simon said, "In my church, we sing from a hymn book that we've used for a good number of years. Most of the songs are translations from Western hymns. Although there are about three hundred songs in the book, the song leaders use only about twenty of them because they are the ones the congregation have memorized. Now that we are using Palapala for the services, we also sing a few songs in our language, but they also are mainly translations from the Kisanu which are translations from English! The result is that people sing very slowly with very little life, and I wonder how much they actually understand the words. The choirs are livelier, but sometimes their words don't make much sense to the congregation. Some of the songs actually teach bad theology! The music in your church is completely different! What happened?"

Zoki said, "Well, it really all started with the Catholic church on the other side of town. You remember Father John who came to the last seminar? We went together to a funeral, and his choir was there to sing. I was fascinated by the way they sang through the story of the raising of Lazarus from the dead using a music style that was traditionally used at funerals. Everyone listened to the song with great attention, and after that I was asked to read the passage aloud from John 11.

"After the funeral, we got the chance to send some of our musicians to a special seminar to help churches use their own ethnic music, and you've seen the result. Not only are people worshipping better in the services, but the music has attracted others to come to church. We've made some recordings of Scripture songs, and even the neighbouring women who never come to church listen to them. We've put a few videos of songs on YouTube. Now they are asking more about Jesus. There has been another advantage. We've been trying for some time to get church people to memorize Scripture but have not had much success with the adults. Since we started using Scripture songs, however, people are remembering lots more Scripture verses."

1. Why do you think the music in Pastor Zoki's church had such a powerful effect on people?
2. Do you have Scripture songs in your language that use local music forms? If not, what could you do about it?

1. Music Is Used in Many Ways

1. What are some ways people use music in your culture?
2. What are some ways people use music in the Bible? Give references.

Add any of the points below that participants did not mention.
Music can . . .

- express many different emotions, including joy, fear, anger, and repentance (Psalms).
- teach by reminding people of God's actions (Exod 15).
- accompany dance (1 Chr 15).
- celebrate cultural festivals (2 Chr 35:15).

- fight spiritual warfare (1 Sam 16:23; 2 Chr 20:21–23; Ps 149; Isa 30:31–32; Acts 16:25).
- celebrate victory in war, for example of Moses and Miriam (Exod 15).
- animate processions (2 Sam 6).
- praise "big men" (1 Sam 18:7).
- worship (Rev 5; 2 Chr 5).
- mourn (Matt 9:23).
- encourage and strengthen people (1 Cor 14:26).

1. In a column, list all of the ways your church uses music (such as for offertory, processions, and so forth).
2. In a second column, list the language(s) in which people usually sing the songs.
3. In the third column, list the type of music that is used (traditional tunes, borrowed music, Western music).
4. Share the results with the whole group.

2. Reclaiming Music and Dance for God's Glory

In order to become all that God intends them to be, individuals must bring themselves to Christ. In the same way, people must bring their culture's music and art forms to Christ so that they can give God glory and become all that God intended them to be.

A. We Need to Bring Our Whole Selves to Christ

Ask someone to read Mark 12:28–31:

> One of the teachers of the law came and heard them [Jesus and the Sadducees] debating. Noticing that Jesus had given them a good answer, he asked him, "Of all the commandments, which is the most important?"
>
> "The most important one," answered Jesus, "is this: 'Hear, O Israel: the Lord our God, the Lord is one. Love the Lord your God with all your heart and with all your soul and with all your mind and with all your strength.' The second is this: 'Love your neighbour as yourself.' There is no commandment greater than these."

We don't want to take God's word only into our heads but into every part of our being and actions. Singing God's word to songs, music, and dances from our own culture can help us love God with all of ourselves and love our neighbours as much as ourselves.

B. Often Music Has Been Stolen by Satan, But We Can Redeem It

Ask someone to read 2 Corinthians 10:5, where the apostle Paul says:

> We demolish arguments and every pretension that sets itself up against the knowledge of God, and we take captive every thought to make it obedient to Christ.

God commands us to obey his word rather than any argument against it. We make every thought that has rebelled against God captive and make every part of our culture obedient to Christ. Developing Christian music and other forms of art in our own local styles reclaims for Christ's good uses whatever Satan had stolen for harmful uses.

C. Sing a New Song

Ask someone to read Psalm 96:1:

> Sing to the LORD a new song;
> sing to the LORD, all the earth.

God wants us to sing new songs to him using musical forms that already exist. Old songs and borrowed songs are not bad, but each culture should also be composing new songs flowing from the unique musical resources that God has given them.

3. Reclaiming Musical Instruments for God's Glory

BITA RECLAIMS HIS BALAPHONE FOR GOD'S GLORY

Bita was a very well-known player of a West African instrument called a balaphone. He played in nightclubs and made a lot of money. One day he went to a special evangelistic meeting and became a Christian. Soon he started attending a church. Many people there had seen him on television and knew he was an expert balaphone player, so they asked him to play in church. At first he refused because he felt the balaphone was tied up with the sinful things he had done before he became a Christian.

Then one day he had an idea. He talked to the pastor of the church, and they agreed on a plan. The next Sunday he took his balaphone to church, and the pastor invited him to bring the instrument up to the front of the church. Then the pastor prayed to consecrate this balaphone for the work of God. He poured some oil on it to show that now it was set aside for God. From then on Bita often played his balaphone in church to praise God. Everyone was encouraged.

Do you think Bita did the right thing? Why or why not?

Have each group read one of the following passages and then answer the questions below: 1 Chronicles 15:16–29; Daniel 3:5; Psalm 150; Isaiah 5:12.

1. Does the passage describe a pagan or godly event?
2. What instruments did the people use at this event?
3. Did people use any of the same instruments for both pagan and godly events? Is the instrument itself good or bad then, and if not, what makes music good or bad?

4. What instruments do people use traditionally in your area? At what kinds of events do people use them?

5. What instruments do people already use in your churches? What other traditional instruments could people begin using? Consider whether each instrument would help people worship God more or detract so that people would worship him less.

4. Our Heart Music and Other Art Forms

Our musical language is part of us from our childhood and is the music of our hearts. In addition, dance or other art forms can touch our emotions in a powerful way. Music and art are channels through which the Holy Spirit speaks to us deeply. Often when a church uses local music, movement, and other art forms in services, people feel more closely connected to God and to one another. We can invite musicians, singers, poets, dancers, and other artists to study God's word and create new works for God, for ourselves, for one another, and for celebrations.

1. How can you introduce newly composed Scripture songs and other art forms into the different types of Christian meetings inside and outside the church building?

2. How can we introduce God's word into more parts of our lives?

3. Who are the best dancers, singers, musicians, and performers of local music in the villages and cities you know? If they are Christians, pray for them, and encourage them to compose new Scripture songs. If they are not Christians, pray that God will call them to himself so that they can use their gifts to praise him.

> Our heart music is a channel through which
> the Holy Spirit speaks to us deeply.

Assignments

Think about inviting others into the creative process. Do you know any talented musicians, singers, poets, or other people who could help? Divide into groups to compose new songs. If different language groups are present, divide by language group.

1. Pray and ask the Holy Spirit for inspiration.
2. What are some good kinds of songs, celebrations, and performances we already have?
3. For what events would we like to have new songs, prayers, or performances? Think of a need in our community that you would like God to speak to through song, poetry, dance, or performance at the event you have in mind. Find one or more verses in the Bible that apply to this need for this event. If your church uses a liturgy, consider writing a Scripture-based song to go with an element of it, such as the Confession, Reading the Word, or Offering.
4. Meditate on the Scripture verses you have chosen, and think about how to form them into song lyrics. Choose a type of local music that is culturally meaningful and will communicate the theme of the passage. For example, an advice-giving song style could instruct people from God's word. A song style to praise a leader could worship God, the greatest leader. A love song style may be a good style to talk about loving God. A harvesting or working song style might go well with Colossians 3:17 – "And whatever you do, whether in word or deed, do it all in the name of the Lord Jesus, giving thanks to God the Father through him."
5. Put your words and music together. Your song may use the exact words from the verse(s), or you may say the same idea differently to make it easier to sing. Make the words and music fit together well. If you have changed the words of the passage, check them with a pastor or another wise leader who knows the Bible to make sure that they faithfully communicate the meaning of the passage.
6. Sing your song for the whole group. Ask them for feedback. Make small changes to make it even better.
7. Introduce the new work at the event you chose.

Readings

Collard, Dianne B. "Promoting Arts Awareness and Education in the Church." In *Worship and Mission for the Global Church: An Ethnodoxology Handbook*, eds.

James Krabill, Frank Fortunato, Robin Harris, and Brian Schrag, 358–63. Pasadena, CA: William Carey Library, 2013.

Kindell, Gloria. "Ethnopoetics: Finding Poetry." *Notes on Literature in Use and Language Programs* 50 (1996): 31–46.

King, Roberta R. *A Time to Sing: A Manual for the African Church*. Nairobi: Evangel, 1999.

Neeley, Paul. "Social Factors in the Acceptance or Rejection of Indigenous Hymns." *Notes on Literature in Use and Language Programs* 42 (1994): 29–33.

Olson, Bruce E. "Night of the Tiger." In *Bruchko*, 147–53. Altamonte Springs, FL: Creation House, 1978.

Petersen, Michelle. "Arts Development for Scripture Engagement." *Global Forum on Arts and Christian Faith* 5 (2017): A58–A86. http://www.artsandchristianfaith.org/index.php/journal/article/view/31.

Saurman, Mary E. "Music: A Bridge to Literacy." *Notes on Literacy* 19, no. 3 (1993): 34–42.

Saurman, Todd, and Mary Beth. "Encouraging the Development of Relevant Arts in the Lives of Believers." In *Worship and Mission for the Global Church: An Ethnodoxology Handbook*, eds. James Krabill, Frank Fortunato, Robin Harris, and Brian Schrag, 380–88. Pasadena, CA: William Carey Library, 2013.

Schrag, Brian. *Creating Local Arts Together: A Manual to Help Communities Reach Their Kingdom Goals*. General Editor, James R. Krabill. Pasadena, CA: William Carey Library, 2013.

Scott, Joyce. *Tuning in to a Different Song: Using a Music Bridge to Cross Cultural Differences*. Pietermaritzburg: Cluster Publications, 2007.

25

Engaging People with Scripture through Drama

Introduction

Many different forms of live and recorded dramas can engage people with God's word. This chapter helps you consider ways to use live and recorded drama in churches and communities.[1]

A CHRISTMAS DRAMA GONE ASTRAY

It was Christmas Eve. Pastor Simon's church always had a service on Christmas Eve that went on into the early hours of Christmas morning. One part of it was almost always a drama of the Christmas story performed by the youth. This year they had not prepared much because they had been practising for an important football match.

They started the drama, and Pastor Simon was glad to see that this year they were talking in their mother tongue, Palapala. In the past, they had performed in English, which meant that many people had not been able to understand it. They started the drama at the point at which Caesar Augustus imposed a census on everyone in the Roman Empire. This part took thirty minutes, and as each person came to have his or her name written down, the soldiers joked with them and demanded small bribes. The part when Joseph and Mary arrived in Bethlehem and the baby was born was over very quickly. After that, the shepherds came and amused everyone by bringing their rather unwilling dogs with them! The kings came next, and, finally, Herod's soldiers took about forty minutes to kill all the babies, doing it with great enthusiasm.

---

1. This is only an introduction to the subject of drama. If you want to develop this ministry in your church or on the radio, you may want to have an entire workshop or series of workshops devoted to developing dramas. The resources at the end of this chapter can help give you ideas.

After the service, Pastor Simon went home with his excited children. They were talking about the drama, but the parts they remembered and talked about were the census, the shepherds' dogs, and particularly the part when the babies were killed. As he heard them talking about these things, he began to think, "Is this type of drama really communicating the message of the Bible, or was it giving rather strange ideas about which parts of the story were important?"

1. How could Pastor Simon find out what people learned from this drama?
2. In what ways could the youth improve their drama presentation next year?

1. Using Drama for Scripture Engagement

What kinds of dramas have you seen used in your church and community? List them on the board (and add any that are not mentioned from the list below). What purpose or function does each kind serve? How long does each typically take? When do people perform each kind? Where do people perform each?

Many kinds of dramas can be used in church; for example:

- Dramas performed for an audience.
- Acting without words or to the words of a narrator (mime).
- Dramas on Bible passages.
- Teaching dramas on themes.
- Dramas that introduce the subject of a sermon or speech.
- Dramas that tell short stories or long stories.
- Dramas performed in person or pre-recorded audio or videos.
- Dramas done indoors or outdoors.
- Dramas with other art forms such as poems, songs, dances, or visual arts.
- Dramas where the audience participates in action or song.

The Bible is full of examples of drama. For example, each year the Israelites had a special Passover meal when they celebrated their deliverance from slavery in Egypt. According to tradition, this included a small drama which is still used by Jews today as part of the Passover meal.

The youngest child asked four questions which the parents always answered in the same way:

- Why is this night different from all other nights?
  Because on other nights we eat matzo and bread, but on this night we eat only matzo.

- Why on all other nights do we eat many herbs and on this night only bitter herbs?
  To recall the bitter lives of our ancestors, who were slaves in Egypt.
- Why on all other nights do we dip our food only once, but twice on this night?
  It is our custom to dip on other nights. We dip a second time to remember that our ancestors dipped a leafy branch to smear lambs' blood on their doorposts.
- Why on all other nights do we sit up to eat, but recline on this night?
  Because free people reclined in ancient times, and our ancestors became free on this night.

Then the child would go outside to see if Elijah was coming that year or not.

There are many other examples of dramas in the Bible. God told Isaiah to go around naked to show how the nations would be stripped of their power (Isa 20). He told Hosea to marry a prostitute as an illustration of God's marriage to unfaithful Israel (Hos 1 and 3). He told Ezekiel to act out God's message to Israel in a number of dramatic ways (Ezek 4; 5; 6; 12). In Acts 21:11, Agabus acts out a warning to Paul. If God told the prophets to communicate through dramatic means, we certainly can use drama too.

1. Which kinds of dramas on the list you made above have you seen used to communicate Scripture?
2. Which kinds of dramas on your list have people not yet used for Scripture engagement but could?
3. When could people present live or recorded dramas to help people better understand God's word? Which style would be good to use for each opportunity?

2. Preparing Dramas Based on Scripture

Local drama styles are always best because they will communicate most clearly to the audience. Before preparing a drama, talk together as a team.

A. Who Is Your Audience? What Scripture Will You Choose for Them?

Think of your audience as you prepare your drama. What Scripture stories or topics could relate well to their interests and needs? What style of drama would be good for that content and audience? When are they available to come to see a drama or watch a video? Decide how long you would like your drama to be. For how long will people pay attention?

B. What Is the Performance's Goal?

Decide whether you will show one story or a series of several short stories, and which Scripture stories or teaching illustrations would be good for the audience and event. Dramas may be used to evangelize, share stories from the Bible, illustrate main teachings of the Bible, build up believers in their faith, or help a group understand a Scripture passage's application for their lives today. Ask a good reader to read the Scripture passage aloud more than once, perhaps in more than one translation. Discuss the focus of the story. For example, in the story of the prodigal son, the focus is not on the sins of the son but on his father's love for him when he returned. Discuss what happens in the story until all the actors can remember the order of the story events well. Discuss its meaning.

C. Practise and Get Feedback to Improve before the Performance

Practise the play several times before you perform it for an audience or record it.
Ask the actors to face the audience as much as possible so that the audience can see their facial expressions. The audience will understand emotions through

people's faces. Practise speaking loudly enough for the person watching from furthest away to still hear you. For recorded dramas, be sure the voices and sound effects are loud enough to be heard clearly. Be sure that the actors are in good lighting and the audience can see them well.

Before you perform a drama in public, perform it for two or more people who have good discernment. Ask those people to answer the following questions after they have seen a rehearsal. Use their ideas to make the actual performance even better.

1. What did you learn from the drama?
2. What do you like about it?
3. Would any part confuse or offend some people?
4. How can we make it better?

D. How Will You Deliver the Drama?

Discuss where and when you'll perform the drama in person or how to record it for radio or video. Arrange a time to perform it. Discuss how you will invite people to come and who will introduce it and close the performance. Talk about ways to follow up with the audience after the performance to help meet the goal.

If you want to record the dramas, you'll need recording equipment and a way to share the recording. You can record and edit dramas on computers or mobile phones. If you need to record sound effects, you can make them using ordinary household items. For example, small stones falling on a piece of aluminium roofing can sound like a heavy rain storm. (See appendix 4 for more recording ideas.)

Perform the drama, or distribute the recording. Talk with people afterwards about what the story meant to them, what they liked, and what could have been done better. Use these ideas to make the next performance or recording better.

1. Divide into two groups. One group is to perform the parable (example teaching story) of the wedding feast in Matthew 22:1–14 and the second group the historical narrative of Elisha and the Aramean army from 2 Kings 6:8–23.

    First pick two group leaders. For each group, ask a good reader to read the story aloud twice while everyone listens. Discuss the main point of the story. Choose roles in each group. For the parable from Matthew, choose who will play the following roles:

- the king
- the man who came to the wedding without appropriate wedding clothes
- the king's servants and soldiers
- the guests who refused to come
- the guests who did come

For the story of Elisha and the Aramean army, choose who will play the following roles:

- Elisha
- his servant
- the king of Aram
- the Aramean army (modern Syrians)
- some angels
- Jehoram the king of Israel
- some Israelites

2. Each group rehearses their story until they know it well. Come back together and get each group to perform the story for the other group. Ask what people learned from the drama.
3. Break into two groups again. One group should prepare a narrated drama of the story of blind Bartimaeus (Mark 10:46–52). The other group should prepare a modernized drama of one of Jesus's parables such as the rich fool (Luke 12:13–21). Follow the process described in points 1 and 2 above.

3. Drama Showing Applications of Scripture

Scripture Relevance Dramas show the application of Scripture to life today. A main character has a problem and changes in some significant way by the end of the story. One of the characters tells a Bible story that shows the solution to the problem. During the drama, the characters should ask the same questions as the audience would be likely to ask, and answer these questions in a way that the audience would find satisfying. The concluding scene should show how people put Scripture into practice to make a difference in the life of at least one character. Alternatively, it could show the consequences of not putting Scripture into practice.

The following is an example of a drama on the theme of forgiveness.

Engaging People with Scripture through Drama

A woman tells her son to take an expensive meat sauce she has cooked to his father, who is selling in the market. On his way there, his neighbour's daughter bumps into him and the food is spilled on the ground. The dish breaks. His mother refuses to forgive the neighbours even though they reimburse her for the loss. Later, her son is trying to hit a bird in a tree with a slingshot. The rock misses and hits the neighbour's daughter in the eye. She is wounded. The family who refused to forgive now need forgiveness from the people they had refused to forgive. They pay the neighbour's hospital bills, but there are still ill feelings between the two families.

One of the fathers calls an elder to intervene. The elder brings the two families together and tells them the parable of the unforgiving servant (Matt 18:23–34). The two families apologize to each other and forgive each other. The concluding scene shows the children of the two families playing together, the two women going to the market together, or the two men chatting together. A neighbour asks one of the women why she is singing so happily and she explains that it is because the other woman has forgiven her.

Another way to show the relevance of Scripture to life today is to show a modern version of a Scripture passage. This kind of drama takes the main point of a biblical passage and acts it out as if it took place in today's setting.

Divide into groups to prepare a short drama that shows the relevance of a Scripture passage to the audience.

1. To start with, decide on a theme that the intended audience and the Bible both value, such as neighbours getting along with one another, gratitude, or forgiveness. Later, go on to biblical themes that ask people to change their values and act differently.
2. Develop a written script or plan an oral outline to help performers remember.
   (a) Describe a problem exactly using these questions as a guide: Who? What? When? Where? Why?
   (b) Describe the cultural and biblical views on the topic. Select one or more Scripture passages that address the theme. Study the passage(s) well.
   (c) What style will you use for this drama? Think about the story you want to tell.
   (d) Develop the main character's problem, the biblical solution, and the application. A character may become a Christian, but this does not need to happen in every drama. A Christian may learn how the Bible can help him or her in a way he or she didn't know before. A character may refuse to change, and this is all right as long as another character shows a better example.
   (e) Think about how the story will begin and end.
   (f) Add a song or other artistic elements suitable for the chosen drama style as appropriate.
   (g) Check to make sure your message is sensitive to all who are likely to see it.

3. Assign roles.
4. Rehearse and get feedback. Improve it.
5. Perform it, or record it, and play the recording.

Assignments

1. What are the benefits of using drama in evangelism?
2. What can be some good results of using drama in teaching?
3. Listen to or watch a video of a local drama, and think about the main ideas, characters, actions, and emotions. Identify what you think was good and what could make future work even better.
4. Practise and perform a passage of Scripture that you believe would interest your intended audience. Ask a few people who saw it what they learned from it, what they liked about it, and what could make it even better next time. Perform the improved version for more people.

Readings

Banale, Apep. "Using the Luke Video Script for Dramas." *Scripture in Use Today* 6 (2003): 9–11.

Brown, Rick. "How to Make Oral Communication More Effective." *International Journal of Frontier Missions* 21, no. 4 (2004): 173–78. http://www.ijfm.org/PDFs_IJFM/21_4_PDFs/Oral%20Comm%20Brown-2.pdf.

Datson, Mark. "Advice for Scripture and Drama Recording: A Guide for Narrators and Actors." Forum of Bible Agencies International, 2009. https://scripture-engagement.org/wp-content/uploads/2020/09/Datson-M-2005-Advice-for-Scripture-and-Drama-Recording.pdf.

Ernst, Andreas. "Audio Dramas for Scripture Engagement: A Participatory Oral Approach." Forum of Bible Agencies International, 2018. https://scripture-engagement.org/wp-content/uploads/2020/09/Ernst-A-2018-Audio-Dramas-for-Scripture-Engagement.pdf.

La Rivière, Leen. *Creative – and Christian! Biblical Principles*. Carlisle: Piquant Editions, 2005.

Petersen, Michelle. "Arts Development for Scripture Engagement." *Global Forum on Arts and Christian Faith* 5 (2017): A58–A86. https://scripture-engagement.org/content/arts-development-scripture-engagement/.

———. "Scripture Relevance Dramas." *EthnoDoxology* 4, no. 4 (n.d.). https://scripture-engagement.org/wp-content/uploads/2020/09/Petersen-M-2010-Scripture-Relevance-Dramas.pdf.

Prettol, Joyce. "Drama Productions for Scripture Use." *Notes on Literature in Use and Language Programs* 22 (1989): 21–24. Republished by the Forum of Bible Agencies International. https://scripture-engagement.org/wp-content/uploads/2020/09/Prettol-J-1989-Drama-productions-for-SU.pdf.

Schrag, Brian. *Creating Local Arts Together: A Manual to Help Communities Reach Their Kingdom Goals.* General Editor, James R. Krabill. Pasadena, CA: William Carey Library, 2013.

Other Resources

https://www.jesusfilm.org/watch.html – Find the *Jesus* film and many other Scripture films in many languages. Click on a film and then click "Language List" to see the languages available. Download any of them free of charge by clicking "Download."

https://thekingdomfilm.com/ – A video of the prodigal son parable can be downloaded for free in several languages.

ScriptureEarth.org – Has links to dramatized audio and video Scripture in many languages.

26

Engaging People with Scripture through the Visual Arts and Media

Introduction

Throughout the centuries, visual arts have helped people engage with Scripture. In places where most church members didn't know how to read, the church has used paintings or stained glass windows of biblical scenes as a means to communicate the message of the gospel. People remember a message better when they experience it in a variety of ways, through pictures as well as words. Christians today can use arts and media in a variety of ways to help people engage with Scripture. We can research our community's arts and work with local artists and others to make Scripture-based works that encourage people to follow God.

OUR CREATOR MAKES US CREATIVE IN HIS IMAGE!

Pastor Simon was chosen to attend an area conference of his church, and he knew he had a long journey ahead. The bus he was on broke down a couple of times, and he didn't arrive at his destination until 11 p.m. By that point he wasn't interested in much more than getting some food and finding a bed, but as his host took him through the big church where they were meeting, he did look in amazement at all the interesting things he could see.

The next morning, having had a good night's sleep, he went into the church where they were meeting and started looking around. He could see beautiful woven cloths on the walls, big posters showing scenes from the Bible, and lots of flowers and plants arranged around the sides of the church. As he sat listening to the speakers, he was also thinking, "How can we make our church inviting, hospitable, and beautiful? How can we better remind ourselves of God's presence with us through the beauty we see?"

A week later he was back home having a meeting with his deacons. He told them about the church where the conference was held and said, "We have people in our church who are weavers of cloth and baskets, embroiderers, tailors, painters, ceramic makers, potters, jewellery makers, and people who design signs, decorations, books, and cards. How can we encourage them to use their gifts for God?" They talked and prayed about this and finally decided to start with a special woven cloth to hang near the door of the church. So Pastor Simon asked a weaver in the church to make a design for the entrance of their church in the colours people especially liked. The weaver sketched several design possibilities. Pastor Simon talked with the deacons about which design they liked the best. Together they agreed how much money they could set aside from the church budget to pay the weaver. They agreed on their favourite colours and design. In the middle, the main part would say, "God is with us."

The weaver completed the commission, and the deacons hung it in the entryway. When people arrived at church the next Sunday, they talked about how beautiful and inviting it was. They felt encouraged as they remembered how God was there with them and with their people.

At their next meeting, the deacons talked about how much everyone had liked the new woven cloth. Pastor Simon asked them to think about other kinds of local arts that could be used to decorate the church. They were very excited as they talked about different creative possibilities.

1. Think about the kinds of visual arts found in your community. There are different kinds of art:

    - Art without words – paintings, murals, sculpture.
    - Art with words – posters, banners, Bible pictures, wall paintings.
    - Visual recorded media – videos, films.
    - Digital images – pictures with text, memes.

    Who do you know in your community who is good at creating things? How can you encourage that person to use his or her skills for communicating God's ideas?

2. What different types of visual arts are used in your church building, Sunday school, or other meeting places? What kinds of art forms are found in your community's meeting places? What kinds of visual arts do people use in our community that we could start using in our churches?

3. What kinds of art forms do people use in their homes to make them beautiful and welcoming? How can we design our homes to remind ourselves of God and to welcome people?

    Report the answers back to the large group and list them on the board.

1. Visual Arts in Scripture

In the Bible, God used visual images to communicate with the Israelites. They were told exactly how to construct the tabernacle. Its different parts communicated different messages. For instance, the beautiful curtain dividing off the Holy of Holies showed the holiness of God. Moses was told to find craftsmen who had been given artistic gifts by God to do this work.

> Then the LORD said to Moses, "See I have chosen Bezalel son of Uri, the son of Hur, of the tribe of Judah, and I have filled him with the Spirit of God, with wisdom, with understanding, with knowledge and with all kinds of skills – to make artistic designs for work in gold, silver and bronze, to cut and set stones, to work in wood, and to engage in all kinds of crafts. Moreover, I have appointed Oholiab son of Ahisamak, of the tribe of Dan, to help him. Also I have given ability to all the skilled workers to make everything I have commanded you." (Exod 31:1–6)

Just as God gave Bezalel and Oholiab artistic gifts in Moses's day to make the temple beautiful, so he continues to give his people gifts to make places of worship beautiful today. These works can invite more people to recognize God's presence with us.

2. Producing and Using Visual Arts and Social Media

Many kinds of visual arts can encourage the people who see them to remember God. Some works are for temporary use, like a flower arrangement or a beautiful meal, while others, such as a woven cloth or a video, last longer. Works that last a short time as well as those that last a long time can encourage and strengthen people who see them.

Try sketching three or four possible designs or ideas on a piece of paper. Before you make a final version, ask a few people which of these ideas they like best and would like to see developed further. Check your idea with someone you respect. Decide which you like best, and create a larger version of it, or work with a local artist to make a final version.

A. Walls Can Speak

To decorate houses or community spaces, people could make posters, carvings, paintings, or woven fabrics with text or visuals reminding us of Scripture, and hang them on the wall of a church or house. You could try your hand at creating your own or work with a local artist to make one or more new works. Choose together a short verse, or part of a verse, or a scene from a Bible story. Pair Scripture words with a drawing or design that fits the theme of the verse. Take one session to make Scripture posters on paper during Scripture engagement seminars. If you like, glue things on the poster – for example, dried grasses or seeds.

B. Calendars

In many areas, calendars are very popular. A calendar with Bible verses keeps Scripture in view all year long. If the verses are in the mother tongue, the calendar can be good publicity for mother-tongue Scriptures.

There are many ways to make a calendar. You could have one large picture with twelve smaller tear-off sheets, each showing a month and its text, or you could have a page for each month with its own picture and text. The texts could be Scripture verses or proverbs from Scripture with a relevant proverb from your own culture. To have the calendars ready for sale in December, you will need to start working on them in August.

C. Banners

Banners are made of cloth or woven mats and have a verse or part of a verse of Scripture and some sort of art work. They are more durable than posters. Some communities use banners when they parade around town to praise God with songs, instruments, and dance as a witness to people there.

Making banners with a group of people can be fun. Here is the process.

1. Pray together for God to guide you to a Scripture passage. It should have fewer than eight words. You may need to shorten the text for the banner. Think of where the banner will hang and decide on the language(s) that would be most appropriate for that place.

2. Cut the letters of the text out of some fabric or felt that contrasts with the colour of the background. Make the letters big enough to be read easily from across a room.

3. Put the text on the background and check that it looks good and is easy to read.

4. Decide on the decorations. Objects such as rice, maize, millet, cow peas, dried flowers, small remnants of cloth, ribbon, or cord

can make the banner more interesting. Let each person work on a separate part.

5. Assemble the banner. Lay out all the parts to check that they will all fit, and then sew, glue, or paint the words onto the banner. In some cases, you might write the letters on the banner using a wide felt pen. Make a hem at the top of the banner but leave an opening at each end. Put a stick through the hem and use it to hang up the banner.

6. Find out if people understand what you were hoping to communicate by your banner, especially if you are using symbols to represent things. Make any changes that are necessary to get your message across clearly.

D. Paintings

A painting attracts people's interest and can remind them of biblical truths. It can also serve as a focus for meditation. For example, the Dutch author Henri Nouwen meditated a long time on a picture that showed the return of the prodigal son and then wrote his reflections in a book that has blessed many people. How would you show a prodigal son returning in your context?

If a church is engaged in Bible storying, a series of pictures hung around the church showing key stories from God's plan of salvation can help people remember these main stories. Some key illustrations could include the creation of the world, the fall of humankind, Noah and the flood, the birth of Jesus, Jesus calming the sea, Jesus healing people, Jesus casting out the Gadarene demons, the crucifixion, the resurrection, and the Great Commission.

Some paintings have a Scripture verse as a caption. If the verse is in the mother tongue, it helps raise the prestige of the language. If the picture is a meditation on what Scripture means to the artist or a testimony of what God has done for him or her, the artist can place a card next to the work sharing briefly what the work means.

Ask each participant and staff member to make a poster or a banner and show it to one another or to sketch a picture that can later be painted on a church wall. It could illustrate a Bible story, have a Bible text on it, or help people engage with Scripture.

E. Bible Story Illustrations

Read the following paragraph written by a person working in Asia:

One day a local partner and I were in a village meeting people and giving out tracts. We gave out about twenty and decided to return in a week or two to gauge the response. When we went back, no one could remember the nineteen tracts that were all text. However, numerous families in the village had read the one tract with illustrations and could describe its message. Based on this information, we began to develop Bible stories and booklets that only used words to describe the illustrations. The number of people who read these tracts skyrocketed.

People are far more likely to read Bible stories or Bible portions with pictures than those without them. Many types of Bible pictures are available, so find out what kind of picture is best understood by local people. Illustrations need to be sensitive and accurate. The following are two areas of concern:

- Followers of Islam may find some kinds of illustrations in books containing Scripture offensive. They usually believe a holy book ought to include calligraphy and beautiful ornamentation, especially on the cover. They usually expect a holy book to put ornamental borders around sacred text. If they accept illustrations of people in Bible stories and videos, make sure that the people in the illustrations or videos are well clothed, particularly prophets such as Abraham. Always community check drafts with a few wise people and make revisions as requested before making many copies.
- Both contextual illustrations using local art and historical illustrations documenting the look of the original time and place can be helpful. Scripture illustrations may either take the audience back in time or bring the story forward in time. The intended audience should decide what kind of art they like for each purpose: they may approve a different kind of art in a Scripture illustration for adults than in one for children, for example.

Look at a variety of Bible story pictures: some line drawings, some in colour, and some cartoons. Ask the group to discuss which they think would be the most suitable in their area for adults, youth, and children.

> Try out all audio-visual methods with a small audience before using them on a large scale.

F. Videos and Films

Christian films and videos can be great evangelistic tools as they draw interested crowds to see and hear Bible stories. They can also help Christians learn important scriptural truths. When people learn in a combination of ways, using both their ears and their eyes, they remember better than by using their ears alone.

Perhaps the best-known video is the *Jesus* film produced by Cru. This uses parts of Luke's gospel to show the life of Jesus. The *Jesus* film and many other Scripture films are available to download or watch for free in over 1,800 languages at https://www.jesusfilm.org/watch.html. Many people become Christians after seeing such films. Viewers who are already Christians benefit by seeing many stories from the Bible. They see how Bible stories relate to one another. They also get a much better idea of what life in Israel was like. Films also help people realize that Israel is a real country on this earth. Show a video to a few people before you show it to many people. Ask what people understand, what they like about it, and what people may misunderstand. For example, if you are going to make the *Jesus* film in your language (see below), and if people think of the left hand as unclean, producers will let you show a group scene at Communion instead of showing Jesus serving Communion with his left hand.

Preparing the *Jesus* film in your language requires a commitment of time. You also need to have a translation of Luke's gospel in your language that has been checked by a consultant. Once you have that, follow these steps:

1. Contact your country's *Jesus* film director to begin the process.
2. Translate the script of the film. This involves getting the number of syllables of the script in your language to match those spoken on the film, if that is possible. You can use different beginnings and endings for the film in areas where Islam is strong or where there is very little understanding of Christianity.
3. Select people gifted at reading the language to record the script. Rehearse the readings until everyone can read his or her part well with expression.
4. Plan on taking ten to fourteen days to do the recording and using between seventeen and twenty-five people. *Jesus* film staff take care of the technology, mixing music and sounds with the voices and getting it all on film.

5. Once the film is ready, do a test showing of it with a small group and watch their reactions. Ask them about what they have seen. Occasionally, a group of people may seriously misunderstand a part of the film. If this happens, you can either add a special introduction or not show the film in the area because it is not suitable.

6. Arrange to show the film. This involves obtaining the equipment and contacting the leaders of the village. If the film is used for evangelism, the church needs to have a plan for following up with people who commit their lives to Christ. One ministry that is effective for this is Faith Comes By Hearing. This ministry records the New Testament in various electronic formats such as CDs, MP3s, and podcasts, and it organizes people into groups to listen to the Scripture and discuss it.

7. If people are not used to watching films, explain that actors are playing the various parts. It may be good to show a short locally made video before beginning to show the *Jesus* film. This allows the audience to get used to watching the moving images and to concentrate by the time they see the foreign film.

8. If possible, have a book or booklet of passages from Luke to sell at the showing of the film. The film may motivate non-literate people to learn to read and the books or booklets can reinforce the message.

Making and Sharing Short Videos

We can record actors performing Bible stories, music groups singing Scripture songs, or people sharing testimonies about how God has helped them. Make a programme that is so interesting it attracts non-Christians as well as Christians. Ask a wise Christian leader or leaders to check your ideas and to give you ideas on how to make the video better before you make it, or show leaders a draft and then make an improved version. You can create your own videos using mobile phones or dub videos from other cultures in local languages.

Research how people share videos and what file formats are optimal for sharing in terms of size and quality. People may have limited data plans or poor Internet connectivity that would make HD videos a challenge to download, but short mobile phone videos may be popular.

G. Sharing Scripture in Art and Videos on Social Media

With mobile phones and tablets becoming more affordable and Internet connectivity growing more accessible, it is no wonder that social media is becoming a very popular platform for engagement of all kinds.

The following are a few things to consider as you look at using social media for Scripture engagement:

- With what social media does your intended audience engage – Twitter, Instagram, WhatsApp, Facebook, or others? Different service providers may have special packages that may give unlimited Facebook or YouTube access for a minimal monthly subscription.
- What types of posts get the most traffic? Check out what gets the most likes and comments. Ask a few people what they like about them. What good elements could we use in our own posts or videos? For example, if people like to watch music videos, could we make Christian music videos, leaving out the bad things but keeping the good things, or making them better?
- Consider having a regular schedule of posts so that people anticipate what is new each day of the week. For example, you could set up a Facebook page for your language and follow a schedule like this:

    Daily Scripture Posts or Daily Devotions

    Monday: Community announcements in which people share practical information about events, news, health, classes, training, scholarships, or job opportunities.

    Tuesday: Testimony Tuesday, when people in the community share testimonies such as how the literacy programme has impacted their community, how God has answered their prayers, how the Bible storying groups are seeing people grow in their faith, or other positive changes in the lives of individuals.

    Wednesday: A chapter of Scripture.

    Thursday: Throwback Thursday, posting pictures and videos of past workshops, meetings, and other gatherings.

    Friday: Scripture song videos.

- How can you make posts more engaging and interactive? Are online polls and surveys effective? Do people actively discuss and debate online? Are competitions attractive?

- Are there security concerns? If so, you may want to use a social media account with a name that is not identifiable with a person, such as the name of your language or the topic of the page.

Assignments

1. What kinds of visual arts and media are present in your community? Make a list. Which of these do people use in your church? Which of the others would you like to introduce? What could each be helpful for, and for whom?
2. Think about Bible storytelling or singing using chapter 13 of this book, meditating on Scripture. Draw the story and show it to children you know. Tell the story to the children while showing them your drawing. Ask them what they have learned.
3. Look for a visual representation of a Bible verse where you are. For example, a lamp can help us remember that Jesus is the light of the world (John 8:12) and that we are the light of the world (Matt 5:14). Ask God to help you see his light and share his light. Or, when you see flowers, think about how God promises to care for us (Matt 6:28–31). Share your idea with your family or friends.
4. Talk with local artists. Appreciate what they do well. Ask them to listen to Scripture and portray its ideas through their art.

Readings

Corbitt, J. Nathan. "Soften Your Media to Put Community in Communication." *Notes on Scripture in Use and Language Programs* 31 (1992): 9–15. https://missionexus.org/soften-your-media-to-put-community-in-communication/.

Dye, T. Wayne, and Tim Hatcher. "Video Translation: Opportunity and Challenge." *Global Missiology* (Jan. 2014). Republished by the Forum of Bible Agencies International. http://www.scripture-engagement.org/content/video-translation-opportunity-and-challenge.

Fujimura, Makoto. *Art and Faith: A Theology of Making*. New Haven, CT: Yale University Press, 2020.

Jordan, Ivan, and Frank Tucker. "Using Indigenous Art to Communicate the Christian Message." *Evangelical Missions Quarterly* 38, no. 3 (2002): 302–9.

Merz, Johannes. "How to Watch and Evaluate Bible-Videos Critically for Cultural Evaluation and Script Preparation." 2016. https://scripture-engagement.org/content/bible-videos-cesp/.

Petersen, Michelle. "Arts Development for Scripture Engagement." *Global Forum on Arts and Christian Faith* 5 (2017): A58–A86. http://www.artsandchristianfaith.org/index.php/journal/article/view/31.

———. "Avoiding Visual Miscommunication." Forum of Bible Agencies International, 2016. http://www.scripture-engagement.org/content/avoiding-visual-miscommunication.

———. "To Engage Audiences with Scripture, Illustrate Stories, Not Dictionaries." Poster Session presented at the Bible Translation 2011 International Conference, Dallas, 15 October 2011.

Sayers, Dorothy L. *Mind of the Maker*. Victoria, BC: Reading Essentials, 1941.

Schrag, Brian. *Creating Local Arts Together: A Manual to Help Communities Reach Their Kingdom Goals*. General Editor, James R. Krabill. Pasadena, CA: William Carey Library, 2013.

Swiss Mission of Peru. *Teaching the Bible to Children*. Translated and adapted by Mary E. Peterson, Linda Potter, and Robin Rempel. Updated ed. Nairobi: Bible Translation and Literacy of East Africa, 2014 (1999).

Weber, Hans-Ruedi. *The Book That Reads Me: A Handbook for Bible Study Enablers*. Geneva: WCC, 1996, 37–47.

Other Resources

https://www.deafmissions.com/tv – Deaf Missions: this page has Bible videos in ASL for the deaf community.

https://www.jesusfilm.org – *Jesus* film.

https://www.lumoproject.com – Lumo Project. Their website says, "The lumo project is a groundbreaking multi-language biblical resource that is set to transform the way in which people engage, discover, and study the life of Jesus through the Gospels."

https://actinternational.org – Artists in Christian Testimony International: this is a ministry that mobilizes and equips artistic and innovative ministries and missionaries for Christian work around the world.

27

Mother-Tongue Reading and Writing for Literates

Introduction

Many people who speak a minority language already know how to read in a majority language. These people are a key resource for helping a community to use their mother-tongue Scriptures.[1] Often they can learn to read their own language very quickly and can then read Scripture in church services and lead Bible studies. They can also learn how to teach others to read. This chapter explains how to help these key people become fluent readers in their mother tongue.

NOT ENOUGH READERS!

Pastor Simon was reading Palapala quite well now, but few others in the church could read the language. When he wasn't present at a meeting, there was rarely anyone to read the Palapala Scriptures, and people went right back to reading in Kisanu. He realized that he should be teaching people to read, but it seemed like a huge task that would take months.

Pastor Zoki happened to be in the village attending his uncle's funeral, so he took the opportunity to visit Pastor Simon. After visiting for some time, Pastor Simon said, "Zoki, you're my friend and a very wise man. Can you help me? I want to use Palapala in my church services, but very few people know how to read it. I don't see how I can

---

1. Teaching literates to read their language can be done in a Scripture engagement seminar if the writing system resembles that of the majority language. If it is very different, you may need to hold a separate seminar devoted to learning to read and write in the mother tongue. If this is the case, the first Scripture engagement seminar can concentrate on oral methods of communicating the message of the Bible.

possibly begin teaching literacy classes. It will take months for people to learn to read and write in Palapala, and I'm already too busy. I don't know what to do!"

Zoki smiled. He knew exactly what Pastor Simon could do. He said, "It's true, this is a big challenge. You need to break it down into parts. I know that many of your church members already read in Kisanu. The differences between Kisanu and Palapala aren't that great. Within a short time, these people could be reading Palapala fluently and writing it too. Then they can teach the others. What is more, if you start by teaching the illiterates to read Palapala, the educated people will probably decide reading Palapala is only for those with little education. So start at the top, and everyone will want to learn."

Pastor Simon felt a ray of hope. "That's a great idea. Why didn't I think of that? It's good to have good friends like you." They went on talking, and Zoki explained more about how to prepare materials for such a reading class.

1. If you speak a minority language, have you learned to read it? If so, how did you learn?
2. What percentage of your congregation already knows how to read the majority language?
3. If literate people in your church speak a minority language and want to learn to read it, how would they go about it?

1. Making a Transfer Guide

Teaching people who are literate in the majority language to read and write in their own language involves two main skills:

- Helping them learn letters and tone marks that do not exist in the majority language or how to pronounce letters that are pronounced differently in the majority language.
- Teaching any necessary conventions connected with the writing system, such as where to divide words and when and how to mark tone.

Write down the alphabet of your language and that of the majority language of your area and compare them.

- Are there any letters that occur only in your language?
- Are there any letters that have different sounds in your language?
- Are there other symbols used in your language?

The best way to teach this material is by using a transition guide. This is a book that has a series of lessons covering the differences between the local language and the majority language. For example, the first lesson may cover the sounds and letters that look the same and sound the same in the two languages, such as *k*, *p*, *t*, and *a*. The second lesson might introduce an implosive *b* written as 'b and contrasted with a non-implosive *b*. The next lesson might teach the letter combinations *kp* and *gb*, and so on.

Each lesson should have lists of words that compare the sounds and letters being taught. There should also be illustrations of some of the words. The exercises should be laid out in such a way that the student can write in the correct answer. For example, here is an exercise teaching the difference between *b* and 'b and *d* and 'd.

Fill in the missing letters with *b*, 'b, *d*, or 'd.

1. _ _ _ili	4. _ _ _ako	7. _ _o
trap	sadness	wait
2. _ _ _u	5. _ _afa	8. _ _ _okolo
ten	fix	behind
3. _olo	6. _ _ _ _ua	9. _ _ _ete
war	goat	palm tree

The lesson should also have a short story that uses many words with the letter or tone being taught in that lesson. This can be followed by an exercise that gives the participants sentences to translate that are based on the story. At the end of the book there may be any or all of the following for extra reading practice: a test, a model letter, a story, riddles or proverbs, a short Scripture passage, or a word list.

If the lessons are being taught during a seminar, give assignments each day. The first page of each lesson in the transition guide might be done in class, and the second page as an assignment to complete before the next morning. At the beginning of the next class, check the answers. A transition guide can be used in various types of seminars and by individuals who are well motivated to learn.

If possible, find a literacy expert to help you make your transition guide. This is particularly important if your language has a very different writing system from that of the major language of the area.

1. If a transfer guide is available in your language, is it used? Could it be used more? Does it need to be improved in any way?
2. If there is not a transfer guide, who could help produce one?

2. Teaching People to Read and Write Their Language

1. Do you think it's important for people to be able to write their language in addition to being able to read it?
2. Why? (Add any of the following points that were not mentioned by the group.)

It helps people if they are able to write their own language.

- Learning to write reinforces reading and improves reading fluency.
- Where church services have been entirely in a major language, if leaders switch to the mother tongue they will need to be able to write such things as the announcements and sermon notes.
- Once people realize that their language can be written, it raises its status.

Although people learn to read more rapidly than they learn to write, teaching writing along with reading from the start helps people learn both skills better. This is especially true for people who learn best by oral means. After the participants have learned to read each lesson, dictate some words or texts for them to write down. For example, for the lesson on ɛ, dictate five words with ɛ and some with e. Correct these words, and then give another five words. People need lots of examples before they will be able to write the language confidently and correctly.

It usually takes more than one seminar to teach people to write their language well. During the first seminar in an area, you can teach only the essential parts of the writing system. With each successive seminar, increase the difficulty of the writing tasks. Help participants to begin to write their language by giving them useful assignments, such as the following:

- To write a letter.
- To write the order of a church service.
- To write announcements to be given in church.
- To write exercises on the more difficult parts of the writing system, such as tone marks.
- To write folk tales, riddles, or songs.
- To write about their experiences.
- To write a story they make up (creative writing).
- To produce a newspaper or a newsletter as a group.

If a number of people who come to the first seminar are able to read and write the language, put them in an advanced group. To identify those who belong in the advanced group on the first morning, give a quick evaluation, such as reading a paragraph or taking a dictation of ten difficult words.

3. Teaching People to Read Aloud Well

One of the main reasons churches do not use newly translated Scriptures in services is that pastors are afraid that they will not be able to read them aloud properly. They need a way to practise reading aloud that will not shame them publicly. Holding seminars that are open only to church leaders can provide good opportunities for such practice.

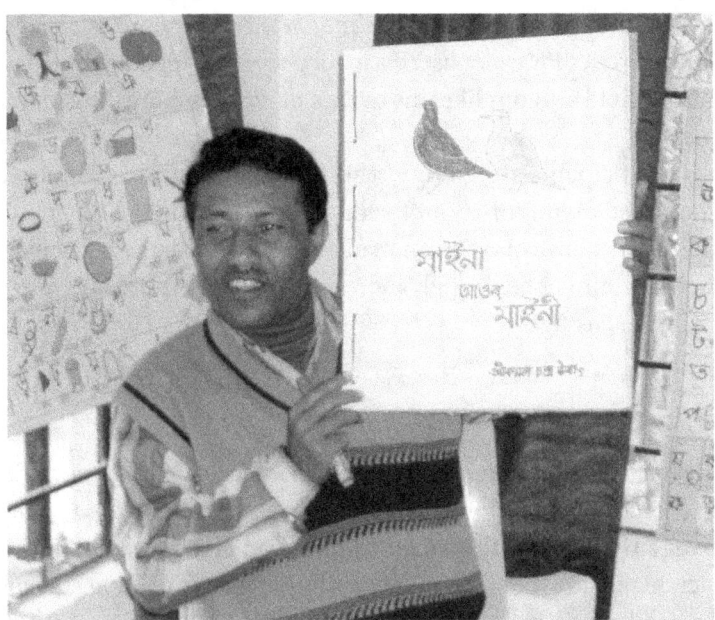

A. Beginning to Read Aloud

If you are running a Scripture engagement seminar for church leaders who have not learned to read their language but who can read the majority language, the first teaching session should be designed to give them confidence that it is possible to read the mother tongue. To do this, have a speaker of the language demonstrate briefly (ten minutes maximum) the symbols in the writing system that the participants need to know. For example, these could be unfamiliar vowels, tone marks, ways of writing nasalization, or two sorts of *b*s or *d*s. Teach only the things that are essential for reading the language at this point.

After this demonstration, divide the participants into small groups so that everyone has a chance to read aloud. Put slower readers in one group and faster readers in another. If older pastors typically read more slowly than younger ones, or if they would lose face by making mistakes in front of them, keep the two age groups apart. Give them an easy, well-known folk story and have everyone read a sentence in turn. Usually they are willing to try in this kind of situation. If they are afraid to get started, read the first part together as a group to build their confidence.

Observe the groups and move anyone who should be in a different group, unless this would embarrass that person. Follow the folk story with an easy passage from Mark, such as a healing miracle of Jesus, or an easy narrative passage from the Old Testament. You may want to produce a leaflet of these stories and exercises for wider use. If a lot of people are reading the language for the first time, hold sessions like this twice a day, using more difficult materials each time.

If any participants are finding reading difficult, have a fluent reader in each group read aloud for about twenty minutes while the others follow in their books. Then have one person read a phrase and all the participants read it together after him or her. Supply more easy reading materials before moving on to Scripture passages.

B. Speed Reading

Once most of the participants can read their language without much difficulty, do some exercises in speed reading to improve their ability to see more of the sentence at a time. This will enable them to read aloud well. As they learn to read faster, make sure they still understand what they're reading. The following exercises will help them to learn this.

1. Prepare a series of sentences for the participants to read. The first few sentences should have just a few words; the later ones should be longer and have a number of parts divided by commas. If all the participants share the same mother tongue, prepare the sentences in that language. If they speak different languages, prepare the sentences in a language that everyone understands. The language used isn't critical since the skills they learn can be applied to reading in any language. Here are some examples of sentences in English:

    - The man went to the market.
    - The old man went to the market quickly.
    - The dog chased the cat all round the streets of the town.

Mother-Tongue Reading and Writing for Literates

- The woman who arrived yesterday was the one I saw in the market earlier today.
- When you go to your field, don't forget to take your hoe, your basket, your machete, and some water to drink.
- If it doesn't rain this afternoon, I think I will go to the market with my three children, but if it does rain, I will stay at home and make some bread.

2. Write each sentence on the board or on a PowerPoint slide before the session begins, but don't let anyone see them. If you use an overhead projector, write each sentence on a separate slide. If you use a blackboard, ask the participants to close their eyes while you write the sentence on the board.

3. Tell the participants that they will be shown a sentence for a few seconds, and they should try to see all the words they can, in chunks or as a group of words, rather than read one word at a time. Ask them to try not to move their lips while reading. Then let them see the sentence just long enough for about half the participants to read it. Have a blank slide to move over or erase the sentence and have everyone write down what they saw. When they have finished writing, have everyone look at the sentence again. As you move to longer sentences, most of the participants will improve their speed and no longer mouth the words.

1. Another way to help people learn to read faster with comprehension is to give a copy of a paragraph in the language to each participant. Start with the papers face down. When it's time to start, have them turn over their page and read the paragraph as fast as possible. When they finish, have them turn the paper back over and signal that they have finished. Note down each person's name and the time they took. After everyone has finished, read out comprehension questions on the passage and have everyone write down the answers. Correct the answers together, being careful not to shame the slower readers. At the end, tell each student how long he or she took to read the passage. Their papers show them what their comprehension scores are.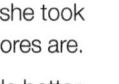

2. The next time, use a different paragraph and encourage everyone to try to do better. Once most of the participants are reading their language fluently, the time has come for a session on how to read well in public.

> Reading Scripture aloud well takes practice.

4. Reading Scripture in Public

When Scripture is read publicly, people should be able to follow it easily. To read well, it's important to practise reading the passage out loud at least four times. Practise reading the passage to your family or to a friend. Learn how to pronounce difficult names or terms so you don't stumble on them. Think about the meaning of the text, and let God speak to you through it. If you don't believe or understand what you are reading, you will communicate this without intending to. Before the service, put a bookmark in your Bible, or save the place in the app to mark the passage so you can easily find it.

At the service, arrive early, and get the order of the service. If you're nervous, breathe deeply to relax. Go up to the front slowly, and read slowly, paying special attention to enunciate clearly. If you feel you are reading too slowly, you're probably doing it just right. Project your voice so that those farthest away can hear. Look up to establish eye contact with the congregation and to see if they are following. If you are using a microphone, keep your mouth about two inches away from it. If you are closer, your voice will be distorted and harsh.

Some people begin stuttering when they read in public. Research has shown that if stutterers can stop stuttering in their mother tongue, they will also stop stuttering in other languages. On the other hand, if they learn not to stutter in the majority language, it does not seem to help them in other languages. To help stutterers, encourage them to take deep breaths between sentences and to practise singing first what they want to say in public later.

Use easy passages to practise reading. Here are some from Mark:

Mark 1:21–39	Mark 9:14–29
Mark 3:7–12	Mark 10:46–52
Mark 5:1–20	Mark 12:41–44
Mark 8:1–9	Mark 16:1–8

Here are some easy passages from elsewhere in the New Testament:

Matthew 2:1–12	Acts 12:4–11
Matthew 8:23–27	Acts 16:16–34
Matthew 18:22–35	Acts 23:12–22
Luke 10:25–37	Acts 28:1–6
Luke 15:11–32	Ephesians 6:1–4
John 2:1–10	Hebrews 13:1–6
John 8:1–11	James 2:1–4
John 11:17–43	Revelation 22:12–17

Here are some easy passages from the Old Testament:

Genesis 24:10–26	1 Samuel 3:1–10
Genesis 37:1–11	Esther 1–10
Joshua 2:1–7	Job 1:1–12
Judges 16:23–30	Ecclesiastes 3:1–8

1. Assign one of the following examples of bad reading to each small group and ask them to demonstrate it:
   (a) Reading too fast or too slow.
   (b) Reading too softly or shouting.
   (c) Reading with no expression.
   (d) Reading in words not phrases while paying no attention to the punctuation or the meaning.
   (e) Stopping at the end of the line, even mid sentence.
   (f) Hesitating over the words.
   (g) Backtracking or rereading phrases or words.
2. Divide into groups of four and practise reading Mark 1:21–28. First read it aloud together. Then have each person read it to the rest. The group should help each person to improve his or her reading. After fifteen to twenty minutes, tell everyone to come back together, and ask for volunteers who think they can read the passage really well. Listen to two or three people.

Assignments

1. Make up a speed-reading exercise in your language, and try it out on a group of people.
2. What do you think are the most important points to remember when reading aloud in public?
3. If reading and writing in the mother tongue is a problem in your area, what could you do to teach literates to read and write it well? Make a list of steps to follow.

Readings

Kutsch Lojenga, Constance. "Transition Primers." *Notes on Literacy* 60 (1989): 31–35.
Loveland, Nancy Jean. "Transition Literacy Workshops in the Peruvian Andes." *Notes on Literacy* 18, no. 1 (1992): 33–40.

Marsch, Angelika. "It's All a Question of Practice! A Scripture-in-Use Project in the Central Andes of Peru." *Notes on Literature in Use and Language Programs* 46 (1995): 48–55.

Remple, Robin. "Transition Primer Manual for Trainers and Teachers." *Notes on Literacy* 24, no. 3 (1998): 18–47.

Trudell, Barbara. "Making Readers Literate: Transition Literacy in Sub-Saharan Africa." *Notes on Literacy* 21, no. 3 (1995): 47–58. https://scripture-engagement.org/wp-content/uploads/2020/09/Trudell-B-1995-Making-Readers-Literate.pdf.

Walters, Leah. "A Back Transition Primer: National Language to Vernacular." *Notes on Literacy* 48 (1986): 22–27. https://scripture-engagement.org/wp-content/uploads/2020/09/Walter-L-1986-Back-Transition-Primer.pdf.

28

Basic Literacy and Scripture

Introduction

Adults who don't know how to read sometimes feel that it would be impossible for them to learn, but this isn't the case. Learning to read can take months, but it is worth the effort. One of the strongest motivations found among Christians in adult literacy classes is to be able to read the Bible. This chapter talks about how Scripture can be part of a literacy programme.

PASTOR SIMON'S LITERACY CLASSES

Pastor Simon had successfully helped start classes for educated people in his church to read Palapala, and after a few weeks many of them were reading fluently. A few months later a Christian organization came to help start literacy classes in Palapala for those who couldn't read at all. After the classes had been going for about three years, Pastor Simon went to a meeting of all the pastors in the northern part of Sanatu.

One of the subjects the pastors discussed was how to get good literacy programmes in the churches so that more people could read the Bible. While they were together, Pastor Simon heard various tales of woe from his fellow pastors. Pastor Baji from an area in the south said, "We've started literacy classes in English two or three times. The first week we have twenty-five students, but after three or four weeks only two or three people come. They find it so hard learning to read in English."

Pastor Mambo had a different problem. He said, "An organization came to our area and started literacy classes. They teach people to read in our language, but the materials they read are all about cotton production. Some of the women in my church have gone to the classes, but they get bored after a while."

Pastor Mark had yet another problem. "A new organization has come to our region and started some special sort of literacy classes. Some of our church members go to them. They thoroughly enjoy the classes, which consist of long discussions about matters that touch the local community. The problem is that none of them ever actually learn to read!"

When Pastor Simon heard all of this, he began to be happy about the literacy classes in his church, even though they were always having small problems, such as a lazy teacher who often didn't come to teach. He told the other pastors, "We have literacy classes in the church three times a week. The students begin by learning to read and write in Palapala, then in the later classes they go on to learn to read and write Kisanu, and the most advanced class is learning to read English. Anybody can come to the classes, whether they come to our church or not. In fact, the advanced class is held in the Catholic church. Each of the classes has some Bible reading because we find that many of our students want to learn to read in order to read the Bible, but we make sure they have plenty of other things to read as well."

1. Have you had any of the problems expressed by these pastors?
2. Have you had different problems with literacy programmes that were not mentioned?
3. What solutions has Pastor Simon found to the problems stated by the others?
4. Would any of these solutions be helpful in your area?

1. Types of Basic Mother-Tongue Literacy Programmes

There are two main types of literacy programmes for adults: community-based and church-based. A community-based programme may be organized by the government, the local community leaders, or another organization. It often meets in a local school. A church-based literacy programme is organized by a church or a group of churches, sometimes with help from other organizations.

Church-based literacy programmes should include Scripture reading in all their classes. This not only helps church members to use Scripture, but also reinforces their motivation for joining literacy classes. The leaders of these programmes should encourage Christians and non-Christians alike to come and learn to read. Non-Christians may well become Christians through hearing and reading the Scriptures for themselves, but they shouldn't be pressured to do so.

Scripture can be used at all levels of a basic literacy programme. If the literacy classes consist of people from different church denominations, it is very important that the study of the Scriptures is non-sectarian. The following are some things to bear in mind when organizing such classes:

- Give church leaders an opportunity to study the materials before the classes begin so that they agree with what is being taught.
- Avoid divisive subjects, such as baptism or the end times.
- Instruct literacy teachers to encourage students to stay in the students' own church rather than join another!

Even if the classes are not church-based, it may be possible to have a Scripture component in the programme, but this needs to be researched carefully before it is even suggested. If it is not possible to include Scripture as an integral part of the programme, it might be possible to arrange optional sessions for reading Scripture.

2. Stages in a Literacy Programme

There are four stages in a literacy programme. When people who don't know how to read finish the programme, they should be at the point of being able to read fluently. At the same time, they will have learned to write their language.

Depending on the difficulty of the particular alphabet used to write the language and the dedication of the teachers and participants, it can take people between one and two years to complete all of the stages.

Stage 1: Pre-reading and Basic Primer Stage

At Stage 1 of a literacy programme, students will not be able to read the translated Scriptures, so the teacher should begin each lesson by reading a short passage of Scripture aloud, and the class can pray and sing together. This opening part should not take more than fifteen minutes. It is not the time for a sermon.

A primer is the main reading material for this stage. Some primers are based on Scripture. The first lesson may have "Jesus" as one of the key words. By the sixth lesson, people will be reading short, simple Bible stories – for example, one about Jesus healing a person. The advantage of this sort of primer is that Christians who join a reading class to read the Bible immediately feel that their goal is in sight. Another advantage is that non-Christians may come to Christ. There are some disadvantages, however. The first few lessons of any primer are challenging to write as only a limited number of letters can be used. Scripture-based primers limit the number of letters even more as the stories have to be from the Bible. This may result in unnatural or uninteresting stories. In addition, these primers can only be used in church-based programmes. Another primer has to be prepared if there is also a community-based literacy programme. Non-Christians may find the approach overly aggressive and so reject both the message and the chance to learn to read.

Other primers teach reading by using stories based on familiar themes from the language group. People master the primer before they begin reading Scripture. These primers are easier to develop and can be used in all kinds of programmes but may be less appealing to Christians who want to read the Bible.

A combination of these two types of primers is possible. The first lessons can concentrate on finding the best words to teach the most frequent letters and helping the students read meaningful material as quickly as possible. By the time the students have mastered about half of the primer, the lessons can begin to include Christian concepts. By the last quarter of the primer, the lessons can have simple adapted Bible stories as some of the reading material.

Other combinations are also possible. A programme known as Literacy for Life was developed in Ghana. It takes a primer without Scripture content and adds Bible studies for each lesson based on the key word. For example, if the key word is "well" in a story on drawing water, the story might be about Jesus meeting the Samaritan woman at the well. In the first stages of the literacy programme, the teacher reads this material to the students. Later, the students read it for themselves.

> Scripture can be used at all levels of a basic literacy programme.

1. In your situation, what kind of primer do you think would serve your community best? Why?
2. Which kind of primer is used at present?
3. Would an approach such as Literacy for Life help you?

Stage 2: Post-primer

Students at the beginning of Stage 2 need small booklets of simple Bible stories. These could also be available orally on an app on mobile phones. Each story should contain no more than four to six new words. Choose stories that build on the vocabulary learned in Stage 1. Prepare exercises on these new words before you teach the story. The New Readers' Series of Bible booklets published by the United Bible Societies is suitable for the second part of this stage. By the end of this stage, students should understand the idea of a chapter and a verse and be able to look these up in a book such as Mark's gospel.

By the middle of Stage 2, students are ready to receive a New Testament if it is available. If not, they should receive at least a gospel or a book of the Old Testament, such as Genesis. The average student at this stage will be able to make a reasonable attempt to read any narrative passage in the Bible but will still find teaching material, such as the epistles, difficult to read.

During this stage, it should be possible to teach students how to do Bible studies. One way to do this is to prepare workbooks of twelve Bible studies on simple passages in the New Testament or on one book of the Old Testament. Each study should have a series of questions for students to answer and lines on which they can write their answers. Each lesson should also have a verse to memorize. Teachers lead the study, but they don't tell the students the answers. Instead, they help the students to find the answers in the Bible passage. (See chapter 11.)

The following are some passages that may be good for beginning Bible studies from the New Testament:

- Matthew 1:18–25 – Birth of Jesus
- Matthew 4:1–11 – Satan tempts Jesus
- Matthew 6:5–15 – Jesus teaches about prayer
- Mark 1:29–39 – Jesus heals people
- Mark 6:35–44 – Jesus feeds five thousand people
- Luke 8:4–15 – The parable of the sower
- Luke 10:29–37 – The parable of the good Samaritan
- Luke 19:1–10 – Jesus and Zacchaeus
- John 5:1–9 – Jesus heals a paralytic
- John 20:24–31 – Jesus and Thomas
- Acts 1:6–11 – Jesus returns to heaven
- Acts 16:16–34 – Paul and Silas in prison

1. Does your church have classes for people who are only partially literate?
2. If so, which Bible stories would you recommend they read?
3. Do they need more materials at different levels of difficulty, from easy-to-read to difficult?
4. Who could prepare these materials?

Stage 3: Adult Education

By Stage 3, students are fluent readers and can do many types of Bible studies and activities suggested in this manual. For example, you could prepare a booklet of helpful passages of Scripture for good news encounters, as suggested in chapter 17, or a booklet on relevant themes, as suggested in chapters 9, 14, and 15.

If more than one denomination is working on the literacy programme, circulate a draft version of any Bible study books among the church leaders to be sure that everyone agrees with the content.

If the whole Bible is available, have the students learn the order of the books of the Bible at this stage.

Stage 4: Advanced Adult Education

By Stage 4, students should have a Bible if it exists in their language, and they should have acquired a habit of reading and studying it. During this last stage, it is important that the class is able to do their Bible study with minimal help from the teacher. They should study some of the harder books of the Bible, choosing those that are particularly relevant to the problems they are confronting. For example, if there is a lot of misunderstanding of the Christian's power over Satan, Ephesians is a good book to study. If the whole Bible is available, they could study one of the minor prophets.

3. A Well-Rounded Programme

Literacy programmes aim to give a broad education to students so that they can use their literacy skills in everyday life and go on learning for the rest of their lives. A programme should have many parts to it: learning to read and write, writing letters, learning how to balance a budget, using arithmetic in everyday tasks, knowing something about the wider world through geography and history, and so forth. If the literacy programme draws its material solely from Scripture, it will not result in a well-educated person.

Assignments

1. Does your church have a literacy programme? If so, describe how Scripture is used in it.
2. Is more than one church involved in your literacy programme? If so, what topics do you need to avoid to make the classes acceptable to all?
3. If you were planning a Bible study book for Stage 4 students, which book of the Bible would you like them to study, and why?
4. Imagine that a number of non-Christians who are semi-literate have just joined Stage 2 in a church-based literacy programme. Make a list of easy passages in the New Testament that you would like them to study. Prepare six questions for the first study.
5. A large church where everyone speaks the same minority language has about a hundred students in literacy classes. The pastor continues to read from the majority language Bible every Sunday.
   (a) Why might the pastor be doing this?
   (b) What problems will this cause?
   (c) What can be done about it?

Readings

Herbert, Pat. "Literacy for Life." *Scripture in Use Today* 13 (2006): 24–30. https://scripture-engagement.org/wp-content/uploads/2020/09/Herbert-P-2006-Literacy-for-Life-Ghana.pdf.

Hill, Margaret. "Ngbaka Adult Literacy Program in Northwestern Zaire." *Notes on Literacy* 21, no. 4 (1995): 38–55.

———. "Scripture Impact and Literacy." *Scripture in Use Today* 7 (2003): 8–10.

Levinsohn, Stephen. "Literacy and Scripture Materials in a Bilingual Environment." *Notes on Scripture Use* 3 (1982): 24–25.

Margetts, Richard. "Literacy for Life: Teacher's Guide." 2006. https://scripture-engagement.org/wp-content/uploads/2020/09/Margetts-R-2006-Literacy-for-Life-Teachers-Guide.pdf.

Trotter, Cynthia. "Using Feature Phones to Promote Literacy and Scripture Engagement." 2020. https://scripture-engagement.org/content/using-feature-phones/.

Other Resources

https://bloomlibrary.org/bible – "Bloom makes it easy to create simple books and translate them into multiple languages. . . . Bloom's Book Library offers books from around the world for you to translate into a local language. This includes over 500 Bible story books." These can be very helpful for the development of a literacy programme. Booklets can also be created as "talking books" in the Bloom Reader app, so people can read them on their mobile phones. (See "Bloom Bible Story Books," https://scripture-engagement.org/content/bloom.)

https://www.literacyevangelism.org – Literacy & Evangelism International (LEI) "helps people connect better with their world and with God's Word by assisting churches and missions with materials and training for basic literacy or English teaching ministries [and] by developing Bible-content teaching materials in multiple languages." (See "Literacy & Evangelism International," https://scripture-engagement.org/content/literacy-evangelism-international/.)

29

Research, Marketing, and Distribution

Introduction

One test of relevance for a Scripture product is the degree to which people voluntarily use it. For people to use it, they need to know that it is available, find it attractive, and be able to get hold of a copy. Research can help us know whether people are currently using Scripture, how they are using it, what kinds of Scripture products they are using, and in which languages and media. This can help us evaluate needs and interests and develop marketing and distribution programmes that will improve Scripture engagement. This chapter explores these issues.

WHERE ARE THE BIBLES?

The Southern Anglican diocese of Bingola had just declared the coming year to be the Year of the Bible. Every parish was asked to make plans as to how they would help their church members read, listen to, and study the Bible in a language they could understand well. This got off to a good start with a special dedication service.

Bishop Joseph decided to visit all the parishes in February to find out how things were going. Three weeks later, he returned home having travelled many miles and talked a great deal. He was warmly welcomed home by his wife and three children. That evening, after his bath and a good meal, he relaxed in the house and started to tell his wife about the trip. "I visited thirty-five churches," he said, "and they all know about the Year of the Bible. But what is actually happening on the ground is very different from church to church. I counted five churches where the Scriptures are read in languages that most of the congregation don't understand. Another ten churches have no programme to help their ordinary church members study the Bible, and only five are offering Scripture in audio form for those who can't read. I'm not sure exactly what the problem is. I feel discouraged."

His wife said, "My dear, you need a good night's sleep. Then maybe you will be able to pray and think about it."

The next day, as the bishop was sitting in his office and praying for guidance, he thought about reports he had heard of a certain Pastor Simon from Sanatu, who had helped a number of churches engage with Scriptures in various local languages. "Perhaps I should invite him here," he thought. So, after negotiations, Pastor Simon's denomination lent him to the Anglican Church for three months. Pastor Simon started travelling around and assessing the situation. After a couple of weeks, he returned to discuss his findings with the bishop and a group of pastors. After some preliminary discussion, Pastor Simon stood by a blackboard and wrote three words on it: "research," "marketing," and "distribution."

He explained each one, giving examples from the churches he had visited, being careful not to say which church it was! "First," he said, "you need to do some research. One church I visited had no idea at all how many members were able to read the Bible or which language they would prefer to read it in. The New Testament had just been published in that region, but no one could tell me how many copies had been sold or whether they were in use in the churches. Getting information from anyone was like groping around in the fog!

"Second, in some places there is a marketing problem. I met one poor pastor trying to sell some Bibles that were in tiny print. I watched the people in his church open the Bible, take one look at the words, put it back on the table, and immediately walk away. Then in another place I found a pastor selling Bible study books. They really would have been very useful for Bible studies, but unfortunately they had been published with a picture on the cover that looked like something you find in a children's colouring book! People looked at the cover and wouldn't even pick it up! I found another pastor who had posted a digital copy of the New Testament on the Internet, but very few people knew to access it."

Finally he addressed the issue of distribution. "You all know about the new revised version of the Likali Bible that was published a year ago? Everywhere I went, people asked me where they could buy it. People were still using old tattered Likali Bibles with half the pages falling out! I was curious as to what had happened and finally managed to track down all the stock in a church office. I asked the man in charge there why they were stored away when people were asking to buy them. He told me, 'No one had told us how much to sell them for or what we do with the money.'"

1. Share any experiences you have had of Bibles or Scripture portions being marketed in the wrong way. For example, they may have had a cover that no one liked.

2. Where would you go if you wanted to buy a Bible, New Testament, or Scripture portions in

    - English?
    - the majority language in your area, if not English?
    - your mother tongue?

3. Where would you go on the Internet to access a Bible, New Testament, or Scripture portions in any language?

1. Why Do Research?

In the course of daily life, we all do research. For example, if we want to buy a bike, we look at the options and decide which one is best. When working in Scripture engagement, we should also do research so we can know which strategies are the most effective.

What are some good and bad reasons for doing research? (For answers, see 7. p. 294.)

The Ghana Evangelical Commission researched whether there was a church in each of the ethnic groups of Ghana. Everyone assumed that all the groups in Ghana had been reached with the gospel. To their great surprise, they found that one people group didn't have any Christian witness at all. When they discovered this, a church sent missionaries to the area.

A language group in Côte d'Ivoire had the New Testament in their language, but it was not being used by individuals or churches in the area. When some church leaders were asked about this, it became clear that they didn't even know that the New Testament existed in their language. If there had been attempts to tell people about it, they were not adequate.

Imagine that you want to start producing and marketing a new soft drink called Fantastic Fruit Flavour, or FFF for short. What would you need to find out before you started? Make a list (and add any of the following points if they have not been mentioned).

- Find out about present sales of soft drinks.
- Find out what type of soft drink people like.
- Decide where the distribution points will be.
- Research the type of label that will appeal to people.
- Research the price people would pay for the product.
- Find out what size and shape bottle appeals the most to the general population.

2. Researching Scripture Use

Church leaders need to know whether the people in their churches are receiving enough spiritual food to grow in their faith. Two ways of assessing Scripture use are (1) to monitor the distribution of Scripture products, and (2) to find out how the Scripture products are being used.

A. Monitoring the Distribution of Scripture Products

To monitor the distribution of Scripture products, make an inventory of the Scripture products you have prepared for your audience. Include printed, digital, audio, and video products. Below is an example of a form. Copy out the form (leaving out the numbers) into a notebook, onto a computer spreadsheet, or on a mobile phone. Leave enough blank spaces to record all your information.

Scripture Products Inventory			Date:	
Title	Date Printed	Number Printed	Total Number Sold	Number in Stock
Luke (printed)	2016	1,500	700	800
Transfer primer	2012	1,000	899	101
Luke (audio)	2016			

When you have completed the inventory, take some time to think about the information. Discuss the following questions:

1. Which products have sold quickly? Why do you think they did?
2. Which products have not sold quickly? Why do you think they didn't?
3. Which products should be reprinted?
4. What kinds of Scripture products should you invest in next?

Digital Scripture Products Inventory			Date:
Title	Date Posted	Number of Social Media Engagements (Likes, Shares, Clicks)	Number of Downloads of Apps or Other Files
Luke (pdf)	2018	-	157
Luke (audio)	2018	-	342
Luke (app)	2019	-	409
Scripture songs	2021	22,421	-
Bible verse images	2021	14,398	-

5. What kinds of phones do people have? How do they use them? What kinds of websites do they go to frequently? How do they share digital content?

6. What strategy could reach people who use their phones in this way?

After six months, do the inventory again and see if the situation has changed. If sales have increased, this would most likely indicate that people are becoming more interested in reading or listening to Scripture.

B. Finding out How Scripture Products Are Being Used

People may have a copy of a Bible, but they need to be using it regularly to grow in their faith. To find out who is using which Scripture products in which contexts, languages, and media, fill out the following form for each church in your language area. Involve church leaders or their designates in collecting this information.

Researcher's name: _____ Date: _____
Church name: _____
Location: _____
Mother tongue of local church leaders: _____
Are local church leaders able to speak the main mother tongue of the congregation? _____
Mother tongues represented in congregation. Indicate the approximate percentage of the people who speak them – for example, Palapala, 50%
_____

Approximate percentage of congregation that is able to read in any language:
_____

Approximate percentage of congregation that is able to read in their mother tongue: _____

List all of the meetings of the church and find out what Scripture products are used at each one. The title of the product will indicate its language and media. If Bible storying groups are meeting, include these in the list and write "oral stories" in the second column.

Event	Title of Scripture product used
Mass	
Catechism	
Sunday school	
Women's meeting	
Bible Studies	
(add others)	

Gather information on these events in all of the churches in the target area. This may include both urban and rural churches. If there are too many churches to visit them all, write the names of the churches on slips of paper and divide them into two piles, one for urban churches and one for rural. Mix up the papers in each pile and take some slips from each, selecting a number proportional to the number of churches in each group. For example, if the Methodists have forty rural churches and ten urban ones, pick at least ten slips from the pile of rural churches and at least three slips from the pile of urban churches. By picking slips this way, you're far less likely to go only to the churches that are using Scriptures well or the ones with which you're already familiar.

After gathering the information, compile it for each kind of church (Catholic, Baptist, etc.), keeping the results from urban and rural churches separate. Analyse it, and look for a pattern in the way the churches use Scripture. For example, eight of the ten churches may use mother-tongue hymnals but not use mother-tongue Scriptures; or the Catholic churches may use mother-tongue Scriptures for Scripture reading, but the Protestant churches may not.

After analysing the information, meet with the church leaders and report on the findings. Discuss the following questions, being careful to do so in a way that does not shame any church or church leader.

1. How much Scripture are the churches using?
2. In what contexts are they using Scripture?
3. Which churches are using Scripture in the language(s) spoken by most of the congregation?
4. In what contexts are they using mother-tongue Scripture?
5. Which Scripture products are being used?
6. If audio, digital, or video products are available, are churches using more audio, digital, video, or printed Scripture products?

With this information in hand, think about the kinds of Scripture engagement activities that seem to be most effective and what can be done to increase Scripture use where it is weak. Agree together on the best strategies to use. After you have tried these new strategies for a period of time, collect information again, and see if there has been any increase in the amount of Scripture churches are using.

1. In a certain group of rural Baptist churches, research showed that in every congregation, over 80 percent of the people spoke Wezi, but the churches used Wezi only for the announcements and songs. Most of the Baptist pastors there were not Wezi speakers. What Scripture engagement activities would you recommend to the senior pastor of the area?
2. In an urban group of Assemblies of God churches, research showed that all the churches were multilingual and multicultural but that there were two sizeable groups of monolinguals in every church – one group that spoke Wezi and the other Bamama. The main services were all held in English. What Scripture engagement activities would you recommend?

3. Marketing

Research may show that some or all of the mother-tongue Scripture products are not being used by most people. This may well be a marketing problem.

A. The Appearance of the Product

Hold up samples of a variety of attractive and unattractive Scripture products. For each, describe the product and its intended audience.
1. Do you think this product would be appealing to the intended audience?
2. Why or why not?

People judge a book by its cover. They decide what kind of product it is: a Bible, a children's book, a book only for Christians, for women, and so forth. They decide whether it looks interesting enough to pick up and look inside. If the cover looks shabby, dull, or uninteresting, or is simply in a colour that people don't like, they are unlikely to buy it. Businesses spend a lot of money making the packaging of their goods attractive. For something as important as Scripture products, we need to put effort into packaging as well.

If people find the pages of Scripture products filled from one edge to the other with text in a very small font, they may well set the product aside, especially if they are not used to reading or reading in that language. Leave plenty of blank space around the text, and if culturally acceptable, include illustrations.

People also make quick judgements about digital, audio, and visual products. They need to hear a voice that they enjoy listening to and trust. With videos, viewers often decide in less than one minute whether they want to watch the whole thing or turn it off, so those first minutes need to capture their attention. With both videos and audio products, the labels on the covers are also very important. Test what people perceive to be attractive and interesting.

B. Advertising the Product

Before people can use a product, they need to know that it exists. Develop a plan for advertising the available Scripture products widely and in all parts of the community. Mass media is helpful at this stage.

What are some ways to advertise Scripture products?
(Add any points below that have not been mentioned.)

Scripture products can be advertised through the following means:
- Local radio stations
- Television programmes that give the news of each ethnic group in the country
- Billboards
- Flyers or brochures
- Announcements and/or banners at church conferences and pastors' meetings
- Dedications of New Testaments or other Scripture products
- Church announcements
- Town criers

- Facebook ads
- Google ads

1. What communication channels are available in your community to advertise your Scripture products?
2. What parts of the community are reached by each one?
3. What costs would be involved with each one, in terms of both money and effort necessary to prepare the advertisement?
4. Which channels do you think would be most effective to use?
5. What efforts have you made to market Scripture products? Which have been successful?

C. The Appropriateness of the Product

The content of Scripture products needs to attract the audience's attention. Some products may not be used because they don't meet a need the audience feels it has. Sometimes a very small thing can keep people from using a product. For example, they may find an illustration offensive, or they may wrongly assume that the Scripture product is intended for only one church, or it may cost more than they are willing to spend, and so forth. Find out why a product isn't being used, and determine if changes can be made to correct the problem. If the product can't be salvaged, use what you learn about your audience to design more relevant products in the future. It is helpful to do several "test versions" of a product before spending lots of money to publish it. Ask people's opinions of them. This can help you discover problems before they are published in their final form. This can also show you what kinds of things excite people.

4. Distribution Channels

The most carefully prepared book or recording is of no use if it remains in a storeroom or unaccessed on a social media platform. Distributing and selling Scripture products depends on successful distribution networks and money management.

A. Distribution Networks

The way products can be distributed successfully will differ from one community to another. Find out how things are distributed successfully in your community, and reflect on the distribution of your Scripture products.

1. What kind of product sells well in your area? Coca-Cola? Baseball hats? Mobile phones?
2. Why does it sell well?
3. Who sells it?
4. Where is it sold?
5. When is it sold?
6. Are there places where books are sold?
7. Are there places where CDs, DVDs, and videos are sold?
8. How is the money from these sales managed?

In many communities, Scripture products can be distributed in bookshops, mission offices, church offices, markets, shops, and at conferences, church services, or meetings. In some communities, colporteurs sell Scripture products door to door with great success. They buy the products at a reduced cost and are able to share God's word with people and make a small profit for their efforts.

> The most carefully prepared book or recording is of no use if it remains in a storeroom!

B. Money Management

Printing and recording Scripture products costs money, and this money must be managed properly.

NO REPRINT FOR THE IKARI

The Ikari language committee were very happy when the Bible was finally published in their language. The stock of Bibles was put in their care, and they were told that when all the copies had been sold, the money would be used to pay for the next printing. The committee appointed a treasurer to keep track of the money. Things got off to a good start at the dedication of the Bible as many people bought a copy. Many of the pastors asked if they could have copies of the Bible to sell in their churches, so soon after the dedication the committee sent boxes of Bibles to pastors throughout the language community.

The committee kept some boxes of the Bibles, and as time went on they gave out free copies to friends, visiting officials, and pastors. Some of the boxes were kept in a small, damp room, and before long the termites began eating them. Gradually some money started to trickle in from the boxes given to pastors, but no one had a list of those who had actually taken Bibles. Without any record of where the Bibles had gone, there was no way to keep track of the money.

One of the committee members tried hard to get in the money from the sales, and every time he met pastors who had received some Bibles to sell, he asked if they had sold any. Most said that they had given the copies to people and were still waiting for the money. This went on for some months until all the copies had been distributed except those that had been eaten by termites. People started to ask for a reprint as the original print run had been insufficient for all the people who wanted one. When the committee met again to discuss this and hear a report of the money available, the treasurer was absent. After some time they found out that his wife had been ill, and he had used the Bible money to take her to the hospital. No reprint was done for many years, and many Ikari people are still without Bibles.

1. How did distribution affect Scripture engagement?
2. How could this unhappy ending have been avoided?
3. What are some ways to distribute Scripture products successfully?
4. Discuss responses to the third question in the large group. (Add any points from below not already mentioned.)

The following are some policies for distributing Scripture products.

- The best policy may be no cash, no book! This needs to include even pastors and priests!
- A sustainable financial system may need outside funding to print the first publication. After that, money from the sales of that product must be used to pay for reprinting.
- Accountability is needed for managing any type of finances. It is often best if two people control the cash. This could involve a cash box with two locks. Many communities have ways of ensuring that money is not misused.
- Books or other media must be stored in a place that protects them from theft, termites, water, and mould.

Assignments

1. Choose two Scripture products available in your area, one product that you know sells well and one that is difficult to sell. List some of the reasons for the differences.
2. Who should make decisions about the appearance of Scripture products? What process should be used to make these decisions? This includes cover colour, type of illustrations, and so forth.

Readings

Collins, Wes. "Selling Books from a Bookstore." *Notes on Scripture Use* 8 (1984): 35–36.

"Facebook Ads for Scripture Promotion: How to Leverage the Power of Facebook Ads to Promote the Translated Scriptures and Other Scripture Media." https://scripture-engagement.org/content/facebook-ads-for-scripture-promotion/.

Hill, Harriet. "How to Know When Scripture Use Is Succeeding." *Notes on Sociolinguistics* 5, no. 2 (2000): 81–87.

Hill, Margaret. "How to Use a Dedication Event to Improve Scripture Engagement and Use." 2009. https://scripture-engagement.org/wp-content/uploads/2009/04/Hill-M-2009-How-to-use-a-dedication-event.pdf.

Lange, Martin. "Digital Distribution Strategy for Bible Dedication Celebrations: A Step-by-Step Guide for Using Wi-Fi Media Boxes at Your Event." 2020. https://scripture-engagement.org/content/digital-distribution-bible-dedications.

———. "Using Your Wi-Fi Media Box: 28 Ideas for Digital Distribution." 2020. https://scripture-engagement.org/content/using-your-wi-fi-media-box/.

Lauber, Ed. "SIU and Funding the Translation Program." *Notes on Scripture Use and Language Programs* 37 (1993): 15–21.

Margetts, Richard. "Our Bible Has Arrived! Organizing a Dedication Event to Celebrate the Publication of a New Testament, Bible or Other Translated Books." 2018. https://scripture-engagement.org/content/our-bible-has-arrived/.

McKinney, Carol V. *Globe Trotting in Sandals: A Field Guide to Cultural Research*. Dallas: SIL, 2000.

Porter, Doris. "Area-Centered Promotion-Distribution: The Concept and Some Suggestions for Guidelines." *Notes on Scripture Use and Language Programs* 37 (1993): 32–35.

Showalter, Catherine J. "Getting What You Ask For: A Study Of Sociolinguistic Survey Questionnaires." In *Survey Reference Manual*, ed. T. G. Bergman. Dallas: SIL, 1990.

Søgaard, Viggo. *Research in Church and Mission*. Pasadena, CA: William Carey, 1996.

There are also many other good articles on and tools for research, marketing, and distribution on the Scripture Engagement website: https://scripture-engagement.org.

30

How to Bring about Change

Introduction

This book is full of ideas about changes you can bring to your community to help them engage more with Scripture. It particularly addresses the issue of helping people use newly translated Scriptures. To introduce these changes successfully, it's helpful to understand how people adopt changes and what makes them resist change.

GOOD ENOUGH FOR OUR FATHERS, GOOD ENOUGH FOR ME!

One afternoon Pastor Simon was sitting talking with the local Catholic catechist, Lambo. They were talking about the way that the new Palapala Scriptures were really helping their Christians to understand the Bible. As they talked, Pastor Simon thought about one of his deacons called Ngulu Mba. He told Lambo, "Ngulu refuses to buy a Palapala New Testament. He always has his Kisanu Bible with him, and if he is leading the service, we go back to using Kisanu for almost everything except the announcements. I asked him why he doesn't want to use the Palapala translation, and he had various reasons. One of them is that he thinks it will cause disunity in the church. Another one is that he needs the Kisanu for the Old Testament and doesn't like carrying two books. But really I think he just doesn't want to change!"

Lambo replied, "If you have only one leader in your church who feels like that, you are lucky! I have a whole group of church leaders who don't want anything at all to change. Not only do they find it hard to use the new translation, but they even resist changes like having the morning service at a different time! One of them said to me, 'What was good enough for our fathers is good enough for me!'"

They discussed this and thought about other changes that had come into their community. "Remember when they first introduced the idea of planting beans between the corn?" said Pastor Simon. "Some people accepted those free seeds and started planting beans right away. Other people started doing it once they saw that the first group were enjoying the beans and that the corn was growing better. Some other people waited a couple of years, but then they eventually planted beans as well. But there are still a few people who won't touch a bean! You know old Papa Gambo? He is still saying that the beans are some foreign plot to poison us all!"

"Yes," said Lambo, "and do you remember that organization that tried to introduce oxen for ploughing? That never worked because no one could really imagine taming those big cows, and no one could show us how to do it."

They discussed the whole problem of bringing about change and decided they needed to know more about it. Lambo said, "After all, becoming a Christian brings a big change to people's lives, so maybe some people who won't listen to the gospel are actually just resisting change."

1. What types of change have come to your community?
2. How have people reacted to them?

1. Is Change Good or Bad?

People have one of three basic attitudes towards change.

A. Change Is Bad

Some people think change is bad. They think that if anything in a culture changes, the society will fall apart. This type of person thinks cultures are like car engines: you can't just take one part out and put a different part in its place because then the engine won't work any more. Such people want to preserve the past.

Sometimes people cling to their traditions for fear that they will lose their identity. For example, many French people feel that if their language changes or accepts words from other languages, they will lose part of their heritage.

B. Change Is Inevitable

Change is all around us, and some people see change as inevitable. If agriculture and farming were the same now as they were three hundred years ago, Africa would not have any pineapples, mangoes, corn, cassava, goats, or chickens, and Europe would not have potatoes, tea, or coffee. When people find that their neighbours have something that they think might be useful to them, they borrow it. Cultures also change in response to significant events, such as war, tsunamis, disease, and conquest. Where there is life, there is change.

With globalization, people say that the world is getting smaller. This means that what happens in one part of the world affects people in another part of the world much more quickly than before. Whether we want it or not, even remote villages in Majority World countries are affected by the wider world.

C. Change Is Good

Some people see change as a good thing because they believe it helps people. All cultures suffer from the effects of sin. None is perfect. They need to change so that they become all God intended them to be. For example, in some cultures, getting drunk is the norm. This leads to problems, such as alcoholism, unemployment, poverty, divorce, abuse, and so forth. The gospel brings change. When people become Christians, they may stop getting drunk, and gradually their way of life may improve. They may develop other ways to have a good time with friends that are less destructive.

Yet good practices in a culture can be corrupted by sin. For example, God told Moses to hold up a bronze snake so that those who had been bitten by poisonous snakes would be healed. This was right and God's will for them. However, by the reign of King Hezekiah, the people were worshipping this bronze snake, and so he destroyed it (2 Kgs 18:4). Something good became bad.

Good practices in a culture can also become obsolete. For example, men's ties were intended to keep them warm in very cold climates. Buildings and vehicles are often heated now, and in tropical climates men have no need to try to keep warm, so the reason for wearing ties has become obsolete in many places. Men are gradually wearing them less.

On the board, list some changes you see around you to illustrate each of the following statements:
- Change can be bad.
- Change comes whether we want it or not.
- Change can be good.

2. Determining the Need

If you intend to introduce a change in a community, you are a change agent. You may have some ideas about the kinds of changes that might be helpful, but you need to do research in the community to find out if your ideas are correct. This research can involve the following:

- Understanding the culture.
- Discussing with people and getting their opinions.
- Observing what is going on in the community, including observing other development organizations that are working in the area.
- Observing what is going on in the larger world that will affect the community – for example, AIDS, COVID-19, war, and so forth.

The main goal of this research is to understand the felt needs of people. Another goal is to understand real needs that the community may not be aware they have, such as their need for Christ, AIDS education, and so forth. Change will be accepted only if it responds to a need in the community.

If in a typical village in your area you asked a young man and an older woman what they felt they needed, what do you think they would say?

3. Levels of Difficulty

Some changes are more difficult to introduce than others.

- Changes in beliefs and values (what is considered right and wrong) are the most difficult to introduce. For example, people may have very different and very strong beliefs about polygamy or female excision.
- Changes in activities are less difficult to introduce – for example, queuing to buy bus tickets.
- Changes in technology are the easiest to introduce – for example, using plastic buckets instead of clay pots.

Because things are interrelated in a culture, any change in one area may affect other areas. For example, if people believe that water comes from a deity in the river, using a well would require them to change that belief. They might fear offending the deity and being punished. Getting the water would no longer require the long walk to the river, and this would affect who got water, when, and how. They would also need to learn the new technology of using a bucket on a rope or a pump instead of simply skimming water out of the river.

Things may also fall into different categories in different cultures. For example, farming methods are on the level of technology and activity in the West, but in many traditional cultures, strong religious beliefs surround farming, such as the belief that divinities or ancestors are in charge of the earth's fertility. When people resist a simple technological change that would provide obvious benefits, it may be due to their underlying beliefs. For example, in

Democratic Republic of Congo, a development mission wanted to introduce a new type of tree that produces fruit with a high protein and vitamin content. One ethnic group accepted the saplings with joy, and soon the trees were growing all over the area. The neighbouring group with the same climate and soil also took some saplings, but they all died in no time. The second group didn't take care of the newly planted trees because they believed that if you planted a fruit tree, you would die before you could eat the fruit.

When you begin getting ideas about changes that might improve life, test them with several small pilot projects. It's impossible to predict which changes will be adopted and which will be rejected. Pilot projects are the only way to find out. Once you know which things are accepted, you can promote them more widely.

From the beginning, think through how the change could be sustained long term when the change agent is no longer investing resources and energy in the process. The more the local people can do with their existing resources, the more likely the change is to spread throughout the community and continue. Finding ways for local communities to sustain their own programmes takes a lot more creative thought and hard work than simply finding an outside donor, but it is well worth the effort.

4. Increasing the Appeal of Change

As Christians, we are all change agents. We want people to turn to Christ and to let him change their lives. How can we increase the appeal of new things, whether this is turning to Christ, using the mother-tongue Scriptures, or any other new thing? The following are some characteristics that make change more appealing:

- *Imaginable:* people have to be able to imagine themselves adopting the new thing. For example, taking pastors to see how a multilingual church functions will help them to imagine the possibility for their own churches.
- *Advantageous:* the advantages of the change should be greater than the pain of making the change. If there is no advantage that makes sense to people, they probably won't choose to adopt the change. Advantages are not only material benefits. Prestige and power provide surprisingly strong motivation.
- *Compatible:* the innovation must fit (or be made to fit) into existing values and experiences. This may mean emphasizing different aspects

of the change with different groups. For example, you might present literacy in a church setting as helping people to read God's word. When speaking about the same literacy programme to a university, you could present it as developing the country's languages.

- *Simple:* keep the new idea as simple as possible. There are three kinds of knowledge: awareness knowledge, user knowledge, and theoretical knowledge. At this stage, people need only to be aware of the change. Keeping the message simple may be difficult because what seems simple to you might seem very complex to your audience. Explain the change you're promoting to someone from your intended audience to get feedback. Keep working on the message until your explanation seems simple to the other person.
- *Able to be sampled:* if people can try out the new thing, they are more likely to adopt it. For example, people are more likely to buy a Bible in their language if they can first sample a small brochure with some key passages from it. If people can try out the new thing without having to abandon their present practice, the chances of them adopting it also increase.
- *Positive:* changes that prevent something bad from happening are more difficult to introduce than those that result in immediate positive differences. One implication of this is to introduce things in a positive way whenever possible. For example, rather than saying that people should boil water so that they don't become ill, say that boiling water makes you very healthy.
- *Incentives:* people can be motivated to change if rewards are given to those who adopt the change or penalties to those who do not. This kind of motivation will work only in the short term, however. Eventually, the change needs to spread on its own merits.

1. Choose one change you would all like to see come to your community.
2. Choose three of the above ways to increase the appeal of this change, and discuss how this could be done.

5. Stages of Change

Change occurs in stages, not all at once. If you understand these stages, it will help you know how to introduce change successfully. The change agent's involvement in the process is different at each stage.

A. Knowledge Stage

People cannot adopt changes they don't know about. Letting them know about the change is the first step. This may involve radio, newspaper, television, flyers, billboards, town criers, social media ads, and so forth. Mass media is the best way to get the information out to the widest possible audience.

When people hear about a new thing for the first time, they need the information to be simple and clear. For example, if you're trying to get the pastors in your community involved in a translation committee, don't tell them about all the fifteen steps involved in getting a translation ready for publication. Give them a summary, the big picture. Too much information can overwhelm them, and they will stop listening.

The information also has to catch people's attention and do so in such a way that they go on thinking about it. This is referred to as making your change "sticky." There is always too much going on around us for us to pay attention to everything, so we have to choose what we give our attention to. Find out what grabs your audience's attention. People often pay attention to those they respect. If respected people in the community have adopted the change you're proposing, publicize this in the mass media.

B. Persuasion Stage

Once people know about a change, they need to be persuaded to adopt it. This requires personal interaction. They need to be able to ask questions and get answers about exactly how the change will affect their lives. Feelings become more important than facts. If someone they know and trust recommends the change, they are much more likely to adopt it.

C. Decision Stage

At this point, the change agent needs to leave people alone to decide whether they want to adopt the change. If a change agent pressures people to accept a change, they may decide to do it just to please him or her. Later, they will not follow through on their decision.

D. Implementation Stage

As people adopt a change, the change agent needs to be on hand to help solve any problems that might arise. Many changes have been abandoned because one small piece of equipment or one small bit of knowledge was lacking. For example, a project in Democratic Republic of Congo was set up to teach people how to make reading glasses. This went well for a few months until a clip on the side of one of the tools broke off. No one knew how to mend it or how to use another method, so the whole project stopped until someone with the right knowledge came and solved the problem.

Often people adjust a new thing to make it fit their situation better. For example, one community adopted the change of planting beans in rows between their corn plants. After a while, they found it was easier to plant the beans in patches rather than in rows. Now almost everyone does this. When people adjust a change to fit their situation, it is a good sign because it shows they have personalized it and made it their own.

As a change agent, you need to be able to recognize the adjustments that will help, or at least not ruin, the change you're introducing, and the things that will ruin it. Be flexible enough to encourage good adjustments and discerning enough to spot adjustments that will cause problems.

When a change has become a part of the routine, it is adopted. The change agent is no longer needed on a full-time basis.

E. Confirmation Stage

Whenever people adopt a change, it upsets the way things are done. Like a stone that is dropped into a pond, change causes a ripple effect. This can make people feel insecure because life isn't as predictable as it was before. For example, when women attend literacy classes in the evenings, their other chores may not be done, and this may cause trouble in their marriages. Or they may find new self-confidence and defend themselves against abuse they had previously always accepted.

If tensions become too great, people may give up and go back to their old ways. For example, literacy classes may be tried for a year and then abandoned. During the confirmation stage, the change agent needs to make occasional visits to encourage people and help them solve unexpected problems.

Discuss a change that has happened recently in your community – for example, the introduction of mother-tongue Scriptures.

1. Which stage are you at in the stages of change given above?
2. What do you need to do to arrive at the confirmation stage, if you are not there already?

6. Kinds of Adopters

In any society, some people are adventurous and others cautious. They don't all adopt a change at the same time.

1. Think of a change that most of the participants have been exposed to – for example, using a mobile phone, a computer, or an agricultural innovation. Ask them to arrange themselves in a line according to the year they adopted this change. At one end of the line there will be those who adopted it first, and at the other end those who adopted it last or not at all. Then divide the line into the five sections shown below. The first 3 percent of the group are the innovators, the next 13 percent the early adopters, and so forth. Do this in a way that doesn't cause embarrassment.

First 3 percent	Innovators
Next 13 percent	Early adopters
Next 34 percent	Early majority
Next 34 percent	Late majority
Last 16 percent	Laggards

2. Now tell them about the typical characteristics of each group, as explained below.

A. Innovators

Innovators are people who are known to be risk-takers, willing to try anything. Others don't follow them because many of the things they're excited about never work out. They are often on the fringes of a community. If you are trying to introduce a change, don't concentrate on this group.

B. Early Adopters

Early adopters are progressive. They are able to make a decision to try out something new more quickly and take more risks than others in the community, but they're more sensible than the innovators, and so they make good role models. They have more connections with the outside world, so they are exposed to new ideas more quickly and more often than others. They are often better educated and richer than average.

Change agents should focus their attention on the early adopters, and more precisely on the opinion leaders who are in this category. These are the few people who influence the opinions of others. They are not necessarily in formal leadership roles, but the eyes of the community are on them, watching to see if they will adopt or reject the change.

C. Early Majority

The early majority are slightly more conservative than the early adopters. When people in this group see those they trust adopting a change, they begin to feel that they could adopt it, too.

Often a change has to be adapted in some way to make it appealing to the early majority. For example, the early adopters may be willing to meet five nights per week for literacy classes, but the early majority may be interested only if the classes meet two nights per week. Certain people sense what would appeal to others and are good at "translating" the change in a way others will accept. Try to identify these "translators."

When 25 percent of the people have accepted a change, then what is called "the tipping point" has been reached. From then on, the change will continue to filter through the society largely on its own momentum. For example, a literacy programme in Democratic Republic of Congo started with fourteen students. During the first six years it grew steadily, totalling about five thousand students at the end of the sixth year. Suddenly, for a combination of reasons, the next year it grew to twenty-five thousand students![1] At this point, the programme had taken on a momentum of its own that nothing could stop.

D. Late Majority

The late majority are more cautious. When they see the positive effect the change has had on those who have adopted it, they are willing to accept the change too. By the time the change has reached this group, it will be accepted by most of the community without any further work from the change agent.

E. Laggards

Laggards are people who are very slow to adopt new things, if they do so at all. Change agents should not worry about this group. There will always be some, and they don't have much influence on the larger group.

1. Among Jesus's disciples, who do you think was an opinion leader? Give evidence for your opinion, especially from the time of Christ's death and resurrection.
2. Who do you think was part of the late majority? Give evidence.

---

1. Some of the reasons for this growth were that the Ngbaka realized that the classes were the equivalent of primary school, two volunteers publicized the schools throughout the area, and the government schools were no longer functioning.

7. Important Gifted People

We have already seen that the early adopters are important people in the change process. Other people with certain character qualities are also important in the change process. We refer to them as connectors, information specialists, and salespeople. Identify these people, and focus your energy on getting them on board!

A. Connectors

Some people are naturally good at connecting with many different people in and out of their communities. Because they know so many people, they hear of new ideas and spread them far and wide. Information travels best by word of mouth. If the connectors are involved in the change you're proposing, it will spread rapidly.

B. Information Specialists

Information specialists are people who enjoy collecting information and sharing it with others. They are databanks of knowledge and remember facts correctly. When they recommend something, people listen. People trust them and go to them for information. Be sure they know the facts about the change you are proposing.

C. Salespeople

Salespeople can convince people to do things. These are generally optimistic, energetic, likeable people who have good social skills. If you can convince them of the change you're proposing, they will sell it to the masses.

1. Identify people in your group who are early adaptors, connectors, information specialists, and salespeople.
2. How can you interest these people in the changes you want to bring about?

Assignments

1. Write a short description of different ways two ethnic groups you know have responded to change.
2. Think about a change you would like to introduce to a community. What are the three most important things you have learned from this chapter that will help you introduce it better?
3. If you are working in a community where witchcraft is common, discuss how witchcraft accusations can work against people accepting change.

Readings

Bradshaw, Bruce. *Bridging the Gap: Evangelism, Development and Shalom*. Monrovia, CA: MARC, 1993.

———. *Change across Cultures*. Grand Rapids, MI: Baker, 2002.

Carlson, Joyce. *The Stranger's Eyes: Best of Ethno-Info*. Edited by H. Hill and J. Arensen. Nairobi: SIL Africa Area, 1995, 159–63.

Crickmore, Mary. "Change: How It Happens, How to Understand and Promote It." 2008. https://scripture-engagement.org/content/change-how-it-happens-how-understand-and-promote-it.

Cromartie, Michael. "How to Infect a Culture." *Christianity Today*, 7 August 2000, 64–66.

Elkins, Richard E. "Conversion or Acculturation?" *Notes on Literature Use and Language Programs* 46 (1995): 1–13.

Gladwell, Malcolm. *The Tipping Point: How Little Things Can Make a Big Difference*. New York: Little, Brown, and Co., 2000.

Godin, Seth. *Unleashing the Ideavirus*. New York: Hyperion, 2001.

Johnson, Scott, and James D. Ludema. *Partnering to Build and Measure Organizational Capacity*. Grand Rapids, MI: Christian Reformed World Relief Committee, 1997.

Johnson, Spencer. *Who Moved My Cheese?* New York: G. P. Putnam's Sons, 1998.

Rogers, Everett M. *Diffusion of Innovations*. New York: Macmillan, 1983.

31

Preparing for Scripture Engagement Seminars

Introduction

Scripture engagement seminars have been discussed and described throughout this book. They are one of the best ways of helping church leaders to translate the Bible into action in church and personal life. This chapter discusses some of the practical details of running these seminars.

PASTOR SIMON PASSES IT ON

One year, Pastor Simon was asked to go to a Scripture engagement seminar to be held in Retali, the capital of the country. He was excited at the opportunity, though he wasn't looking forward to the journey by public transport over some very bad roads. One of the Palapala Catholic priests was also invited to the seminar. Happily for Pastor Simon, Father James could use a mission car, so they were able to travel together in much more comfort.

Right from the start, they discovered that the emphasis of the seminar was on teaching what they learned to church leaders back home. They learned more about how to reach people who were not only resistant to following Christ but also uninterested in learning how to read. They listened with interest to presenters who talked about using songs, stories, recordings, radio, and films to reach such people. They spent most afternoon sessions improving their Bible storying skills.

On the last day of the seminar, participants worked in language groups to plan the seminars and other activities that they hoped to run when they got home. Pastor Simon and Father James sat down together. After praying for wisdom, they discussed who should be invited to the seminars, which subjects they would choose to teach, and how they could finance the event. Before the closing meeting, each language group had the chance to present their plans.

On the way home, Pastor Simon said, "There still seem to be a lot of things to decide. Where do we start?"

Father James replied, "I think we need to form a small group of people to help arrange this. We should be involving the other churches in the area, and I'm sure the Palapala Old Testament translators will want to help."

After about two weeks, they were able to get a small representative group together and discuss a possible seminar for church leaders to help them use the Palapala New Testament. In addition, they agreed that everyone would be interested in learning about oral ways of telling people about Christ. Then they needed to agree on where it would be held, who would teach, when they would hold it, and other practical details. They found that this couldn't all be decided in one meeting and that other people needed to be consulted.

Finally, after a couple of months, the plans were made for a seminar in three months' time. Pastor Simon thought about it all night and wondered, "What if no one comes?" He needn't have worried! Fifty church leaders came from five different kinds of churches. They really enjoyed learning together. At the end, they left feeling very happy to have new skills and with new confidence in their abilities to help people engage with the Palapala Scriptures.

1. Do church leaders from different kinds of churches in your area come together for other kinds of seminars? If not, will there be a problem in getting them to come together?
2. If there is a problem in getting leaders from different kinds of churches together, can you think of any solutions that will help to overcome it?

1. Overview of a Scripture Engagement Seminar

A seminar may last from a day to two weeks. Each day is usually made up of four or five sessions. As you plan the first seminar, keep in mind that it will be the first of a series. Change takes time! During a seminar, there are two sorts of sessions:

- Those in which the participants work in small groups for the whole time – for example, when they are learning to write the language.
- Those in which the subject is introduced by a short lecture with discussion in the large group, followed by smaller groups or by individuals working to put what they have learned into practice. For example, a talk on Bible studies may be followed by the groups doing a Bible study on a specific passage. Or a talk on studying topics in Scripture may be followed by each person studying a topic and filling in answers on a sheet.

If participants have the chance to discuss and to put new information into practice, they are far more likely to remember it and apply it to their lives. So each session should include some exercises and discussion groups. Plan these first, and then plan to teach only what is necessary to prepare the participants for the exercises or discussion. Try to keep to the ten-minute rule: no one should teach for more than ten minutes at a time without having exercises, discussions, or questions.

> People learn much more by doing than by only hearing!

2. Preparing for Scripture Engagement Seminars

There are several things to do before the start of a Scripture engagement seminar. They are listed here in the approximate order in which they need to be done.

A. Form a Planning Committee

To hold a Scripture engagement seminar, you'll need a planning committee. This committee prepares for and makes decisions about the seminar. It should consist of three to six people. Top church leaders from the churches that are expected to attend the seminar should be on this committee as well as people who have already attended a Scripture engagement seminar. This group should discuss the ways people are presently engaging with Scripture in the churches and the barriers to that engagement. They should also discuss ways they hope to break through those barriers during the seminar.

B. Address Practical Arrangements

The first issues that the planning committee needs to address are practical ones:
- *Location:* if the seminar is for one language only, a village setting may be more hospitable and less distracting than a city.
- *Timing:* check that there are no conflicts with the dates of other conferences and events.
- *Length:* typically, local courses last from three to six days.
- *Food and lodging:* work out who will arrange food and lodging and how the finances will be managed.
- *Timetable:* decide when the programme will start and stop each day. This depends on local conditions and customs.

C. Choose the Participants

The participants invited to come should be people in leadership roles in the church and should include the pastors and priests. A suitable number for one of these courses is somewhere between twenty and sixty people. Once the committee decides how many churches to involve, it can calculate how many people each church may send. For example, if the course is meant for a church region that has forty-five churches, each church should be asked to send only the main leader, so as not to make the group too large. If too many people want to come to the seminar, it will be difficult to keep it participatory. Arrange to have another seminar later so you can include everyone.

> Always aim to train trainers of others!

D. Choose and Train the Leaders

Once you know how many participants to expect, you will know how many leaders you need to help with the training. There should be one leader for each group of six to eight participants. If this is the first seminar in which you are promoting written mother-tongue Scripture, you may need more leaders as people are likely to need help to read their mother tongue. One member of the planning committee should serve as the overall organizer, with the other members serving as small-group leaders.

Group leaders should be people who are well respected and have good Bible knowledge. If you are using written Scriptures, they should be able to read their mother tongue fluently. To find these people, look among the top church leaders, members of a translation team, reviewers, schoolteachers, missionaries, and so forth.

Decide who will train the small-group leaders and draw up a programme for this. Different members of the planning committee can take it in turns to teach. Include the following in the training:

- If reading and writing will be part of the seminar, check that each person can read and write the language correctly. If necessary, give spelling lessons.
- Go over all the sessions, explaining what will be done in the small groups and how to lead them.
- If there is time, and if the leaders can read English, read through parts of this book and discuss it.

- Decide who is going to give each talk, and let each person practise the talk in front of the other leaders.
- Pray and sing together.

This type of leadership training is especially necessary when you run your first seminar. Later on, it may be possible to do the training in a short session just before the seminar begins.

E. Plan the Content of the Course

To plan the content of the course, the committee needs to decide which subjects are most important in the churches at the time. Your seminar should be lively and stimulating and give the participants several new tools to use in their churches. They should go home wanting to come back to future seminars.

It takes about half a day to teach a chapter of this book, so in a seminar of three days do not try to cover more than six subjects at the most. If time needs to be spent practising reading and writing the local language, then choose fewer subjects. Don't give your participants mental indigestion! Break up the daily schedules into one-hour or one-and-a-half-hour blocks. Often it's possible to have three sessions before the noon meal and two sessions in the afternoon. Begin the day with a thirty-minute devotional time, and take time for singing during the day. If possible, use a variety of local music.

Aim to have variety in the programme each day of your seminar. Follow a session that requires a lot of concentration with something easier. Have sessions in which participants are learning something new followed by sessions in which they practise what they have learned. Include enough time for the participants to practise new skills to be able to master them. For example, teach about Bible studies on passages during one seminar and introduce Bible studies on themes at the next.

It may be possible to meet in the evenings, particularly if everyone is housed at the same place. The evening sessions should not require great concentration and should be fun! The following are some suggestions:

- Show a video such as *How the Bible Came to Us* (a United Bible Society production), the *Jesus* film (see chapter 26), videos of life in Israel today, and so on.
- Share, learn, and record new Scripture songs.
- Demonstrate finding mother-tongue Scripture materials on websites, download Bible apps, or use Scripture App Builder.
- Pray and share together.

- Have the participants present skits or dramas they have developed.

The workshop should end with a closing ceremony. This can be a time to invite others in the community or local churches to see what has been learned. The workshop participants can share their Bible studies, songs, dramas, and testimonies of what they learned. Awarding certificates to the participants can be a joyous time after many days of hard work.

> The details of the seminar schedule and timetable all depend on the local situation.

3. Preparing the Materials

Once the programme is settled, draw up a list of all the materials that must be translated and made available to the participants. These could include the following:

- All the Scriptures that are available in the language, in print, recorded media, or Scripture apps.
- A hymn book or a sheet of hymns.
- Certificates for the end of the course.
- A writing manual or a series of exercises to teach writing.
- If liturgical churches are involved, the passages for the next group of Sundays, including Old Testament passages, if possible.
- If learning to read the mother tongue is a goal, easy reading material such as folk stories.
- Invitations to the closing ceremony.
- Computers or equipment to record stories and songs.
- Large sheets of paper for posters, marker pens, glue, and tape to hang posters on the wall.

Additional materials will be needed according to the subjects that have been chosen for the programme. Once a list of all the necessary materials has been prepared, the next step is to be sure you have all of the materials in the appropriate language. If the seminar is promoting mother-tongue Scripture, this may involve translating materials that do not already exist in the language. This takes time. The people who do this should have already received training in translation principles. If you need help, contact a Bible translation agency in your area.

Certificates need to be prepared in advance in the appropriate language. They could look something like the example shown.

Scripture Engagement Seminar

_____(Name)_____ has attended a Scripture engagement seminar held at _____(location)_____

from ___(beginning date)___ to ___(end date)___

and is able to ___(insert main teaching goal of workshop)___

in ___(language)___, and is able to teach this to others.

Signed _____   Date _____
         Seminar director

---

4. Assembling the Materials

The materials for the seminar need to be assembled in such a way that they can be distributed quickly to the participants. The best way to do this is to put them in plastic bags to be sold during the first session on the first day. If some Scripture has just been published, include it in the bag. If not, sell it separately to those who do not have it. In some countries it is very helpful to include a pencil and a small exercise book.

In addition to the bags for the participants, the following things also need to be ready:

- Chalk.
- Blackboard(s).
- Cloth to clean the blackboard.
- Prizes for the competitions, where appropriate.
- Answer sheets for the leaders, where needed.
- Programmes for the leaders.
- A register book or sheet for the participants to write down their names and any other information about themselves that is needed.

5. Preparing for Follow-Up Scripture Engagement Seminars

Plan for a follow-up seminar to happen about a year after the first one. Invite to the follow-up only those who have put what they learned into practice. (Knowing this will happen can motivate participants to hold local seminars within the year.)

When you plan the timetable for the follow-up seminar, include time for participants to report on how they have put ideas from the previous course into practice. Some may have some good ideas to share with the group. They may also have problems that need to be discussed.

Remember that some participants will be there for the first time while others will have already attended a seminar. For some sessions, you may need to schedule beginner and advanced classes at the same time. For other subjects, it is good to have everyone together. Those who have heard the presentation before may benefit from hearing it again, or they may be able to help teach part of the session.

Each seminar should include fresh material and approaches. Basic subjects, such as Bible studies and reading aloud well, should be taught at every seminar until they are completely mastered, but these subjects can be taught in slightly different ways. For example, if the first course had Bible studies on Mark, the second course might have Bible studies on James. It should not be necessary to repeat any sessions in exactly the same form. If most people have phones, help them to download any new Scripture available on the Scripture app.

If church leaders can attend a seminar every twelve to fifteen months, this will almost certainly increase their ability to help people in their churches to engage with Scripture. Courses need to continue until the majority of church leaders and church members are using Scriptures in appropriate languages and media in all aspects of their lives.

These courses require a lot of work, but you will find it is worth the effort when you see men, women, and children studying God's word in a language they understand well and applying it to their lives.

Make tentative plans for a Scripture engagement seminar for your area. Think about the following questions as you make your plans:

1. If you were planning a Scripture engagement seminar in your home area, who do you think should be members of the decision-making group?
2. Who would you invite to the seminar as participants?
3. When would you hold it?
4. How long would it last?

5. What chapters would you teach?
6. How would you arrange for the participants to be housed and fed? How is this done for other types of training in your area?

Assignments

1. There are two ways to change the ideas and practices of church leaders. One is by holding a seminar for them; the other is by giving them the same information individually or in written form. Give at least three reasons why the seminar is more likely to be successful than giving the information individually or in writing.
2. You can teach a topic either by using discussion and exercises or by a lecture. Which do you think is the better way, and why?
3. How many courses would have to be held in your area to enable all church leaders to participate without needing to travel more than 20 miles (32 kilometres)?

Readings

Hill, Margaret. "Are Workshops Useful?" 2011. https://scripture-engagement.org/wp-content/uploads/2020/09/Hill-M-2011-Are-Workshops-Useful.pdf.

Vella, Jane. *Taking Learning to Task: Creative Strategies for Teaching Adults*. San Francisco: Jossey-Bass, 2000.

The scripture-engagement.org website has many articles about Scripture engagement seminars and workshops.

Appendix 1

Good News for Muslims

Certain things in the Bible are especially attractive to Muslims. This appendix provides key biblical themes, important questions from the gospels, and important characteristics of Jesus which you may find helpful to use when engaging with Muslims.

1. Key Biblical Themes

There are a number of biblical themes that Muslims find attractive. These themes are good news to them and create interest in the Scriptures. These themes and related Scripture passages can be used to make memes and social media messages for Muslims.

1. God's goodness, love, reliability, and care for his servants.	These qualities are demonstrated in the stories of Abraham, Joseph, the exodus, Daniel, Jesus, and the apostles, among others.
2. God's guidance of history towards good ends as he works through events to oppose evil, to train his servants in righteousness and truth, and to fulfil his good purposes for his people.	This is clearly seen in the stories of Abraham, Joseph, Moses, Ruth, David, Jonah, Daniel, and Job, and in Revelation.
3. The portrait of Jesus himself: his kindness, devotion, wisdom, power (including to heal and do miracles), and ongoing reign as saviour and king.	Jesus is presented in all of the gospels, but Luke's gospel is the one that is used the most to introduce Muslims to Jesus.
4. The love and forgiveness exhibited by true followers of Jesus.	This can be seen in stories from the Acts of the Apostles and in the lives of true disciples whom people meet today. A similar theme is present in the life of Joseph.

5. The offer of personal forgiveness and acceptance by God.	This is presented in the gospels and in Acts.
6. The offer of assured and complete salvation from hell and acceptance into God's kingdom.	This is foretold in Isaiah 53, and it comes out in the gospels, particularly in Matt 11:27–29 and Luke 7:36–50; 10:20; 12:32; 23:42–43; John 3:14–16; 11:25–27; and 20:31.
7. The offer of a personal relationship with the Lord, fully realized in the next life.	Matt 18:20; 28:20; John 14:16–20; Acts 18:10; Rev 21–22.
8. The offer of inner cleansing and renewal through God's Holy Spirit.	This is presented in segments of the gospels, Acts, and the epistles.
9. The offer and example of grace to live a godly life through the strengthening and guidance of the Holy Spirit.	This is described in the Acts of the Apostles and in some of the epistles.
10. Power to resist and repel Satan, evil spirits, curses, and the evil eye in Jesus's name.	This is found in the gospels (for example, Luke 10:17–20), Acts, James, 1 Peter.

2. Important Questions in the Gospels to Ponder

- Luke 5:21 "Who can forgive sins but God alone?"
- Luke 7:49 "Who is this who even forgives sins?"
- Luke 8:25 "Who is this? He commands even the winds and the water, and they obey him."
- Mark 6:2 "Where did this man get these things? . . . What's this wisdom that has been given him? What are these remarkable miracles he is performing?"
- Mark 10:18 "'Why do you call me good?' Jesus answered. 'No one is good – except God alone.'"
- Luke 24:26 "Did not the Messiah have to suffer these things and then enter his glory?"

3. Important Characteristics of Jesus to Ponder

- Jesus declared that he came from God.
- Jesus creates matter from nothing.
- Jesus controls the forces of nature.

- Jesus has authority over evil spirits.
- Jesus has the power to heal all sicknesses and diseases.
- Jesus proclaims he is lord of all and has all power on heaven and earth.
- Jesus issues commandments on his own authority.
- Jesus knows the thoughts and hearts of people.
- Jesus sits on the throne of God in glory.
- Jesus sends and commands his angels.
- Jesus judges the nations.
- Jesus forgives sins.
- Jesus bestows eternal life.
- Jesus condemns people to hell.
- Jesus receives and accepts worship.
- Jesus receives and accepts prayer.
- Jesus receives and accepts being addressed as God.

Appendix 2

Researching Song Styles

Each culture has its own music. To begin learning about your culture's music, choose one kind of song from your language group and answer the following questions.

1. At what events, for what occasions, and under what circumstances is this kind of song sung?

2. At what times of the day or in what seasons of the year are these songs sung?

3. Where are they typically sung?

4. Do you know where and when this kind of song originated?

5. Are there still people who compose new songs in this style?

6. How do people learn this kind of song? In what contexts? Has it changed over time? What changed?

7. Why are these kinds of songs sung? What emotions are expressed?

8. Who typically sings these kinds of songs? (Women? Men? Children? Adults? Everybody? Specialists only?)

9. What instruments typically accompany these kinds of songs? How many? Who plays them? (Men or women, adults or children, anyone or specialists?)

10. Does performing this music require special clothing?

11. Does performing this music require other special objects (e.g. a machete, magical objects)?

12. How do people feel during the performance?

13. Does dancing accompany these kinds of songs? How many dancers? Are they men, women, adults, children, or specialists?

14. Are there observers? How many? Who?

15. How are these songs composed? (Spontaneously? Improvised? With pencil and paper? While dreaming or thinking under a tree? Another way? Who composes them?)

16. What social or religious connotations, positive or negative, are associated with these kinds of songs? (Sorcery? Immoral acts? Initiations? Virtuous acts? Amusement? Neutral? Youth only? Drunkenness? Other?)

17. Considering the positive, negative, and neutral associations in the question above, would it be appropriate to adapt this genre of song to biblical texts for use in the church? Why or why not?

18. Has this kind of song style already been adapted to Bible texts currently sung in the church?

Appendix 3

Example of Sunday School Lesson

Title of lesson series: Miracles of Jesus
Title of this lesson: Ten healed of leprosy
Bible passage: Luke 17:11–19
Main teaching point: We should say thank you to God.

Opening activity: Play the game "Simon Says."
Review last week's lesson: Split the class into two teams and do a quiz – ask them questions about last week's lesson.
Introduction to today's lesson: Ask the children if they have ever felt ill. How did they feel when they were ill? Tell them that today we will learn about ten people who were ill with leprosy. Do any of them know what leprosy is? If not, explain it to them. Explain that people did not like to go near people with leprosy because they thought that they might get it too.
Pray: For God to help the children to understand his word.
Tell the Bible story: Tell the Bible story – ask ten children to help. They will act out the parts of the people with leprosy.
Teach and apply the Bible story:
Ask a few questions about the story to make sure they have remembered it.
Invite ten children to the front. Give each one a sweet. See if they say thank you. Talk to the children about what happened (if the children said thank you or not and how it made you feel).
Ask, "How many of the sick people came back to Jesus to say thank you?" and "How do you think Jesus felt about that?"
Explain that it is important to always say thank you when we receive something, whether it is something big like healing or something small like a sweet!
We should say thank you to other *people*: Give an example – when their parents give them food, what should they say?
We should say thank you to *God*: Ask the children to mention things that we can thank God for, e.g. food, family.
Ask the children, "How can we thank God?" (We can thank him through prayer, through giving an offering, through singing.)

Memory verse: Psalm 118:29 (Compose a tune and sing the verse.)

A review activity to help them remember what they have learned: Sing the song "Thank you, Lord, for this new day." The children can create extra verses, such as "Thank you, Lord, for my mum and dad."

Prayer: Give one or two children a chance to pray and say thank you to God for good things in their lives.

Closing activity: Children draw pictures of things they are thankful for.

Appendix 4

Recording Scripture and Dramas

Introduction

In chapter 25, we discussed the various types of dramas that are possible and how to develop them. The quality of a Scripture recording can either make people want to listen to it, or put them off completely. Good recordings can be made locally with very simple technology. This appendix tells you how.

1. Preparing for Recording

Before recording, the actors should come together and rehearse the script. Speak as though you are speaking to one person or one family, even though you are aiming to communicate to a large group.

The art of the radio actor is to read without sounding as if you're reading. Here are some suggestions to help you prepare your reading well:

1. Read your script two or three times to familiarize yourself with the whole story and all the characters.

2. Take a pencil or marker and underline or tick all the lines your character speaks. Write yourself notes about where to talk more loudly or more softly, or to show an emotion or a reaction.

3. Read each line to yourself and then look up and say it to someone. Alternatively, ask a friend to read your line to you and then repeat it after your friend with the right expression.

4. Make sure you understand what you are reading. If you don't, you won't sound believable. Think about how this scene is contributing to the story. What does this character want in this scene? How is he or she working at getting it?

5. If there is something in the text you would like to change, make a note in the margin. Then, at a pause, ask the others if they agree. The only thing that cannot be changed is the translated text of the word of God, although this may be interrupted with questions and explanations. If it is interrupted, the narrator needs to say something like "so God's word continues . . ." when it resumes. This helps the audience know which parts of the drama are God's word.

6. Imagine you are the person you are playing. Live in that person's shoes. Think about his or her character and mannerisms, temperament, likes and dislikes, strengths and weaknesses. Much of this will be evident in the story from your script. You can complete it with your own character traits or those of someone you know well.

7. Find the emotion needed for each scene. At this time is this person happy? Sad? Angry? Suffering? Stunned? Avoid speaking in a monotone unless you want your character to be boring. Vary your volume, speed, and emotion. Even though the audience will not see your gestures, feel free to use them. Your listeners will be able to tell from your voice that you are using your hands properly when you speak. A programme is interesting if the speakers are enthusiastic. If the performers are not involved in the programme, you can't expect the listeners to feel involved either.

8. Listen to the person speaking to you and respond with "mmm" or "m-hm" or "hm"! These small reactions keep you in the scene in the listeners' minds.

9. Sound effects can liven up a recording and make it more real. Look through the script to decide what sound effects might be appropriate (rain, a car door slamming, a rooster crowing, and so forth). Figure out how you can make these sounds. Many of these can be downloaded for free.

10. Ask others to critique your acting. You will learn more from others than from evaluating yourself. You can always learn something from feedback, but remember that you can't please all the people all the time. Stay balanced when thinking about the critiques you receive.

1. In groups of six, think of a three- to five-minute drama. Decide on a theme and develop it through a storyline, involving conflict of some sort.
2. Decide who will act each part.
3. Without any rehearsal, perform this for the large group.
4. Get the group to give feedback on what they found to be believable and what they would have liked to see more of.

2. Recording the Programme

You will need a quiet room to record in. To get rid of echoes while you record, make everything in the room which is made out of metal or cement soft by covering it with cushions, rugs, wood, fabric, or mats.

Most computers are able to make excellent recordings. These recordings are easy to edit with free programs available on the Internet, such as Cool Edit or Audacity.[1] Reaper is another good option although it is not free. A simple microphone can be used and passed between the actors, or you may be able to use several mikes that are all plugged into the computer or recorder.

When you are recording the script, the following tips will help you produce a good-quality recording:

- Sit opposite those you are talking to, and look at them often. This will help you sound more natural.
- Read your line quickly and silently, and hold it in your mind. Look up, and say it to the person you are talking to with the right expression and intonation.
- Stay close to your mike, but don't touch it. Be careful not to breathe heavily into your mike. Try to breathe quietly unless your character is tired or in pain. Hold the mike a bit to one side of your mouth so the "p" and "b" don't make a loud puffy noise. If you back away from your mike, you will sound further away from the person you are talking to. Turn the pages of your script during the moments when you are not being recorded, or else the noise will be heard.
- Pronounce all your words clearly rather than swallowing them. The listener can't ask you to repeat anything he or she hasn't understood.
- Take a drink of water when your mouth is dry. Take breaks when you get tired. If the group is making a lot of errors, take a break. Go outside and walk around, or take a drink or eat a snack and try again later.
- Replay and listen to each scene as soon as you have recorded it. Rerecord any lines that you're not happy with. If there are many changes, you may want to redo a whole section.

Find a computer or other machine that can record, and a mike.

In groups of six, practise reading the story of the rich young fool (Mark 10:17–30). Have one person be the narrator, another the rich young fool, another Jesus, another Peter, and others some of the other disciples.

---

1. Audacity is a free program available at http://audacity.sourceforge.net.

1. Practise until you feel you are ready. Try to "put your face in your voice."
2. Record your drama.
3. Play it for the large group. Ask for feedback.

3. Editing and Distributing Your Recording

After you have made your recording, someone with technical skills should listen to it and remove any undesirable sounds. If you have access to a computer, this can be easily done with simple, free programs.

Give each recording you make a number and a name. Make copies of the recordings to distribute. Keep a chart of which recordings you have given to whom, so you know what other recordings they may want next.

Assignments

1. Choose one passage of Scripture that God has used to speak to you in the past. Practise reading it, and then record it very carefully. After you have recorded the passage, record yourself explaining why you chose that passage.
2. Make up a programme for a ten-minute radio broadcast. Say why you have chosen the subject and how you would get people to help you make the recording.

Appendix 5

Answers

1. Some Answers, Page 23

For example, Acts 8:30–35; 2 Timothy 3:16–17; Deuteronomy 6:6–7.

2. Sample Answers, Page 37

Question	Original Meaning	Underlying Principle	Application
1. John 13:14–15	Gentile slaves or women would wash guests' feet to welcome them hospitably. Jewish men, even if they were slaves, would never be expected to perform this task.	Leaders should humble themselves to the point of assuming the role of a slave to serve one another.	?
2. Exodus 23:19	Perhaps this was a protest against a Canaanite pagan ritual (NIV Study Bible).	Don't join in the worship practices of pagans.	?
3. 1 Timothy 2:8; 1 Kings 8:22	This was the usual Jewish posture for praising God.	Praise God and pray in a culturally appropriate way.	?
4. Leviticus 19:13	Farm workers were poor and had no cash reserves. They counted on getting paid at the end of each day to be able to eat. Employers needed to provide for the needs of their workers in a timely manner.	Be sure that the needs of those who work for you are met in a timely manner.	?

3. Sample Answers, Page 72

If witchcraft didn't exist, the world would be perfect: only very old people would die, and there would be no illness, sterility, or misfortune.	Genesis 3
Spirits and spiritual forces are more powerful than humans.	Genesis 1:28–30 Psalm 8:4–8
Evil is stronger than good.	1 John 5:4–5
Misfortune is due to others, not to any fault of mine. For example, if I drive while I'm drunk, crash my car, and kill a passenger, it's because someone was working witchcraft on me, not because of my drunk driving.	1 John 1:8–10 Galatians 6:7–8
People need to protect themselves from spiritual attack.	1 John 5:18 Psalm 121
A person can become a soul-eating witch without wanting to and can do evil without knowing it.	James 4:7 1 Peter 5:8–9
It is right and necessary to take vengeance on those who harm family members.	Romans 12:17–19

4. Answers, Page 82

The Herodians supported the colonial Roman government. The Pharisees considered anyone who supported it to be a traitor to their faith in God.

5. Answers, Page 92

Joshua 1:8; 2 Timothy 2:15; and other passages.

6. Answers, Page 120

1. What do the letters in the word AIDS stand for?
   A: Acquired – you get it
   I: Immune – the system that protects your body from disease
   D: Deficiency – you are missing something
   S: Syndrome – a group of symptoms

2. What does it mean to be HIV-positive?
   HIV stands for Human Immune-deficiency Virus. If you are HIV-positive, it means the HIV virus is already in your body.

3. How do most people get HIV/AIDS?
   Through having sex with an infected person.

4. What is the second most common way?
   A mother giving it to her baby through childbirth.

5. Is there a medical cure for this disease?
   No!

6. Is there treatment for HIV/AIDS?
   Yes. Antiretroviral medicines (ARVs) are available in many places. ARVs keep HIV from destroying the body's ability to fight off infections so that AIDS cannot develop. People who take ARVs cannot get the other diseases that HIV-positive people often get, such as TB or malaria.

7. If a person starts taking ARVs before he or she gets seriously sick, and continues to take them every day, how long might that person live for?
   If a person takes the drugs faithfully, he or she can live in good health for many years.

8. Can you get HIV/AIDS in the following ways:
   (a) Hugging a person with HIV/AIDS? *NO*
   (b) Sharing the same razor blade with a person who has HIV/AIDS? *YES*
   (c) Using the same toilet as a person who has HIV/AIDS? *NO*
   (d) Having sex with a person who has HIV/AIDS? *YES*
   (e) Through an injection using a used needle? *YES*
   (f) Sharing food with a person with HIV/AIDS? *NO*
   (g) Through receiving a blood transfusion? *YES*
   (h) Kissing a person with HIV/AIDS on the cheek? *NO*
   (i) Drinking out of the same cup at Holy Communion? *NO*
   (j) Treating the open sores of a person with HIV/AIDS? *YES*
   (k) Through insect bites? *NO*

9. How can you tell if you have HIV/AIDS?
   By having a blood test.

10. If a person takes the ARV medicine regularly and the blood tests show the virus is not active, can that person give HIV to others? Why or why not?
    No. When ARVs are taken regularly they lower the amount of HIV in the person's body fluids so much that he or she cannot pass it on to others.

11. If an infected person cannot get ARVs, what else can that person do to protect his or her spouse who is not infected?
    The couple can either avoid having sex at all or use a condom every time they do have sex.

12. What are the church's responsibilities in connection with HIV/AIDS? Name at least three.
    Teach young people about Biblical principles of marriage and avoidance of sex before marriage.
    Look after orphans and widows in practical ways.
    Develop trained people who can give help and comfort to those who are dying.

7. Answers, Page 247

Possible answers: Good – to understand the situation, to be able to take appropriate action. Bad – to prove someone hasn't done well or is wrong.

Langham Literature and its imprints are a ministry of Langham Partnership.

Langham Partnership is a global fellowship working in pursuit of the vision God entrusted to its founder John Stott –

> *to facilitate the growth of the church in maturity and Christ-likeness through raising the standards of biblical preaching and teaching.*

Our vision is to see churches in the Majority World equipped for mission and growing to maturity in Christ through the ministry of pastors and leaders who believe, teach and live by the word of God.

Our mission is to strengthen the ministry of the word of God through:
- nurturing national movements for biblical preaching
- fostering the creation and distribution of evangelical literature
- enhancing evangelical theological education

especially in countries where churches are under-resourced.

Our ministry

Langham Preaching partners with national leaders to nurture indigenous biblical preaching movements for pastors and lay preachers all around the world. With the support of a team of trainers from many countries, a multi-level programme of seminars provides practical training, and is followed by a programme for training local facilitators. Local preachers' groups and national and regional networks ensure continuity and ongoing development, seeking to build vigorous movements committed to Bible exposition.

Langham Literature provides Majority World preachers, scholars and seminary libraries with evangelical books and electronic resources through publishing and distribution, grants and discounts. The programme also fosters the creation of indigenous evangelical books in many languages, through writer's grants, strengthening local evangelical publishing houses, and investment in major regional literature projects, such as one volume Bible commentaries like *The Africa Bible Commentary* and *The South Asia Bible Commentary*.

Langham Scholars provides financial support for evangelical doctoral students from the Majority World so that, when they return home, they may train pastors and other Christian leaders with sound, biblical and theological teaching. This programme equips those who equip others. Langham Scholars also works in partnership with Majority World seminaries in strengthening evangelical theological education. A growing number of Langham Scholars study in high quality doctoral programmes in the Majority World itself. As well as teaching the next generation of pastors, graduated Langham Scholars exercise significant influence through their writing and leadership.

To learn more about Langham Partnership and the work we do visit **langham.org**

www.ingramcontent.com/pod-product-compliance
Lightning Source LLC
Chambersburg PA
CBHW060554230426
43670CB00011B/1824